Fanon

For Aidan's Eye

Fanon

The Postcolonial Imagination

Nigel C. Gibson

polity

First published in 2003 by Polity Press in association with Blackwell Publishing Ltd

Editorial office:
Polity Press
65 Bridge Street
Cambridge CB2 1UR, UK

Marketing and production:
Blackwell Publishing Ltd
108 Cowley Road
Oxford OX4 1JF, UK

Distributed in the USA by
Blackwell Publishing Inc.
350 Main Street
Malden, MA 02148, USA

Library of Congress Cataloging-in-Publication Data

Gibson, Nigel C.
Fanon : the postcolonial imagination / Nigel C. Gibson.
   p.   cm. – (Key contemporary thinkers)
Includes bibliographical references and index.
ISBN 0-7456-2260-7 – ISBN 0-7456-2261-5 (pbk.)   1. Fanon, Frantz, 1925–1961.   2. Fanon, Frantz, 1925–1961 – Political and social views.
3. Blacks – Race identity.   4. Racism.   I. Title.   II. Key contemporary thinkers (Cambridge, England)
CT2628.F35 G53 2003
320.5'092 – dc21

2002014158

Typeset in 10.5 on 12 pt Palatino
by SNP Best-set Typesetter Ltd., Hong Kong
Printed and bound in Great Britain by TJ International, Padstow, Cornwall

For further information on Polity, visit our website: www.polity.co.uk

Key Contemporary Thinkers

Published

Jeremy Ahearne, *Michel de Certeau: Interpretation and its Other*

Peter Burke, *The French Historical Revolution: The* Annales *School 1929–1989*

Michael Caesar, *Umberto Eco: Philosophy, Semiotics and the Work of Fiction*

M. J. Cain, *Fodor: Language, Mind and Philosophy*

Rosemary Cowan, *Cornel West: The Politics of Redemption*

Colin Davis, *Levinas: An Introduction*

Simon Evnine, *Donald Davidson*

Edward Fullbrook and Kate Fullbrook, *Simone de Beauvoir: A Critical Introduction*

Andrew Gamble, *Hayek: The Iron Cage of Liberty*

Nigel C. Gibson, *Fanon: The Postcolonial Imagination*

Graeme Gilloch, *Walter Benjamin: Critical Constellations*

Karen Green, *Dummett: Philosophy of Language*

Espen Hammer, *Stanley Cavell: Skepticism, Subjectivity, and the Ordinary*

Phillip Hansen, *Hannah Arendt: Politics, History and Citizenship*

Sean Homer, *Fredric Jameson: Marxism, Hermeneutics, Postmodernism*

Christopher Hookway, *Quine: Language, Experience and Reality*

Christina Howells, *Derrida: Deconstruction from Phenomenology to Ethics*

Fred Inglis, *Clifford Geertz: Culture, Custom and Ethics*

Simon Jarvis, *Adorno: A Critical Introduction*

Sarah Kay, *Žižek: A Critical Introduction*

Douglas Kellner, *Jean Baudrillard: From Marxism to Post-Modernism and Beyond*

Valerie Kennedy, *Edward Said: A Critical Introduction*

Chandran Kukathas and Philip Pettit, *Rawls: A Theory of Justice and its Critics*

James McGilvray, *Chomsky: Language, Mind, and Politics*

Lois McNay, *Foucault: A Critical Introduction*

Philip Manning, *Erving Goffman and Modern Sociology*

Michael Moriarty, *Roland Barthes*

Harold W. Noonan, *Frege: A Critical Introduction*

William Outhwaite, *Habermas: A Critical Introduction*

Kari Palonen, *Quentin Skinner: History, Politics, Rhetoric*

John Preston, *Feyerabend: Philosophy, Science and Society*
Chris Rojek, *Stuart Hall*
Susan Sellers, *Hélène Cixous: Authorship, Autobiography and Love*
Wes Sharrock and Rupert Read, *Kuhn: Philosopher of Scientific Revolution*
David Silverman, *Harvey Sacks: Social Science and Conversation Analysis*
Dennis Smith, *Zygmunt Bauman: Prophet of Postmodernity*
Nicholas H. Smith, *Charles Taylor: Meaning, Morals and Modernity*
Geoffrey Stokes, *Popper: Philosophy, Politics and Scientific Method*
Georgia Warnke, *Gadamer: Hermeneutics, Tradition and Reason*
James Williams, *Lyotard: Towards a Postmodern Philosophy*
Jonathan Wolff, *Robert Nozick: Property, Justice and the Minimal State*

Forthcoming

Maria Baghramian, *Hilary Putnam*
Sara Beardsworth, *Kristeva*
James Carey, *Innis and McLuhan*
George Crowder, *Isaiah Berlin: Liberty, Pluralism and Liberalism*
Thomas D'Andrea, *Alasdair MacIntyre*
Maximilian de Gaynesford, *John McDowell*
Reidar Andreas Due, *Deleuze*
Jocelyn Dunphy, *Ricoeur*
Eric Dunning, *Norbert Elias*
Matthew Elton, *Daniel Dennett: Reconciling Science and Our Self-conception*
Chris Fleming, *René Girard: Violence and Mimesis*
Paul Kelly, *Ronald Dworkin*
Carl Levy, *Antonio Gramsci*
Moya Lloyd, *Judith Butler*
Dermot Moran, *Edmund Husserl*
Jim Murray, *C. L. R. James: Ideas in Social Movement*
James O'Shea, *Wilfrid Sellars*
Nicholas Walker, *Heidegger*

Contents

Acknowledgments   x

Abbreviations for Fanon's Works   xii

Introduction   1
   An Abbreviated Biography   4
   Key Terms   6
   Answering Some Critics   10

1 The Racial Gaze: Black Slave, White Master   15

   The Jew and Black Consciousness   18
   The Triple Person: Merleau-Ponty, Sartre, and Lived
     Experience   24
   Dialectical Impasses: Hegel and the Black   29
   A Negative Dialectic?   30
   The Black and Reciprocity   33
   Unchaining the Dialectic   37

**2 Psychoanalysis and the Black's Inferiority
Complex**   42

   Authentic Love   49
   Outside my Psychoanalytic Office: Fanon and
     Mannoni   52
   One Hundred Thousand Massacred   55
   Dream and Reality   58

3   **Negritude and the Descent into a "Real Hell"**   61

Césaire's Remembrance of Things Past and "Return"
   to the Future   63
Senghor and Negritude Politics   68
Sartre's *Orphée noir*   71
The Dialectics of Black Consciousness   73
Fanon's Critique of Negritude   78

4   **Becoming Algerian**   84

The Algiers School   84
Beyond Ethnopsychiatry?   90
The Collapse of the Division between Politics and
   Psychiatry: Torture(rs)   92
The Deepening Violence   97
The Battle of Algiers   99

5   **Violent Concerns**   103

The Relativity at the Heart of the Absolute   103
Manichean Realities   106
Violence Interiorized   109
Exploding Manicheanism   113
The Qualifications of Violence: Descent from an
   Absolute   118
Dizzy on Violence   120

6   **Radical Mutations: Toward a Fighting Culture**   127

Antibiotic Attitudes   129
The "Absolute Originality" of Women's Actions   139
Wiring Participatory Democracy   148

7   **Crossing the Dividing Line: Spontaneity and
    Organization**   157

The Subject/Object Dialectic   157
Nodal Points   160
The Beginning of the End of Manicheanism and the
   Limits of Spontaneity   162
The Making of a Radical Intellectual   166
Vertiginous Intellectuals   171
Appendix: Fanon's periodization of the intellectual's
   relation with rural society   176

8 Nationalism and a New Humanism 177

The Question of Nationalism 177
Fanon's Theory of Nationalism: Two Types of
   Nationalism or Three? 179
Nationalism$_2$: The Overworked Peasant and the Lazy
   Intellectual 183
Humanism and Ideology 188
Political Education: How National Consciousness
   can Deepen into a Humanism 192
What Type of Organization for the Postcolonial Future? 200
In Place of a Conclusion 203

Notes 206
Bibliography 239
Index 242

Acknowledgments

This book could not have been written without the help, advice, and input of many friends, colleagues, and teachers over a number of years: Robert Bernasconi, Dave Black, George C. Bond, Drucilla Cornell, Mustafa Dhada, Raya Dunayevskaya, Emmanuel Eze, Irene Gendzier, David Johnston, Anne McClintock, Mahmood Mamdani, Manning Marable, Tony Marx, Jon Murphy, Edward W. Said, Ato Sekyi-Otu and T. Denean Sharpley-Whiting. The Institute of African Studies at Columbia University, Afro-American Studies at Harvard University, Africana Studies at Brown University, and the Institute of Liberal Arts and Interdisciplinary Studies at Emerson College provided institutional support. Students at Columbia University and Emerson College have helped refine and clarify ideas, and Joy Hayton at the Department of English and Comparative Literature at Columbia, as well as Gail Tetreault at Brown, and Tabitha Lee at Emerson have been very generous with resources and time.

Especial thanks go to Raymond Guess, Michael Mallick and Lou Turner; Teodros Kiros who read and commented on the whole manuscript; Lewis R. Gordon, who generously shared his office at Brown; and to Anthony Appiah and Skip Gates who made me welcome at Harvard. Friends and family, Patrick Deer, Neville Hoad and John Lawhead nurtured the project in its early days, as did Richard Barnes, of course. Kate Josephson encouraged the project and its author, and also advised me on matters psychoanalytic. Steven Mendel provided mental health and Seven Stars bakery provided sustenance. With great thanks to Alessio Assonitis who comforted me during the worst period of "Aidan's eye"; and to Marcelo Vazquez and Cecelia Blanco who never left our side at that terrible time. And to Aidan who lost his eye to retinoblastoma, but remains the wonder in my eye. I promised that the book be dedicated to that lost nearly four-year-old eye and so it is. Finally, to the memory of "Bantu" Steve Biko, for it was through Steve Biko that I met Frantz Fanon.

Sections of several of the chapters have been reworked and substantially revised from earlier essays. Part of chapter 1 appeared as "Dialectical Impasse: Turning the Table on Hegel and the Black," *Parallax*, no. 23 (2002); part of chapter 2 is based on my essay in *Contested Terrains and Constructed Categories: Contemporary Africa in Focus* (Westview Press, 2002); and different sections of chapter 6 first appeared in earlier forms as "Jammin the Airwaves and Tuning into the Revolution," in *Fanon: A Critical Reader* (Blackwell, 1996), "Beyond Manicheanism: Dialectics in the Thought of Frantz Fanon," *Journal of Political Ideology*, no. 12 (1999), and "The Oxygen of Revolution: Gendered Gaps and Radical Mutations in Frantz Fanon's *A Dying Colonialism*," *Philosophia Africana*, no. 8 (2001).

The author and publishers are also grateful to Grove/Atlantic, Inc. for permission to reproduce copyright material from Frantz Fanon, *Black Skin, White Masks* (New York, 1967) and *The Wretched of the Earth* (New York, 1968), and to Monthly Review Press for permission to quote from Fanon, *Studies in a Dying Colonialism* (New York, 1967) and *Toward the African Revolution: Political Essays* (New York, 1967).

Abbreviations for Fanon's Works

BS   *Black Skin, White Masks* (New York: Grove Press, 1967), translation by Charles Lam Markmann of *Peau noire, masques blancs* (Paris: Éditions du Seuil, 1952).

DC   *Studies in a Dying Colonialism* (New York: Monthly Review Press, 1967), translation by Haakon Chevalier of *L'An V de la révolution algérienne* (Paris: Maspero, 1959).

WE   *The Wretched of the Earth*, preface by Jean-Paul Sartre (New York: Grove Press, 1968), translation by Constance Farrington of *Les Damnés de la terre* (Paris: Maspero, 1961).

AR   *Toward the African Revolution: Political Essays* (New York: Grove Press, 1967), translation by Haakon Chevalier of *Pour la révolution africaine. Écrits politiques* (Paris: Maspero, 1964).

Introduction

When Frantz Fanon died on December 6, 1961, world politics was quite different. A newly independent Africa was emerging. In 1960, 16 African countries gained their independence, and freedom for Algeria, Fanon's adopted land, seemed near. At the same time, the world was locked in perhaps the most frozen moment of the Cold War. Yet, despite the passage of 40 years, the end of the Cold War, and a new stage of global consciousness, the oppressed of Fanon's book, and the dispossessed and discontented of today, speak in remarkably the same language of revenge and envy. The Manichean morality of an eye for an eye, of unequivocal notions of justice and injustice, remains a dominant term of world politics. What has not changed since Fanon's time are the world economic inequalities between rich and poor, with the Manichean framework of thinking and the feelings of desperation and despair that it expresses. Indeed, perhaps those feelings have become more pronounced as we have moved from the epoch of anticolonial struggle to a period of "the West and the rest," when alternatives to the increasing inequalities of capitalist globalization seem increasingly distant.

In this book I argue that Fanon's understanding of the colonial world is *not* Manichean. His categories are not simple binaries of Black and White (I have capitalized these terms throughout), of colonized and colonizer, and of victim and perpetrator. Despite the characterization of *The Wretched of the Earth* (*Les Damnés de la terre*) as a handbook of violence, underlined by Jean-Paul Sartre's influential introduction, Fanon is not simply a glorifier of violence. While he recognized the psychological and symbolic importance of

dépasser
transcend

the anticolonial violence in the context of the exponential imbalance of colonial violence, he indicated that violence was also a *problematic*. Here, I investigate this problematic in the context of Fanon's powerful critique of narrow anti-imperialist and nationalist politics, arguing that only a very distorted reading of his work could conclude that he believed liberation emerged solely from acts of violence. However, over the past two decades, the Fanon of *The Wretched of the Earth*, the political theorist of national liberation and its pitfalls, has been eclipsed by the Fanon concerned with race and representation. Another important preface, this time written by Homi Bhabha to the edition published in London of *Black Skin, White Masks* (*Peau noire, masques blancs*), proved influential by reinterpreting Fanon's work in term of the ambivalences of identity, shifting the focus away from the social and economic "realities" of colonial rule.[1]

If earlier political analysts had privileged the apparent economic simplicity of a violent zero-sum game between colonizer and colonized, the literary and cultural theorists of the 1990s avoided it, while privileging the apparent ambiguities of identity of *Black Skin*. In my mind, both approaches are seriously limited. Over the past few years works such as Lewis R. Gordon's *Fanon and the Crisis of European Man* and Ato Sekyi-Otu's *Fanon's Dialectic of Experience* have challenged this view. This book follows in this critical vein and considers Fanon's oeuvre as a whole. The problems Fanon addresses do not take place in a vacuum, but arise from distinct historical and social situations and the way people think about them. Thus, like other radical thinkers, Fanon engages the world around him in a quest to understand it and to change it. Fanon's move to Algeria, discussed in chapter 4, is a nodal point of the book. Chapters 1 to 3 concentrate on issues developed in *Black Skin*, chapters 5 to 8 address problematics of the anticolonical revolution.

Black Skin (BS) and *The Wretched of the Earth* (WE) appear quite different in that they reflect different experiences of French colonialism. The former discusses the problematic of an inferiority complex derived both from assimilating Frenchness in prewar Martinique and the experience of being Black in the years immediately after the war in metropolitan France; the latter is a product of a revolt against European colonialism in a settler colony. It might be argued that *The Wretched* reflects a more Manichean reality, and that Fanon's insights into the ambiguity of postcoloniality in *Black Skin* are the ones that really provide the basis for any lasting analysis beyond Manichean thinking. I will argue that taking Fanon as seriously as a consistent theorist necessitates a different approach.

Chronos – father god
~~War~~ *but time is father of us all*

In *Black Skin* Fanon insists that he does not come to proclaim "timeless truths." His analysis is rooted in the temporal: "Every human problem must be considered from the standpoint of time." The point is not simply historical, or solely contextual, but one of praxis: "The future should be an edifice supported by [the] living ... This structure is connected to the present to the extent that I consider the present in terms of something to be transcended [dépasser]" (*BS*, 12). It is in this spirit that I approach Fanon.

It has not been hard to categorize Fanon – he has been subject to myriad categorizations from Africa's philosopher king, to a prophet of violence; he has been understood as a Sartrean, a Marxist, a Hegelian, a Lacanian, a negritudist, a socialist, a Pan-Africanist, a founder of postcolonialism – but it is harder to place Fanon's originality. Most recently, Fanon's idea of lived experience (see chapter 5 of *Black Skin*) has been productively engaged as an attempt to engage Fanon on his own terms, for instance by Gordon and by Sekyi-Otu.[2] This is an important development which I entertain here. However, can Fanon be understood simply in terms of a totality of lived experience? Alone, the concept of "lived experience" is unable to overcome the duality of self and the world. For Fanon, the issue was not simply to describe the world of experience. What needed to be overturned was the situation itself, and in doing so the protagonist could become self-determining. Concerned with understanding the "inferiority complex" among middle-class Blacks, *Black Skin* is quite a different work from *The Wretched*, where the concern about inferiority complexes hardly makes an appearance. What makes Fanon's work of a piece is Fanon's dialectic. That is not to say that the dialectic is worked out theoretically in *Black Skin* and simply applied to his later work. Fanon's dialectic itself undergoes development, takes on concretion, in terms of the Algerian revolution: both its radical possibilities and its internal problematics, such as in his prescient critique of the limitations of national consciousness. Nevertheless, his abhorrence of bourgeois society is quite unmistakable in *Black Skin*, which concludes that "intellectual alienation is a creation of bourgeois society ... a closed society in which life has no taste, in which the air is tainted, in which ideas and men are corrupt" (*BS*, 224). And it is not inconsequential that Fanon begins his conclusion of *Black Skin* with a long epigraph from Marx's *Eighteenth Brumaire of Louis Bonaparte* (written as a response to Bonaparte's coup in 1851 and as a summary of the 1848 revolution in France), about the need for revolutions to strip themselves of the past, for it was precisely this suffocating, corrupt nationalist bourgeoisie that became the problematic of *The Wretched*.

pre knowle before takes place

past → revolution

Fanon was not a central figure nor a leader of the FLN (Front de la Libération Nationale – National Liberation Front). He was not involved in leadership decisions. He was not an important diplomat, though he did represent the provisional government of Algeria in Ghana. He was not a military strategist, though he did embark on an important reconnaissance trip to open up a new front in the south-west. Fanon's day-to-day activity as a member of the FLN was as a journalist, or perhaps more precisely a propagandist of the Algerian revolution, for *El Moudjahid*. Many of his articles are addressed to the French left, imploring them to do something to help the Algerian struggle against the French. Fanon's collection, *Studies in a Dying Colonialism* (DC) (*L'An V de la révolution algérienne* – Year Five of the Algerian Revolution)[3] is, I argue, a masterful rearticulation of the dialectic of lived experience in terms of revolutionary transformation; an attempt to communicate the construction of a new Algeria to a largely French audience. Yet just as *Black Skin* is a theoretical polemic, *The Wretched* is an attempt to make a theoretical intervention into the emerging postcolonial Africa. Grounded in the Algerian revolution, the work offers new beginning points to such old issues as agency and organization, and the role of the intellectual in social movements. Fanon's theorization of the organization emerging from within the anticolonial struggle intimates his vision of the post-independence future. While the concept of lived experience gives tremendous insight into Fanon's life and work in order to make sense of his theoretical legacy, to understand Fanon's ability to sum up a period which had still not ended at his death, to comprehend the trajectory of Africa's decolonization, an idea of a dialectic is required.

An Abbreviated Biography

Born in Fort-de-France, the capital of Martinique, in 1925 to middle-class parents, Frantz Fanon grew up speaking and thinking of himself as French. In high school he took classes with the negritude poet, Aimé Césaire, who had made the shocking declaration that it was good to be Black. Before finishing school, Fanon, who had had enough of the Vichy rule in Martinique, as well as its racist sailors in dock at Fort-de-France, joined the resistance. He left Martinique in 1943 to fight for the "Free French,"[4] returning to Martinique in 1945 to help Césaire in an election campaign for mayor of Fort-de-France on the Communist ticket. The war had a radicalizing effect.

He had fought, he had been injured, he had been decorated, but more importantly he had realized that it was not only Vichy France that was racist but French civilization itself. Stationed in North Africa, he experienced the French race–caste system with the Whites at the top and the Senegalese, the first to be sent into battle, at the bottom.

The center still beckoned and in 1947 Fanon left Martinique. While reading philosophy, he studied psychiatry at Lyon medical school, defending his thesis in 1951. His first idea for a thesis, what he called a "sociodiagnostic" of Antillean alienation – *Black Skin* – was turned down by his academic sponsors. *Black Skin* describes the "lived experience of the Black" (discussed in chapters 1 and 2 below), whose body image is associated with the absence of human value through the White (racial) gaze: In France "I discovered my Blackness, my ethnic characteristics; I was battered down by tom toms, cannibalism, spiritual backwardness, fetishism, race defects, slave ships and above all *Y'a bon Banania*" (*BS*, 12).[5] Fanon refused an easy answer. He embraced negritude but was mindful of its definitions of a Black "essence" (see chapter 3 below).

After medical school Fanon took a position at Blida-Joinville Psychiatric Hospital in Algiers, and tried, with limited success, to put some of his radical ideas about hospital reform into practice (see chapter 4). The failure of the experiments led to a fundamental reorganization of his thinking and practice. Though Fanon did not make a detailed study of Arab culture (Fanon's mostly fruitless attempts to learn Arabic heightened his sensitivity to issues of language), he did investigate culturally sensitive approaches that resulted in the establishment of the first "day hospital" in Africa. A year after he arrived at Blida-Joinville, the Algeria war of liberation began (November 1954). Finding it increasingly difficult to practice psychiatry in the context of increasing militarization, violence, and torture, Fanon resigned his position and left Algeria in December 1956. Renouncing French citizenship, he became a full-time revolutionary and editor of *El Moudjahid*. His analyses of the changes that the Algerian revolution had wrought on social relations and on society were collected in *L'An V*, which was published in 1959 (see chapter 6 below). In 1959 Fanon became the FLN's permanent representative in Accra, Ghana. A year later he took part in a field trip to Mali with the intention of opening up a third front and developing anticolonial solidarity across the Sahara. That same year, however, he was diagnosed with leukemia. His experiences in the Algerian revolution, his knowledge of its political tendencies and

What is Manicheanism? (handwritten)

debates, his observations about Ghana, alongside the murder of Patrice Lumumba, the democratically elected Prime Minister of the independent Congo in 1960, provided the backdrop for his final book, *The Wretched of the Earth* (see chapters 5, 7 and 8 below). The work was finished after a ten-week explosion of intellectual energy in May 1961. His was an "intellect on fire"[6] that would only be extinguished by his death at the end of the year.[7]

Key Terms

Though Fanon's formal training was in medicine and psychiatry, he also studied philosophy, and throughout his life he continued an engagement with some of the "great" thinkers of European modernity such as Hegel, Marx, Freud, Sartre, and Merleau-Ponty, testing their ideas through a confrontation with the dehumanized situation created by racism and colonialism (see chapters 1 and 2 below). Fanon's humanist project was to understand as well as to abolish the divisive and hierarchical zones that divide, fragment, and destroy human beings. Thus the thesis of this book is a fairly simple one. Though often remembered for his powerful descriptions of, and prescriptions for, a violent engagement with colonialism and its logic, his project and goal is to get beyond Manicheanism both in its colonial form and as an anticolonial reaction. By *Manicheanism* I mean a binary system of thought that paints the world as split between good and evil. Its roots go back to the religion of Mani (third century of the common era), which viewed the creators of the world, God and the Devil, as still fighting it out.[8] Manichean consciousness appears to be a "rich" kind of knowledge, but is in fact quite impoverished.[9] The roots of racial and colonial Manicheanism in the modern period are found in the European Enlightenment,[10] which viewed Europe as the center of the world and the bringer of light to "distant regions." Both Kant and Hegel developed this idea, describing the "Negro" as childish, lazy, indolent and slow, lacking in history and humanity, and needing coercive measures such as chattel slavery to force them to be productive. In the colonialist's eyes, the native is a bit of laziness stretched out in the sun, thick-skinned like a crocodile, who only responds to force. Colonial thought, from travel literature of the nineteenth century to administrative and psychological services of the twentieth, was built on Enlightenment categories embellished by imperial scientism. It painted the native as the quintessence of evil, and the colonizer as

defined (handwritten margin note)

Enlight (handwritten margin note)

racism (handwritten margin note)

idea of innate racial difference ≠essence? ≈essence? (handwritten margin note)

Scientism pseudoscience (handwritten note)

respect, obligation

the apogee of good: "The Negro is a being, whose nature and dispositions are not merely different from those of the European, they are the reverse of them," said the author of an inquiry into a revolt in Haiti written in 1792. Thus Blacks needed to be treated only with violence and abuse: "Kindness and compassion excite in his breast implacable and deadly hatred; but stripes, and insults, and abuse, generate gratitude, affection and inviolable attachment."[11] A few years later the ideas of the French revolution reached the shores of Haiti, and under Toussaint L'Ouverture a proclamation of liberty and equality was unfurled. The slaves won their freedom and the historical right to be part of the modern world.[12]

Violence not only described the rosy dawn of colonization, but was at the heart of the settler colonist regimes.[13] Anticolonial thought was often an inversion of colonial Manicheanism – that what was good for the colonized was bad for the colonialist. While Fanon appreciated the power of this inversion, especially as it was expressed positively by the negritude poets like Césaire, on the one hand, and by the peasantry or the laborer on the other, his theoretical contribution was to *problematize* the Manichean certainties and at the same time try to develop new concepts out of this problem. By attempting to get beyond Manicheanism, Fanon was part of an emerging postcolonial debate about subjugation and subjectivity, about discourse and agency, about power and identity, about tradition and modernity, *avant la lettre*. His employment of the terms "Black" and "White" and "native" and "colon" are also attempts to understand them: not to be defined by them but to challenge and get beneath them.

Key words

Fanon contested the European liberal humanist view of the *subject*, arguing that in the colonial situation, the natives, the tribespeople, the masses, the peasantry, and so on, are so utterly dehumanized by the violence of colonial reality and its discourses that they seem unable to articulate their own thoughts. Yet he did not abandon the concept of subject nor that of subjugated knowledge. He is not simply a critic of colonial discourse, understanding that the colonized and colonizer are caught up in a complex web of relations; and though silenced, the native is *not completely* silent. Colonialism wills itself to be totalitarian and the foundation of a new way of life, but paradoxically its hegemony is based purely on force – it always prefers the military option – going to great lengths to separate the native and the European. And so it turns out that colonialism is not, in fact, as omnipresent as it first appears. Cultures that were practiced before colonial domination have been destroyed, but just as importantly, they have remained. Yet what remains is also drawn into the Manichean vortex produced by colonialism, making even the most retrograde "precolonial" cultural practices "anticolonialist." Aware of this dilemma, Fanon emphasized the reinvigoration of culture during a liberatory struggle which gives birth to new social practices and the recrafting of a possible national identity (see chapter 6 below).

The theoretical problem of getting beyond the categories of race is powerfully expressed in *Black Skin*. Unwilling to be defined by the Other, Fanon does not shy away from it. In other words, there is a moment in *Black Skin* when Fanon embraces Black consciousness as an absolute and doesn't want anyone else to tell him otherwise. The force of Fanon's representation of the Manichean reaction has led many to think that he is in fact simply its advocate. But, in Fanon's mind, it is only by embracing the reaction to White construction of the Black, or the colonial construction of the colonized, that one can deconstruct it and thus begin to get beyond it. Though the reaction to the Other's construction remains within the terms of the first – as a reactive action – it is only through a critique of this necessary kind of action that one gets to a new moment of self-knowledge and thereby an ability to explode Manicheanism. The experience is both psychologically and intellectually liberating. This move, I hope to show, is dialectical and historical. At first, that is in *Black Skin*, Fanon refuses to be "bogged down" by history, to be a slave of slavery. He proclaims that "I am my own foundation" and he insists against Sartre that such a move is profoundly dialectical. Yet it is through his involvement with the Algerian revolution that Fanon's dialectic, with its emphasis on immanence and subjectivity, is a celebration of the genius at once of invention and of liberation.

My emphasis on Fanon's critique, rather than dismissal, of Hegel's dialectic underlines how Fanon's *dialectic* is developed in response to the colonial Manicheanism, a dialectic of liberation which aims at real social change. I consider Fanon's dialectic as a movement through absolute, irreconcilable contradictions. In contrast to a static inert binarism, I want to emphasize how the unstable, critical, and creative element in Fanon's thought is produced in an almost debased struggle with Manicheanism. But such a conceptualization of dialectic, I argue, puts in question the apparent parallelism between Fanon's description of the static colonial/racial Manicheanism and his description of the creativity and movement of national liberation. In other words, there is a difference between

Freud

the colonial period – where the settler is the unceasing cause, the sole subject of history – and the period of national liberation, where "the 'thing' which has been colonized" becomes a historical protagonist. To recognize the difference between the settler's logic and the native's subjective response turns on fleshing out the meaning of a dialectic of revolution in Fanon's thought.

Fanon's engagement with Freud and *psychoanalytic theory* will also be explored. Because, in the Manichean world of race, there is no possible agreement on the level of reason, Fanon chooses "the method of regression" (*BS*, 123). If Fanon's dialectic of self-consciousness includes a movement backward, that movement is also expressed psychoanalytically.[14] In the colonial situation, Fanon maintains that the native acts in a way *akin* to a neurosis. If dream formation is the retrogressive movement of a desire, tracing the dream backward reveals the source of the neurosis. It is not Blacks who are neurotics, but the anti-Black society; yet it is an analysis of the neurotic, who happens to be Black, that gives insight into the sociodiagnostic of the quest for recognition. There symptoms are expressed in racial terms. In *Black Skin*, the dream of magically turning White reflects the Martinican reality that one is White above a certain financial level (*BS*, 44). In *The Wretched*, the native still desires to take the place of the colon and achieves freedom during sleep in dreams of running, jumping, and in expressions of muscular activity. Similar to Freud's *Civilization and its Discontents*, Fanon looks to sociogeny, while emphasizing human activity. Yet for Fanon, an understanding of Black experience must highlight the social environment, not the family environment, if one is going to get to the source, because every neurosis is a product of a cultural situation (reflected in books, films, comics, and so forth). Thus, in Martinique, the Oedipus Complex does not exist because the family structure is cast back into the id and the absence of the father is connected with the presence of "the colonial father," represented, for example, by the statue of the White general who "freed" the slaves.

While Fanon argues that the clinical analysis has to be primarily economic (*BS*, 11), it is expressed symptomatically in neuroses. In Freudian terms, economics is understood as a psychic energy that is driven inward when not allowed expression. In a racist society, the channeling of that energy results in an annihilation of presence. Thus, rather than recognition, the slave experiences nonrecognition. The dialectic appears blocked off. Yet driven to "know thyself," Fanon plumbs the painful depths of negritude, which provides him with a glimpse of an alternative (see chapter 3 below).

econo = psychic energy (libidinal)

Fanon's appreciation of dialectic as *lived experience*, namely the actual experience of Blacks living in a racist society, allows him to embrace apparently contradictory positions and work them out. Fanon confronted each alienated situation that he faced – whether in Martinique, France, or Algeria – by getting so thoroughly and deeply involved in it that he was able to analyze the situation without being taken over by it. This is the essence of his conception of the dialectic of experience. Lived experience is central to Fanon's critique of the internalization of the racial gaze in *Black Skin*, yet Fanon wonders by the end of the book how it will be possible to uproot the "inferiority complex" and abolish alienation. Some have argued that violence provides the missing link. I maintain that it is Fanon's conception of lived experience, when considered in the historical epoch of anticolonial struggle, that provides the creative principle. I argue that Fanon translates lived experience of this struggle as a "radical mutation in consciousness." Without a change in consciousness, violence alone can only lead to barbarism. As with other conceptions, Fanon's claims about change – *radical mutation* – affecting social relations, including those inside the family, as well as attitudes to technology, like the radio, or to dress, like the issue of veiling – have been controversial (see chapter 6).

Answering Some Critics

Since his death in 1962, criticisms have been directed at Fanon's analysis of the Algerian revolution and by implication his theory of social change. In its crudest form, the argument is that Fanon could not possibly understand Algeria, Arabs, or Islam, because he was neither Algerian nor Muslim.[15] Fanon's idea of "lived experience" could not apply because the Algerian does not experience colonialism on the basis of corporeal identity.[16] Yet the importance of lived experience of the body-subject is not reducible, I believe, to an essential identity. In *The Wretched*, corporeal experience is expressed spatially, physically hemming the native into "spaces of terror." According to Fanon, these spaces are policed not only by the colonial regime but also by malevolent spirits which are able to keep the people in their place. In their minds this "unreal world" is even more powerful than colonialism. As the colonial regime is challenged, the consciousness of these spatial restrictions breaks up. Additionally, his analyses of the dying colonial body, and the importance of a new, lively motion in the corporeality of the *apparently—as far as one knows or can see.*

colonized, are not simply speculative but based on his observations of dehumanization among the colonized, gained in his work with his patients and with torture victims (see chapter 4 below) and observations during the war of liberation (see chapter 6).

For Fanon, lived experience is empirical and phenomenological. Even if one feels like a foreigner in the world, it doesn't diminish the reality of the world, nor does the reality of the world diminish the feeling of alienation. One does not have to experience torture to understand it, nor does one have to be born in Algeria to empathize with the plight of Algerians under French colonialism. Additionally, what was "Algeria" under colonial rule is contested and open to discussion. As late as 1936, in a debate about assimilation with France, Ferhat Abbas maintained that "the Algerian fatherland" did not exist.[17] Others responded that it did. Some emphasized Islam,[18] while others questioned Islam as synonymous with Algerian identity, and still others insisted on a more secular vision.[19]

During the Algerian revolution, Fanon identified himself as an Algerian, and constructed himself as an Algerian revolutionary. He regarded revolution and Algeria as synonymous, and was not interested in discovering an "essential" Algeria outside of that equation. While this might have put him in the political minority, the position is internally consistent. What is trickier is a general problem that includes Fanon, namely, the relationship of the intellectual and the masses. Fanon makes an important contribution to this question, highlighting how it is the intellectual's consciousness of separateness that is the key to discerning the work to be done. In other words, it is the degree to which the intellectual realizes his or her estrangement from "the people" that fruitfully problematizes the identity of lived experience with knowledge and representation.

Ironically, some of the criticisms of Fanon have remained within the same Manichean frame that he was attempting to break out of. Many of the very issues Fanon was trying to address – the pitfalls of national consciousness, the problematic of Black consciousness, the deficiencies of spontaneous action, the issue of inferiority complexes, the ideas of "modernity" and "tradition"[20] – have been turned back on him. He has been damned from both sides. For example, it has been argued that Fanon is uncritical of "tribal chiefs,"[21] on the one hand, and that he was a political authoritarian who ran roughshod over ethnic difference, on the other.[22] It is argued that Fanon overestimated the degree of change taking place in gender relations,[23] or that he was a cultural conservative upholding traditions like the veil.[24] Some conclude that Fanon, away from the political center, had very little influence on events in Algeria.[25] Others damn Fanon for having too much influence.[26]

Many of these criticisms share the problem not only of decontextualization, but also decontextualization of the sources. My approach is to flesh out Fanon's understanding, not the events themselves, still openly contested over 40 years on.[27]

Fanon was a critic of European racism and African decolonization in a period of radical possibility after World War Two. To begin to grasp Fanon's project, it is absolutely essential to historicize his experiences and his intellectual contexts, and though he still has much to say in our age, he is very much a product of his time and place. In the preceding pages I have alluded to the general question of context. I use the term tentatively, aware of the ongoing debate indebted to Quentin Skinner's work[28] where the invocation of "context" and "intentionality" often function as rhetorical shorthand (or sleight-of-hand) for truth claims. In this forensic context (as it were), my underlying argument could be easily construed as a proposal to supply a fuller intellectual and social context for Fanon and thereby produce a superior understanding; one possessing a greater degree of "reality" because it incorporates subjective intention in a Skinnerian sense – that is, understanding the historical meaning of the text by considering what the author was trying to do in the political (social and ideological) context in which he was writing. I hope it becomes clear in the following that this definition does not exhaust what I am doing. John Keane's point that political argument often comes "into its own only during crisis conditions" finds an echo in Fanon, who developed theory in such a crisis condition where "conventional beliefs and unargued assumptions begin to disintegrate."[29] During such destabilized and potentially creative situations, the very notion of context *determining* the meaning of a text comes into question.[30]

The similarities of experiences under colonization meant for Fanon that the African struggle against colonialism, whether that was British or French, had to take a national form. Other identities such as regional, ethnic, racial, or religious would degenerate into xenophobia and racism. Whether identity has to be national (with a citizenship open to all) in the postcolonial world is open to discussion, but no other unifying concept has yet emerged to challenge Fanon's point. Nevertheless, for Fanon, national consciousness was not the goal but only the ground upon which a new humanism could develop. Part of his critique was that the national bourgeoisie was an unproductive class, a huckstering caste, already senile, who would rip off rather than "develop" the nation.[31] This insight has been proved empirically, yet how did Fanon envision development? Critical of the national organizations which treated the people in a similar fashion to the colonists, Fanon promoted a decentralized organization, staffed by ethically upright and patient militants, where "development" would be a problematic; a long-term human endeavor involving the mass of people in discussion.

Today, globalization and economic liberalization has often engendered a reduction of nation-states to enforcers of transnational organizations and networks of global capital. In quite a different time, Fanon claimed that the end of colonialism would be truly expressed in the reformation and recreation of a vibrant national culture which had its basis in revolutionary transformation rather than ethnic identity, with a future constructed by all who wanted to play a positive part. In other words, it was not the development of a juridical nation, but a social individual that was at issue. To argue that such changes did not occur because of the bulwark of "tradition" or the strictures of the world market does not undermine Fanon's normative argument. For Fanon, anticolonial nationalism was limited as a united front against a common enemy. It was the question of what happened after colonialism ended that needed to be answered creatively. He attempted to address this by developing new concepts and initiating new forms of communication and "political education,"[32] which in the postcolonial society, would be fermented from the bottom up. Fanon died too early to see the concrete outcome of the anticolonial struggle, but he left important critical indicators (see chapter 8).

For Fanon, active resistance was the first stage toward self-discovery, and he was well aware that in its early stages anticolonial action was an inversion of colonial Manicheanism and remained within its framework. The native, formerly battered and dehumanized, jealous, resentful and angry, simply wanted to take the place of the colonizer. Fanon understood this envy but did not judge it.[33] In fact the native's reaction, insofar as it is an understanding that colonialism is a zero-sum game, expressed the truth. Colonialism kept control through violence, but in Fanon's Freudian economy the native's reaction, which had become internalized, was forced to emerge somewhere. Unable to attack the source, natives "beat each other up." "Traditions," including religions, often appease, exhausting the pent-up emotions by appearing even more frightening than colonialism. While such "traditions" serve the function of bringing colonialism down to size, once the period of decolonization has begun they could become a barrier to new cultural developments.

Fanon warns of the barbarity and the tragedy of a political program built on revenge, saying that such a program is a disgraceful thing. Yet he explains how the sense of deprivation and humiliation, the jealousy and the rage, in the context of political and social repression, produce such reactions. These reactions cannot be dismissed simply as politically childish. In fact, sadly, they express a truth and an understanding of the appalling thing about anticolonial violence, that for a community it can be laden with meaning and restore a sense of self-respect. Thus rather than ending the cycle, counterviolence and counterterror, the bombings and shooting merely reinforce the aggressiveness. If in the past the gangster became a hero, today it is the suicide bomber. Fanon's idea of violence engendering counterviolence, which not long ago seemed to have aged so badly, is now (for instance, in Israel/ Palestine) considered "prescient." We remain within a zero-sum Manichean vortex. It is not that a lack of value is assigned to life, but that for the "native," life is already a living death. Rather than resolving this problem, globalization, with the increasing inequalities of the haves and the have-nots, has simply sharpened the resentment and valorized memories of resistance.

At a different point in history, namely the period of decolonization, the problem, Fanon argued, was to gain control of this anger, to explain it and channel it. This channeling demanded a new kind of intellectual work and political education. Today the alternative new humanism, what Fanon called the working out of new concepts, while not on the horizon, seems all the more necessary. If Fanon was an idealist, he was deeply rooted in the "real world" (see chapter 2). Not simply the product of a historical context, Fanon was a visionary whose view of human reciprocity was intimated in the radical mutation of consciousness engendered by the social revolution. That the revolution degenerated does not negate its truth; it simply makes Fanon's critique of its pitfalls all the more compelling. In *L'An V* he attempted to record the social transformations engendered by the Algerian revolution, and though he argued later, in *The Wretched*, that more than recording was required, he never abandoned the liberatory vision. Rather than an artifact of a previous time, Fanon's work, 40 years after his death, still remains compelling. The goal of this book is to bring Fanon's thought back to life and present the vitality of an "intellect on fire."

1

The Racial Gaze: Black Slave, White Master

For my part, I refuse to consider the problem from the standpoint of *either-or* . . . what is all this talk of a black people of a Black nationality. I am a Frenchman. I am interested in French culture, French civilization, the French people. We refuse to be considered "outsiders," we are fully part of the French drama.

Fanon, *Black Skin, White Masks*

When Frantz Fanon arrived in France in 1947 the nation was in flux; shaken by the war, it now faced radical movements for change, including a new "Third World" struggling for independence, as well as the solidifying of the Cold War into spheres of influence. Two years after the end of World War Two French radical critics, no longer outsiders, were becoming a dominant group among the literati and public opinion.[1] The participants in Alexandre Kojève's lectures on Hegel's master/slave dialectic of the late 1930s (Aron, Bataille, Breton, Lacan, Merleau-Ponty, among others) were part of this emergent intelligentsia, Sartre and Merleau-Ponty's *Les Temps Modernes* was the journal of discussion[2] and *Présence Africaine*, founded in 1947,[3] expressed the bringing of the African presence into the very center of French civilization.[4] The African "presence," putting Western civilization on trial, represented a new kind of postwar anticolonial militancy, while Paris "became one of the theaters in which the political and cultural future of Africa was being prepared."[5] In the French constitution of 1946 colonialism disappeared, replaced by a new union of citizenship and parliamentary representation supposedly ending forced labor and the colonial education. Yet the reality of this union was made clear in Madagascar a year later when 100,000 Malagasy were slaughtered.

Black Skin was written in this context. Published in 1952, with references to philosophy, politics, literature, psychoanalysis, film, and popular culture, combined with what seems like an authorial and autobiographical "I," it can create in the reader a certain uneasiness. Nevertheless, the book represents Fanon's profound ability to both synthesize and critically engage phenomenological and psychoanalytic theory through the prism of race.[6] In fact, Fanon's methodology in *Black Skin* is fairly straightforward; race becomes the lens through which social relations and theories of the time are judged. The honesty of his approach is illustrated in his description of the "lived experience" of the Black who "has two dimensions," two ways of being, "one with his fellows, the other with the White man." In other words, Blacks behave differently among Whites than among Blacks. This behavior is not ontological but a product of colonial relations. Among Whites, the Black experiences no intersubjectivity, no reciprocity. The Black is simply an object among other objects. Why is this? How does it happen? These are two questions Fanon tries to ask and which express his quest for reciprocal human relations.[7]

The specific subject of *Black Skin* is the disalienation of the Antillean who, mired in a "dependency complex," wishes to turn White. Fanon's conceptualization of alienation is essentially medical, a neurosis (see *BS*, 204), but he employs it in a social context so that donning a White mask is equated with a false self, an inauthentic self in Sartre's terms, or a false consciousness in Marxian terms. Establishing a process of "disalienation" moves Fanon away from a medical model toward a radical social conception of praxis, which is based on a belief that human beings are reflective and actional, beings of praxis. *Black Skin* can be seen as a painstaking examination leading in myriad ways to the same conclusion, namely the necessity of uprooting the conditions that cause alienation. Disalienation calls for a nihilation, the ripping away of the masks and a *reintegration* of the human being's presence:

> I have been led to consider their alienation in terms of psychoanalytical classifications. The Black's behavior makes him *akin* to an obsessive neurotic type, or, if one prefers, he puts himself into a complete *situational* neurosis. In the man of color there is a constant effort to run away from his own individuality, to *annihilate* his own presence. (*BS*, 60, emphasis added)

Because the Black needs White approval, it is impossible to defend against the lack of reciprocity through ego withdrawal. Consequently the Black's behavior – which is not necessarily neurotic – appears neurotic.

Fanon's attempt to get out of the bind of the inferiority complex is at first psychoanalytic, but then he immediately declares that because the Black's alienation is not an individual question, his approach will be "sociodiagnostic," entailing "immediate recognition of social and economic realities" (*BS*, 11). Thus, diagnostically and proscriptively, the analysis shifts from the individual to the social realm. Thus we begin with Fanon's engagement with the phenomenologies of Sartre, Merleau-Ponty and especially Hegel's master/slave dialectic before moving to psychoanalytic theories.

The Black is a "crucified person," maintains Fanon, who "has no culture, no civilization, 'no long historical past.'" Thus stripped, the existence and Being of the Black is an inferiority complex (*BS*, 216, 34). Such a complex is created in *every* people experiencing the death of their own local cultural originality (*BS*, 18). Civilization is solely French and the Antillean's culture is French.[8] On the scale of humanity, those who write and speak proper French are more civilized. In Paris the Martinican is at the top of the Black pecking order, but it is a *Black* pecking order. The Antillean is seen as Black but the intradistinction of the Antillean pecking order means that the Guadeloupan tries to "pass" as Martinican. The Senegalese is at the bottom and on the other side is the White, the transcendental Other.

Speaking "proper" French is a symbol of authority. Dialect not only places one geographically and socially, but it is a way of thinking. The problem was exemplified by the Martinican in France. Here was a group of people who had grown up speaking, thinking, and looking French. How could Antilleans look French? Because they believed they were, having fully internalized French culture. They had grown up reading Tarzan stories and talking about "our ancestors the Gaul," identifying themselves not only "with the exploiter and the bringer of civilization," but with "an all-white truth" (*BS*, 146–7). At school in Martinique children wrote essays like little Parisians: "I like vacations because then I can run through the fields, breathe fresh air, and come home with *rosy* cheeks" (*BS*, 162 n25). The young educated Martinicans considered themselves White and dream themselves as White. Though Lacan's "Mirror Stage" is clearly suggestive here, it was Sartre's analysis of *The Anti-Semite and the Jew* that provided an important beginning for

Fanon's thinking through of this problem. What attracted Fanon to Sartre's work was both his phenomenological descriptions and his call for action. Authenticity is manifested in revolt, not by accepting the objectification of oneself by others.[9]

The Jew and Black Consciousness

The Jew is a Jew because the Jew is determined by the Other, argues Sartre: "the Jew has a personality like the rest of us, and on top of that he is Jewish. It amounts to a doubling of the fundamental relationship with the Other. The Jew is over-determined."[10] For Fanon this spoke directly to the problematic of the Black.

Fanon found resonances with the types plotted in *The Anti-Semite and the Jew*. He drew out similarities between the anti-Semite and the racist as a Manichean, irrational type and he explicated the French democrat's insistence that the Jew should assimilate in terms of racism. He found equally important Sartre's description of the Jew's attempted flight from others and himself. Alienated from his own body, and "his emotional life has been cut in two," the Jew pursues "the impossible dream of universal brotherhood in a world that rejects him."[11] Sartre argued that Jewish authenticity could not mean assimilation. Assimilation would amount to inauthenticity because it cannot be realized as long as there is anti-Semitism. The same could be said of the goal of assimilation of the educated Black, the évolué, into a racist society. It leads to the inferiority complexes analyzed in *Black Skin*.[12] The assimilation proposed by the White liberal (Sartre's democrat) is, as Steve Biko put it, like "expecting the slave to work together with the slave-master's son to remove all the conditions leading to the former's enslavement."[13] A nonracial approach pretends that racism doesn't exist and ignores its denigrating and derisive psychological effects. In contrast to assimilation, authenticity means realizing one's condition and asserting one's being as "untouchable, scorned, proscribed" and standing apart.

Sartre's claim that the Jew derives pride from humiliation might seem a strange and psychologically damaging basis for subjectivity, but "this haunted man [is] condemned to make his choice on the basis of false problems and in a false situation." Truth is mediated by the anti-Semitic situation. The choice is between the anti-Semite's congenital lie and the Jew's own lie which, in an anti-Semitic society, acquires a dimension of truth. The possibility of authenticity, therefore, can only be fully understood by understanding inauthenticity as a flight from the accusations of Jewishness through a Jewish type of anti-Semitism.[14] This flight powerfully prefigures the action of the educated and alienated Black évolué in *Black Skin* whose life is nothing but a long flight from others and from themselves. As Sartre says, "he has been alienated even from his own body; his emotional life has been cut in two; he has been reduced to pursuing the impossible dream of universal brotherhood in a world that rejects him."[15]

To be a Jew is to be *"abandoned to* the situation of a Jew," yet to "realize one's Jewish condition" in an anti-Semitic world requires a struggle. The authentic Jew fights and *"makes himself a Jew,* in the face of all and against all." Just as inauthenticity is a flight from the world, authenticity can only be realized in the world and though every response has to begin with the individual, there can be no authentic response to anti-Semitism at an individual level. Thus made social by the anti-Semite, the Jew becomes the social man *par excellence,* because "his torment is social."[16]

Putting the Black in the place of the Jew and racist in place of anti-Semite, Fanon felt the power of Sartre's argument. The authentic Jew is condemned to make a choice and "ceases to run away from the obligation to live in a situation that is defined precisely by the fact that it is unlivable . . . [and] derives pride from his humiliation."[17] What is a Jew? The Jew is one whom others consider a Jew. To Sartre's famous quip, "it is the anti-Semite who *makes* the Jew," Fanon adds that it is the White who makes the Black.

How could the Antillean Black make a choice? In the Antilles[18] the Black was French but in Paris the Black found it impossible to be French because, despite arguments to the contrary, Frenchness was equated with Whiteness. The Black was at best a "Black." The characteristic "wandering" diasporic Jew, "never sure of his possessions," found its apogee in the Black who had been systematically enslaved and uprooted.

Authentic assimilation is created not from external pressure but through an openness to the Other as a meeting of equals. In other words, an assimilation which risks self-certainty, which tears off the mask, but in which the self is challenged and sustained. Action implies risk, and authenticity requires giving up insularity. Authenticity needs to be grounded in the historical context, which itself is changing and changeable. Stasis would indicate the end of authenticity.

At the beginning of *Black Skin* Fanon asserted that he didn't think that the Black could accomplish an "authentic upheaval." He realized that such a possibility was itself based on the fact that the Black had not struggled for freedom but had had freedom given by the colonial master. The "liberation of man of color from himself" requires a "descent into a real hell" (*BS*, 10), and an "internal revolution" (*BS*, 198) that had to make meaning for itself, and from the depths of that descent reclaim the subjugated and ongoing history of revolt.

Unlike the Jew, who still has a sense of being unknown, or being able to "pass" in White society, the Black is overdetermined from the outside. The possibility of an existence outside of external appearance is denied to the Black. The Jew is "overdetermined from within," the Black from without.

By becoming an intellectual the Jew can transcend the body. Why can't the Black do the same? "The Jew is disliked from the moment he is tracked down," Fanon says, "but in my case everything takes on a *new* guise. I am given no chance. I am overdetermined from without. I am the slave not of the 'idea' that others have of me but of my own appearance" (*BS*, 115–16). The Jew can escape through a disembodied intellectualism, but there is no escape for the Black. Condemned to the life of the body, there is no memory and no history. The Black is body and the body's death *is* death. The Black is penis. How can you associate Rodin's thinker with an erection? The Black cannot become Phaedro.[19] "The Black symbolizes biological danger; the Jew, the intellectual danger" (*BS*, 165). The Jew is the internal Other, the Black the external Other.

At first this difference, based on skin color, seems obvious. But isn't the Jew spoken of in the same terms? *Because* the Jew cannot be "seen" their ability to pollute gentile society could be far more threatening. They must be marked out. Both the Jew and the Black have to be constructed. The eye does not assign value, "the image of the biological-sexual-sensual-genital-nigger" is a result of socialization. The fact that the site and the sight of difference, the circumcised penis, is also overdetermined signifies more than a fear of castration. Circumcision marks the Jewish male as sexually apart. The Jew is anatomically different, but the Black is purely anatomical, purely sexual, utterly different. Fanon agrees with the Freudian psychoanalyst Marie Bonaparte that the anti-Semite projects onto the Jew all "his own more or less unconscious bad instincts." The same function of "fixation" is assumed by the Black in the United States, adds Bonaparte. What the Jew and the Black share, admits Fanon, is that both stand for "evil."

The association of the Jew with making money (the fetish of money begetting money as if it were alive) is linked to an anthro-

pomorphized phallus, as though it is alive and "out of control."
It is "deviant genitalia," as Sander Gilman puts it. The parallel
between the Jew and prostitute, both economically and sexually, is
mapped on top of an older European topos of Jew as polluting. The
Jew, of course, is also behind the prostitute in more ways than one.
Driving women to prostitution, they are the pimps, brothel owners
and infectors of women: "The prostitute is little more than a Jew
herself . . . Both are on the margins of 'polite' society." The Jew is
the outsider. Associated with disease, the Jew "becomes the surrogate for all marginal males."[20] The Jew has long been associated
with sexual pollution, with syphilis and with other sexually transmitted diseases, just as the Jewish body has long been associated
"with the image of the mutilated, diseased, different appearance of
genitalia." From the Jew's phallus to the Jew's nose, Jews bear their
diseased sexuality on their skin. The stigma of syphilis is dark skin.
Like leprosy, syphilis supposedly turns the skin "Black." In the
Manichean world of anti-Semitism, Blackness marks the syphilitic
and separates the Jew from the White Christian. Because the Jew
is naturally syphilitic, the Jew is "naturally" Black: "their sexual
pathology is written on their skin."[21] Through syphilis the Jew is
associated with Blackness. The Jew is the medium of sexual contagion. The Jew is not Black but *becomes* Black and by turning Black
the Jew is the frightening link to the African's savage and bestial
degenerate sexuality.[22] Thus we are back to the Blackness of the
Black as the mark of the absolute Other. From the standpoint of
European civilization the Black is not a stand-in for the Black, the
Black is Black: "Wherever he goes the Black remains a Black" (*BS*,
173). In the Manichean world of anti-Black racism Blackness marks
and separates the Black.

Enlightenment privileges sight as the basis for calculating difference. Even if it is mapped onto older models, such as the Jew or
the leper, as outsiders within European society, epidermalization
is essential to the "racial gaze." Hegel's description in *Reason in
History* is a remarkable archetype of the colonial project of seeing
the "Negro" and Africa as an absolute Other. Africa is described as
a place of energy and sensations but also as motionlessness and
stuck in time. To describe Africa necessitates a journey not from
sense to reason but rather from reason to sense:

> The Negro is an example of animal man in all his savagery and law-
> lessness, and if we wish to understand him at all, we must abstract
> from all reverence and morality, and from everything which we call

feeling. All that is foreign to man in his immediate existence, and nothing consonant with humanity is to be found in his character. For this reason, we cannot properly feel ourselves in his nature, no more than into that of a dog.[23]

And what is Africa? A continent cut off from history, at least south of the Sahara – the Sahara which "naturally" cuts the continent in two – cut off from the world and determined by its inhumane geography, fauna, and flora: the endless thick forests, climbing creepers, and strangling quick-growing vegetation. The traveler's tales of wild beasts, reptiles, snakes, mosquitos, and especially gorillas, that "hybrid animal par excellence,"[24] provide not only the backdrop but the essence and meaning of Africa.[25] The African is the embodiment of the absolute Other, and the racial gaze of the White judges, humiliates, and deliberately and cruelly denies human recognition to the Black. Paradoxically, the racial gaze produces a twisted recognition. The White racist, who subjugated, enslaved and colonized African peoples, transfers domination into sexual fantasy. He desires and fears the Black, who is perceived as the source of virility. White civilization's sublimation of libidinous drives, primarily sexual, finds an outlet in the production of the Black as sexual Other – deviant, oversexed, and sensuous. The Black is body, a set of external organs – woolly hair, flat broad nose, thick lips, and especially an oversized penis – living in immediacy and sensuousness, which cannot be controlled and thus is beyond morality. The Black male is synonymous with the penis, to be set alongside the "Hottentot venus" with an enlarged clitoris and buttocks, and the veiled Algerian woman with an unseen exotic erotic.[26] The gaze is simultaneously haunted by hate, fear, anxiety, and sexual desire of the Black body. The racist gaze thus suffers from double consciousness, the consciousness of superiority and the consciousness of inadequacy, incompleteness, an incompleteness that is manifest in the visual desire of the Other, the Black Other. For Fanon, the focus is not the revolt against this representation, but its life as it is internalized by "the Black." For example, Sarjie Baartman ("the Hottentot venus") died at 26. Desiring to return home, she could no longer live as an object of the racial gaze; in contrast the alienated Blacks of *Black Skin* do not want to escape the anti-Black world but escape Blackness. Black intersubjectivity is mediated by the White Other even if the White Other is absent.

The racial gaze of the White seals the Black into a "crushing objecthood." "Look a Black," says the French child to its mother. It objectifies and seals the Black's fate as a Black. The White Other puts the Black together as a phobogenic object which expresses the repressed desires of European society:

> In the remotest depths of the European unconscious an inordinately Black hollow has been made in which the most immoral impulses, the most shameful desires lie dormant. And as every man climbs toward whiteness and light, the European has tried to repudiate its uncivilized self, which had attempted to defend itself. When European civilization came into contact with the Black world, with those savage peoples, everyone agreed. Those Blacks were the principle of evil. (*BS*, 190)

Following Freud, Fanon notes that European civilization has an "irrational longing for unusual eras of sexual license." Through the Black, Europeans can realize their imaginary selves, discover their "inner selves," like Joseph Conrad's Kurtz, in the heart of darkness. By projecting these desires onto the Black, and behaving as if the Black really has the desires that the White has projected onto them, these desires and neuroses are allowed expression. The Black is a creation of the White, and in these projections "everything takes place on the genital level." In the White's mind the Black has tremendous sexual powers. The racial gaze is both a polymorphous perverse sexual desire, and sexual projection. The innermost repressed and sadistic and masochistic desires are externalized and projected onto the Black. Lynching is a sexual revenge, and the Black, who is always a threat to White women, is cruelly beaten and castrated.

The racial gaze operates at the level of the body's surfaces. Its size and differences are measured and catalogued with a special interest in the sexual organs. The image of the Black is not only biological but unambiguously sexual. In the colonial world, the colonizer thinks in terms of the phallus and projects it onto the Black: "The black man's sword is a sword. When he has thrust it into your wife, she has really felt something. It is a revelation. In the chasm that it has left, your little toy is lost. . . . Four Blacks with their penises exposed would fill a cathedral" (Michel Cournot's *Martinique* quoted in Fanon, *BS*, 169). The Black is a penis. The preoccupation with the bestial, with sexual prowess, and with the length of the penis expresses the innermost secrets, fears, and desires of the European. "Negrophobia" expresses the European's neurosis and complexes.

The racial gaze operates in the Manichean frame. The Black is the symbol of evil, of Sadism, of Satan, of moral dirtiness, of sin. These symbols, projected onto the Black over and over again, create the basis for an inferiority complex where the White Other becomes the "mainstay of his preoccupations."

The literal translation of "L'expérience vécue du Noir," chapter 5 of *Black Skin*, "the lived experience of the Black," indicates the influence of phenomenology. The lived experience as a "body-subject" facing the world explicates how colonial racism has affected the corporeal existence of the colonized Black and presented "him" with "difficulties in the development of his bodily schema" (*BS*, 110).[27] The idea of "lived experience" alerts us to Fanon's appreciation of different starting points in Sartre's and Merleau-Ponty's methodology. For example, where Sartre argued that the fundamental struggle between consciousnesses creates social relations, for Merleau-Ponty it is the social nature of consciousness that creates the possibility of conflict. This methodological emphasis is repeated in Fanon's critique of psychoanalysis, where he puts the emphasis on the *social* character of the inferiority complex and nonrecognition in an anti-Black racist society.

The Triple Person: Merleau-Ponty, Sartre, and Lived Experience

> The Black is aiming for the universal, but on the screen his Black essence, his Black "nature," is kept intact: always a servant / always obsequious and smiling / me never steal, me never lie / eternally "y'a bon banania." (Fanon, *Black Skin*)

> At the conclusion of this study, I want the world to recognize with me the open door of every consciousness. (Fanon, *Black Skin*)

> By myself I cannot be free, nor can I be conscious or a man; and that other whom I first saw as a rival is my rival only because he is myself. I discover myself in the other. (Merleau-Ponty, *The Primacy of Perception*)

Fanon opens "L'expérience vécue du Noir" by arguing that ontology alone does not "permit us to understand the being of the Black man" because there is not really a Black being or essence. "Being," for Merleau-Ponty, is the sense of a body in a spatiality of situation, or as Fanon puts it, "a definitive structuring of the self and of the world." It is definitive, Fanon adds, because it creates a real dialectic between my body and the world (*BS*, 111).

Merleau-Ponty's description of the spatiality of situation[28] is repeated by Fanon. There is no question of a Black bodily essence:

> I know that if I want to smoke, I shall have to reach out my right arm and take the pack of cigarettes lying at the other end of the table. The matches, however, are in the drawer on the left, and I shall have to lean back slightly. And all these movements are made not out of habit but out of implicit knowledge. A slow composition of my *self* as a body in the middle of a spatial and temporal world. (*BS*, 111)

What happens when the condition is that of Black in an anti-Black situation?

At the end of chapter 5, Fanon refers to a statement in the film *Home of the Brave* (released in France as *Je suis un Nègre*) about the shared perception of the amputee and the Black. "The crippled veteran of the Pacific war says to my brother 'Resign yourself to your color the way I got used to my stump; we're both victims'" (*BS*, 140). In the film the Black character has undergone a psychological trauma. The setting is the South Pacific during World War Two, and five American soldiers (four White and one Black) take part in a dangerous mission. Whereas the White soldiers suffer physical wounds, the Black's wounds, expressed as paralysis and amnesia, are the result of an inferiority complex triggered by racial remarks made by his friend during a firefight. The feelings of betrayal are exacerbated by a feeling of guilt. His friend is shot, but the Black character is unable to help him. Eventually the injured White makes it back to camp, only to die in the Black man's arms.

"Underneath we're all guys" is the positive multiracial message at the end of the film. But behind that message is another message, that the Black's neurosis is an individual not a social problem, created by the individual's sensitivity to racism. Blacks must simply get over these "feelings" and become resigned to their color. Fanon rejects the advice: "I refuse to accept that amputation." Why should he? But should the amputee?

In the *Phenomenology of Perception* Merleau-Ponty spends some time discussing the way the amputee refuses to accept amputation, questioning the creation of and feeling in the phantom limb. The body image of the amputee and that of the Black in racist society is a shared one insofar as there is a degree of collapse of bodily projection. For both, the body (or non-body) becomes a "third" person;

one's relationship to it is like Sartre's "bad faith." What marks the difference between the amputee and the Black, however, is their status in the world. This is not to say that the amputee is not likely to be objectified in the eyes of the Other (though a prosthetic limb may occlude the objectifying gaze), but that for the amputee the task is to *reacquire* an ongoing subject–object relationship between the body and the world.[29] Blacks, on the other hand, wholly determined by the Other, are locked into their Blackness because they are locked into their body *qua* Blackness. Reestablishing a new relationship between body and the world cannot be created prosthetically: for the Black acquiring a White mask expresses a decomposition rather than a recomposition of bodily projection because one cannot hide how one is *seen* by an Other. Racism is a social problem that requires a solution at the societal level.

Thus the phenomenology of being in the world changes when the situation is saturated by color. Where for Merleau-Ponty, "the body image is finally a way of stating that my body is in-the-world,"[30] for Fanon there are times when the Black is not in the world but "locked into his body" (*BS*, 225). Where for Merleau-Ponty, "one's body is the third term . . . as far as spatiality is concerned,"[31] for Fanon the fact that the Black "must be Black *in relation* to the White" means that the consciousness of body for the person of color is not only a "third person consciousness," but a person triply split.

When "the Black man is among own" (which assumes a certain level of equality and recognition), Fanon argues that Merleau-Ponty's conception of intersubjectivity appears correct, yet in a colonial society "every ontology is made unattainable" (*BS*, 109). There is a tension because the relation of Being and Other is determined by the absolute of color and is thus *inauthentic*.

In a racist society where the image of Whiteness has been powerfully internalized, Sartre's conflictual and dualistic philosophy appears a powerful explanatory tool to understand the causes and effects of the child's statement, "see the Black! I am frightened!" (*BS*, 112). Driven back, as it were, into "race," an ontology based on mutual reciprocity is, by definition, sealed off. Though the existence of the Black is dependent on the White, the Black has no ontological resistance in the eyes of the White.

While it is true that for Fanon as for Sartre, existence precedes essence, the Black's existence is defined by the essence of Blackness (evil, lazy, bestial, and biological). The Being is reduced to a corporeal malediction and the body has been snatched away and in its place is put a "racial epidermal schema." Thus, in contrast to what Merleau-Ponty describes as being aware of the body as a "third person,"[32] Fanon replies, my body is "a triple person. . . . It was not that I was finding febrile coordinates in the world. I existed triply. I occupied space" (*BS*, 112). Blacks are not simply individual actors responsible for themselves, they are responsible for their race (culture) and their ancestors (history). Quite an existential load. On top of that there is the racist caricature, the smiling Black who says "sho enough good eating," the smiling Senegalese on the popular breakfast cereal *Banania*, saying "y'a bon Banania."

From the perspective of the Black, Sartre's proposal of an absolute freedom in *Being and Nothingness*, projecting a consciousness which can, as an act of sheer will, tear through inferiority complexes that have structured one's life appears eminently concrete. In the Manichean world of colonialism that Fanon depicts, the very fact that Sartre allows no other perspective, and no space to quibble about shades of gray, is a plus. On the other hand, Merleau-Ponty's perspective that the lived body cannot be divorced from the world as experienced complicates things. These relationships are, according to Merleau-Ponty, "the third term between the for-itself and the in-itself" which Sartre lacks.[33] For Merleau-Ponty, freedom is rooted in the world and mediated through the body. The body appears to limit the possibility of freedom, but it actually makes such a possibility concrete in that it is the relation to other bodies and thus freedom and the limits to freedom that are confirmed through intersubjective relations. Freedom is a social act, not simply an act of individual will (itself a product of social relations), just as values are socially constructed and thus changeable. Where the social world is crucial to Merleau-Ponty's conceptualization of freedom and intersubjectivity, for Sartre the essence of all intersubjective relations are the same "not *Mitsein*, but conflict."[34] For Merleau-Ponty the truth of "the hell of other people" is understanding that the perceiving subject is already an interrelation of subject and object, of self and Other, of body and mind, and is already "open" to other bodies and minds. "The world is not what I think, but what I live through," writes Merleau-Ponty in *Phenomenology of Perception*, "I am open to the world, I have no doubt that I am in communication with it, but I do not possess it; it is inexhaustible." Because consciousness is mediated by lived experience in a social environment, it does not mean that *mutual* recognition exists. In his reading of Hegel's master/slave dialectic, for example, Merleau-Ponty sees the necessity of the struggle for recognition to get beyond "unilateral recognition." Unlike Sartre, and indeed Kojève, who make unilateralism an ontological principle, Merleau-Ponty recognizes there is a processual character in Hegel's master/slave conflict. The conflict is a *moment that must be experienced*. The goal of "mutual recognition" is given content by the drama that consciousness experiences in getting there.

One's experience of the body is part of one's experience of the world. This is no doubt true for the Black who, "walled in by color," has two different experiences of body and being in the world. When race is added to the subject/object dialectic of self and the world, it seems to fall apart, replaced by a dualism that looks remarkably like Sartre's ontology of self and Other: two different species, the Black and the White. In the Manichean colonial world there are no choices, only a series of double binds. If Blacks renounce their bodies as products of their internalization of the gaze of the Other – in other words, the third (who in this case is White) – one is forced into a bad faith[35] either by creating a solipsistic community before consciousness, or creating a make-believe world of assimilated colorless angels (*WE*, 218). In such a bind, how does one become conscious of oneself and in doing so change the world? Merleau-Ponty, grounding consciousness in the social world, offers an insight.

For Fanon, Sartre's dialectic in *Black Orpheus* leads to an intellectualized rather than existential project. Privileging the subjective, existential, over the objective dialectic, Fanon accuses Sartre of forgetting concrete Black experience. Sartre had forgotten that "The Black suffers in his body quite differently from the White man" (*BS*, 138). Though Fanon had almost essentialized the difference between the body experience of the Black and the White, it was grounded in a social and historical context and was the result of a lived experience not an ontological flaw: one is not born Black but becomes Black, to rephrase de Beauvoir. While Fanon criticized the possibility of reciprocity in Hegel's master/slave dialectic when color was added, he rejected Sartre's radical dichotomy between being-for-self and being-for-others. There is a power relation making Sartre's radical dichotomy between myself and others, which he posits as an absolute, seem correct. But Fanon's position is purely contextual, whereas Sartre precludes one *ever* experiencing the Other as intersubjective and reciprocal, seeing it as an expression of inauthenticity and bad faith.

The idea of mutual intersubjectivity is not possible in Sartre's existentialism. For Fanon, mutual recognition remains a goal but because recognition is closed off by the Other (who is White), Fanon is "driven back" into race. He makes reference to Black consciousness but notes that it doesn't change the situation: "The few working-class people whom I have had the chance to know in Paris never took it on themselves to pose the problem of the discovery of a Black past. They knew they were Black and they knew they had to struggle" (*BS*, 224).

Dialectical Impasses: Hegel and the Black

The disaster of the man of color lies in the fact that he was enslaved.
(Fanon, *Black Skin*)

"Since the Black man is a former slave," Fanon writes at the end of chapter 2 of *Black Skin*, "we will turn to Hegel" (*BS*, 62).[36] Though his penultimate chapter contains Fanon's most sustained critique of Hegel's master/slave dialectic, Fanon's concern with reciprocity and his claim that "man is only human to the extent to which he tries to impose his existence on another man to be recognized by him" (*BS*, 216) are central features of the radical humanist project that is repeated throughout *Black Skin*. This section investigates some of the issues posed by the introduction of race into a dialectic of recognition.

The question, "who am I?" is implicit in his first chapter, "The Black and Language," when he writes that "To speak is to exist absolutely for the Other" (*BS*, 17). To possess a language assumes a culture and a world expressed by that language. Just as Hegel cites language as the crucial element of reciprocity, Fanon also finds it necessary to begin with this medium by which the Black experiences "the Other." In Hegel's scenario, reciprocity between individual consciousnesses requires a common tongue. Language and recognition presuppose each other. To speak to others is to recognize them, to acknowledge them as persons. Where this type of language is not present there will be struggle.

Hegel's master/slave dialectic is initially a struggle to the death, and the victor expects service not discourse. In the colonial situation the language used indicates that no real reciprocity obtains. Because the colonizers do not respect the Other's culture, the only language the colonizers speak is the language of violence: "Every colonized people – in other words, every people in whose soul an inferiority complex has been created by the death and burial of its local cultural originality – finds itself face to face with the language of the civilizing nation" (*BS*, 18). If language is one way in which the human being "possesses the world [and] . . . take[s] on the world" (*BS*, 18, 38), in the colonial relationship it is intimately connected with the absence of recognition. The master's language is a *means* of advancement within the White world, but the Black who speaks White is still deprived of recognition. Whiteness is still the measure by which to judge the mastery of *correctness*. Consequently recognition, grounded in an awareness of similarity, is blocked. The slave who embraces the logos of the master can at best hope for only a pseudo-recognition – a White mask.[37] In these circumstances, the master's language does not proceed from a recognized commonality; the imposition of the master's language is a violence whose victim is the indigenous culture. Therefore, the reciprocity at the heart of the Hegelian dialectic is not forthcoming when viewed in terms of Black/White relations.

Fanon has been viewed as simply a Kojèvean interpreter of Hegel. While Alexandre Kojève's influential reading of Hegel is part of the context, Fanon's critique of Hegel is original. An aspect of that originality is his describing the dialectic as "untidy," or open-ended. Fanon's introduction of race into the master/slave dialectic is a profound though largely overlooked original contribution developed in the context of the postwar "Hegel" renaissance in France.[38] Rather than simply dismissing Hegel as a philosopher of imperialism, he engages the methodological core of this key thinker of European modernity – the dialectic.

A Negative Dialectic?

Fanon's project to get beyond Manicheanism also acknowledges that the inversion of colonial Manicheanism is Manichean. Fanon loudly proclaims that Europe is built on the backs of African slaves, that Europe is a Third World creation, but rather than simply dismissing European thought, Fanon critically engages it. Unwilling to be defined by the Other, Fanon does not shy away from it but embraces a Manichean reaction to the construction by Other, following it through to its conclusion. By embracing the reaction to the White construction of the Black, or the colonial construction of the colonized, Fanon believes he can get beyond it. Though the reaction to the Other's construction remains within the ground of the first, that is, it is a reactive action, Fanon believes that it can produce a new moment of self-knowledge and thereby the possibility of exploding Manicheanism.

Just as the eye is not simply a mirror but a "correcting mirror," the racial gaze is not a human condition but a social construction that can be resolved by "correcting cultural errors." The basis for such a correction is by "returning" to what Fanon considers the phenomenologically "real," the lived experience of the Black in a racist society. The method, which Fanon calls a "method of regression,"[39] parodies the colonial ideologue's notion of the primitive Black, a being of sense not reason: "Since no agreement was possible on the level of reason, I threw myself back to unreason . . . out of the necessities of my struggle I had chosen the method of regression" (*BS*, 123). Just as Fanon argues that to get to the source of the Black's alienation psychoanalytically requires going to the stage "preceding" the Oedipus complex, namely the pre-Oedipal stage of socialization, to get to the source of the master/slave dialectic through the prism of race requires "returning" to the moment of self-certainty preceding desire. Paradoxically this "return," while appearing to reproduce the colonial, and typically Hegelian, attitude toward the African as a child mired in sensuousness, is rearticulated in the dialectic of Black consciousness where Fanon insists that consciousness be posited from itself.

In proclaiming the certainty of self in the world of racial Manicheanism, Fanon argues that the dialectic is forced back to a stage "preceding" desire (*BS*, 134–5) and in doing so, "has to create its normativity out of itself," as Habermas puts it. In terms of Black consciousness, Fanon declares, "The dialectic brings necessity into the foundation of my freedom and drives me out of myself." In other words, the movement from self-certainty derives from the historical necessity to struggle for freedom but its form is not already mapped out by Europe's "development." It is, instead, a history posited absolutely from itself which finds its own meaning (*BS*, 134). "Without any possibility of escape," says Habermas, speaking of modernity, it must make a beginning from itself. Thus, moving to a preceding stage does not mean consequently following a prepared route. The originality of this new beginning is Fanon's addition of race, which resituates the struggle of self-consciousness in an unequal situation. Rather than giving up the dialectic, Fanon shifts it, intimating his dialectic of liberation in risk,[41] which "means I go beyond life toward a supreme good that is the transformation of subjective certainty of my own worth into a universally valid objective truth" (*BS*, 218).

The first recasting of Hegel's dialectic in *Black Skin* is negative because, for the Black, dialectical development is blocked off in non-reciprocity; the Black is frozen by the gaze of the White. Sartre's "look,"[42] therefore, seems far more suggestive for Fanon's conceptualization of the racial gaze than Hegel's dialectic of reciprocity. With Sartre, the Other's look becomes a way in which one apprehends oneself as being seen in the world from the standpoint of the world. Sartre's "look" can freeze the Other, but the process is mutual. For Fanon, Sartre is right insofar as one apprehends the world from the standpoint of alienated consciousness, but unlike Sartre, for whom the idea of mutual recognition is a tragic farce, an example of "lack" and impossibility in the human condition, Fanon believes in its possibility (*BS*, 41). Reciprocity has been blocked through the racial gaze but the racial gaze is not an ontological absolute. Implicitly disagreeing with Sartre's position in *Being and Nothingness* that love amounts only to frustration, Fanon connects the idea of "authentic love" with an ethic of reciprocity, "wishing for others what one postulates for oneself" as one of "the permanent values of human reality" (*BS*, 41).

Fanon's discussions of the woman of color's "Manichean conception of the world" (*BS*, 44) are grounded in a belief in genuine reciprocity. That is why, he says, "I endeavor to trace its imperfections, its perversions" (*BS*, 42), which he then attempts to do in the discussion of heterosexual love between Black and White. One particularly striking perversion of reciprocity is his description of how the woman of color's simple "Manichean conception" of reality leads to magical thinking, investing with supernatural powers the topography of the colonial city. Her dream of turning White, of becoming one with the White world and high society, embodies Hegel's "subjective certainty made flesh" (*BS*, 44). The truth of this sense-certain consciousness reflects an inverted world where the view from above dominates life below. The racial economy of the colonial city, which has been experienced since childhood, becomes flesh in the woman of color's Manichean "subjective certainty." She wants to live in a mansion on the hill, dominating the city, and that can be made real by magically turning White. Fanon notes that it would be easy to see the dialectics of being and having in this behavior; for the Black, there is no way out of the social structure except through the White world. Thus the dialectic is insular, anti-social, and blocked off and described by social atomism and alienation: "the Black man is on his own [with] no occasion . . . to experience his being through others," because "every ontology is made unattainable in a colonized and civilized society" (*BS*, 109). In other words, being Black comes into being and has meaning only in relation to the White, though the converse is not so. "This is a form of recognition that Hegel had not envisioned," comments Fanon. The unequal relationship is based on the fact that the indigenous cultures were "wiped out." The dialectic becomes motionless.

Since freedom is "given" by the White, recognition is only possible if the Black man becomes White, or at least extremely light-skinned, but definitely unlike the "real Black" (*BS*, 69). The only realm of freedom for the French Black therefore is the "inner life." Yet the Black does not exist alone, but only in terms of the White: "As everyone has pointed out, alterity for the Black man is not the Black but the White man" (*BS*, 97). Defined in the context of the White, the Black is "an object in the midst of other objects," meaning that the Black has been stripped of identity and "abraded into nonbeing." What is finally at stake in the colonial situation is the replacement of the indigenous consciousness by "an authority symbol representing the master" who is charged with maintaining order and control (*BS*, 145). It is this harsh reality that pervades Fanon's discussion of "The Black and Hegel."

The Black and Reciprocity

A Negro is a Negro, only under certain conditions does he become a slave. (Marx, *German Ideology*)

Fanon's "The Black and Hegel" begins with a quote from Hegel to support his claim that absolute reciprocity exists at the heart of the Hegelian dialectic: "Self-consciousness exists *in itself* and *for itself*, in that and by the fact that it exists for another self-consciousness; that is to say, it *is* only by being acknowledged or recognized" (quoted *BS*, 216). This absolute reciprocity involves mutual recognition and reason where "I am immediately," according to Hegel, "self-related."[43] But the stage of consciousness achieved in the master/slave dialectic arrives only at the threshold of realizing that self-consciousness has to be a unity of "different self-consciousnesses, each for itself . . . An I which is we and a we which is I." The process appears contradictory because the master/slave dialectic starts with the idea of genuine reciprocity, though it does not come to fruition there but only begins its journey. It is the failure to attain reciprocity that drives the dialectic on.

The idea of mutual recognition remains central to Fanon's understanding of Hegel: "Man is human only to the extent to which he tries to impose his existence on another man in order to be recognized by him." Without recognition, the individual remains focused on the Other as the theme of action (*BS*, 216–17). Fanon pursues the question by asking, what would happen if action came from only one side? "If I close the circuit, if I prevent the accomplishment of movement in two directions, I keep the Other within himself. Ultimately, I deprive him even of his being-for-self" (*BS*, 217). Here Fanon interjects: "There is not an open conflict between White and Black. One day the White master, *without conflict*, recognized the Black slave" (*BS*, 217). The turning point of Fanon's discussion of Hegel comes when this is repeated: "Historically, the Black steeped in the inessentiality of servitude was set free by the master. He did not fight for his freedom" (*BS*, 219). The Black slave was acted upon: "The upheaval reached the Blacks from without" (*BS*, 221). The White masters had decided to "be nice to the niggers" (*BS*, 220).

The absolute reciprocity that Fanon emphasizes as the foundation of the Hegelian dialectic appears impossible in the world of Black and White relations. Rather than struggle, the White master grants freedom to the Black slave. Not having "risked" life, the slave cannot attain the truth of "recognition as an independent self-consciousness" (*BS*, 219). Because freedom here is not a result of struggle, new values are not created, nor is the "cost of freedom" known. Instead of embarking upon a changed life where every relationship is radically altered, the Black merely goes from one "way of life to another." Fanon's slave is far different from Hegel's: "Steeped in the inessentiality of servitude," how could there be an affirmation of human possibilities?

Though Fanon returns to the issues of freedom and independence, he believes that any chance for reciprocity is utterly ruptured when color is introduced, because there is absolutely no recognition of the slave by the master. Any relationship between the "civilized" (White) and the "colonized" (Black) is quite unattainable (*BS*, 109). For Fanon, the Black/White division is both naked and absolute. The fact that the White world has barred the Black from all participation is something that has not been given enough attention.

Risking one's life is emphasized in Fanon's citation from Hegel: "The individual who has not staked his life, may, no doubt, be recognized as a *person* but he has not attained the truth of this recognition as an independent self-consciousness" (*BS*, 219). When Fanon argues that a major difference between the Black slave and Hegel's slave is that the former has neither struggled nor risked life for freedom, he assumes that Hegel refers to a physical conflict between the slave and master in the slave's struggle for freedom. However, Hegel maintains that the slave first achieves a "mind of his own" not through a physical confrontation *with* the master but by subverting immediate "desire" and working on the "thing" *for* the master. Yet Fanon argues that when the slave is Black, work provides no opportunity for self-development. Color becomes the sole determinant. Whatever the Black works on, immediacy takes over. The specific experience of Black servitude to the White master induced in the slave a "double consciousness" where everything solid and stable is continually being shaken to its foundations.

In this double life, the Black slave is subservient not only because of servitude but also because of color. Or rather, the slave becomes synonymous with the Black, and vice versa, and the impossibility of changing this position and becoming like the master is enforced by the color line, so that the Black slave's quest for recognition is expressed by remaining dependent on the White master who defines the slave's existence. Unlike the Hegelian slave, the Black slave's slavish regard of the master means that the slave abandons the things worked on as a source of self-awareness. Consequently, Fanon implies that when color is involved the slave cannot "lose himself," as Hegel puts it, "in the object and find in his work the source of liberation." For the dependent Black slave, the only way out of this dilemma is to fantasize about joining, or emulating, the White world. Instead of their own mind there are constant attempts to gain White attention and White approval (*BS*, 51). But this approval never comes, and the Black slave arrives at an impasse which creates ego withdrawal. Fanon records his difference with Hegel in a footnote:

> For Hegel there is reciprocity; here the master laughs at the consciousness of the slave. What he wants from the slave is not recognition *but work*. In the same way, the slave here is no way identifiable with the slave who loses himself in the object and finds in his work the source of his liberation. *The Black wants to be like the master.* Therefore he is less independent than the Hegelian slave. In Hegel, the slave turns away from the master toward the object. Here the slave turns toward the master and abandons the object. (*BS*, 220–1; emphasis added)

Reciprocity in the colonial experience is not so much deformed as closed off by the color barrier. Fanon further maintains that the slave cannot win recognition through labor; since the master wants only work and is not at all interested in recognition. Similarly, in his reading of Hegel, Kojève argues that if the master is not a brute, he will never be satisfied and the master eventually reaches an essentially tragic impasse. He wants service, of course, but he also wants recognition. However, the only recognition he receives is from a slave who is "not a truly human being." "The victor in the bloody struggle for pure prestige will therefore not be 'satisfied' by his victory."[44] Kojève adds that the master's desire incites the pursuit of new conquests, but each subsequent subjugation leads to the same result. Since the master would rather die an honorable death than receive recognition from a slave, there are only two ways to get beyond this impasse: "The Master can either make himself *brutish* in pleasure or *die* on the field of battle as Master, but he cannot *live consciously* with the knowledge that he is satisfied by what he *is*."[45] In Kojève's terms, the colonial master is that very "brute" who just wants work. Not interested in recognition, the colonial master reaches no existential impasse. Instead, he is content to profit from the slave, in whom the possibility of consciousness would be a laughable prospect. Money, in the modern world, has totally displaced honor, or, perhaps more accurately, he knows that money can buy honor and recognition.

The French didn't acquire colonies out of a desire for recognition, unless perhaps from British competitors; from the colonies, however, they sought raw materials and cheap labor. For the colonized, just as for Marx's proletarian, there could be no dignity in labor when labor represented nothing but pure unadulterated exploitation. In Fanon's view, labor unions and reformist parties are only manifestations of a continual turning to the master, who in turn only laughs at the slave and the quest for recognition. The colonial situation presents a polarizing and paralyzing dilemma, immune to reform. The Black slave must eschew the White world and its approbation if he is to find some way to reciprocity.

It is worth pausing to consider why, in Fanon's account, the Black slave doesn't turn toward the object of labor. In Hegel's schema, the turn toward the object is at first compelled through absolute fear and dread of the master. Then, in the course of continued service, consciousness comes to the slave. For Fanon, the Black slave only experiences a general dissolution of being, the wretched result from the prolonged and dehumanizing fear and dread of the master. There is dread but no new beginning through labor. Unlike Hegel's Lord, the colonial landlord or entrepreneur does not want personal service, but only labor that ensures profit. Like the capitalist, he has no immediate interest in the product of the slave (for instance, whether it is bauxite or linen) nor does he recognize anything special about the slave's relation to "nature." He only cares that the "slave" work hard. What Fanon describes seems to have more in common with the "wage slave" than Hegel's slave.

One could argue that Hegel's slave also wants to emulate the master. However, for the Black slave to be like the master means something quite different, namely, *looking like* the master – in other words, becoming White. This internalization of the desirability of being White, Fanon notes, is "a form of recognition that Hegel had not envisaged": the dilemma for the Black slave is that he ideally must "turn White or disappear" (*BS*, 63). How then can the Black recognize the possibility of existence? How then can the Black escape this circle, this "genuinely Manichean concept of the world" where White and Black represent two poles of a world in perpetual conflict? (*BS*, 44).

If we grant the point that the goal of the Hegelian system is mutual recognition, its significance becomes *more not less* important for Fanon. Fanon implicitly agrees with Hegel that what still "lies ahead for consciousness is the experience of what Spirit is." One has to consider the "series of displacements in which self-consciousness fails to recognize itself in another self-consciousness."[46] The inability of the Black to gain recognition from the White necessitated, for Fanon, a displacement, or a "retreat" to a mind of one's own, Black consciousness as a possible ground for mutual reciprocity.

Unchaining the Dialectic

Fanon describes the dialectic of master and slave using the same terms with which Hegel discussed the initial struggle of two equal self-consciousnesses seeking recognition.[47] After portraying the initial "quest for absoluteness" within each self-consciousness which leads to the struggle for mastery, Fanon reintroduces the physical struggle into the later discussion after the master and the slave have been established. For him, color has already determined the outcome and made it absolute. There does not exist a prior moment of two equal self-consciousnesses. In the colonial situation, the Black has no capacity to enslave the Other. Fanon uses the following comment from Hegel, which refers to the initial period of struggle, as the centerpiece of his critique of the master/slave dialectic: "It is solely by risking life that freedom is obtained" (*BS*, 218). Without such risk in the slave's struggle against the master, there can be no genuine recognition, independence, or freedom.

Because Fanon insists on the impossibility of self-consciousness coming to the Black slave through "forced labor" (*BS*, 238), he would seem to agree that the master/slave situation is "only the repetitive fulfillment of the master's wants."[48] Fanon's narrative is dominated by the master because with freedom granted, the slave has no impulse to transcend the slavish condition. As Hegel puts it, "Independence without absolute negativity . . . remains without the required significance of recognition."[49] What is at issue for Fanon is that when the Black slave has occasionally fought, the fight has always been driven by "values secreted by his masters," values such as "White liberty and White justice" (*BS*, 221). The Black slave is "whitewashed" (as it were) and has no memory of the struggle or anguish of liberty. Inasmuch as servility represents an attitude to consciousness, Hegel holds that any emancipation granted by the master, or any other party, does not create freedom for the slave (not even the partially empowering attitude to freedom found in stoicism). Without the slave's own self-secured self-consciousness, no "liberty" will, in fact, create freedom. The Black slave is "doomed" (*BS*, 221)[50] not because self-development through labor is blocked but because the slave has not "aimed for the death of the other."[51] Hegel similarly argues that the slave who has not experienced "absolute fear" will be "still enmeshed in servitude."[52]

What Kojève calls slave ideologies conform with Fanon's idea of the Black slave who has not fought for freedom. For example, Kojève argues that the skeptic "without conflict, without effort . . . obtains – in and through God – equality with the master: equality is but a mirage, like everything in this World of the senses in which Slavery and Mastery hold sway."[53] For Fanon the world of master and slave continues because, instead of an open conflict, the White master acts as God and "grants" freedom: "One day the White master, *without conflict* recognized the Black slave" (*BS*, 217). Just as for Hegel stoicism and skepticism are attitudes that can be assumed by either masters or slaves, Fanon adds that the Black does not become a master, but a "slave who has been allowed to assume the attitude of the master," at a moment when there are no longer supposed to be masters or slaves.

In the Black/White context, a Black consciousness that posits itself as self-certain, even if it does not physically confront colonialism, can to a degree transcend the colonial mind set. As Hegel puts it, free self-consciousness becomes aware of its own truth by the experience of being "forced back into itself" and thereby being "transformed into a truly independent consciousnes."[54] Black consciousness, Fanon writes in *Black Skin*, "is its own follower" and at the same time the very dialectic of internalization "brings necessity into the foundation of my freedom and drives me out of myself" (*BS*, 135).

The imperative now becomes one of recollection and the rediscovery of the suppressed. Yet Fanon concludes *Black Skin* wondering what the existence of a Black philosopher as great as Plato would mean to the eight-year-old child working in the sugar fields? It would not change the child's life. He also speculates whether a change in the self-consciousness of the eight-year-old in the sugar field would make a difference. Fanon praises the worker who knows that Black consciousness is not enough and knows the necessity of a physical struggle. In Hegel's scenario, self-consciousness of freedom only presents a new attitude toward freedom; it does not equal freedom. But this attitude to self, at the same time, denies or rejects the power of the Other. It is a discovery, Fanon argues, that "shakes the world" (*WE*, 45). And, at the conclusion of "The Black and Hegel," he speaks of the different situation of young Africans who "sought to maintain their alterity. Alterity of rupture, of conflict, of battle." The former slave, Fanon adds, "needs a challenge to his humanity" (*BS*, 222). This challenge returns us, in a sense, to the initial stage of the master/slave dialectic where two equal self-consciousnesses fought for recognition. This dialectic is replayed in *The Wretched*:

> He finds out that the settler's skin is not of any more value than a native's skin . . . All the new, revolutionary assurance of the native stems from it. For if, in fact, my life is worth as much as the settler's, his glance no longer shrivels me up nor freezes me. I am no longer on tenterhooks in his presence. (*WE*, 45)

"The native's" certainty during the modern period of decolonization is not really a return but a leap to a reason far more critical than the White master's. This reason, where consciousness is "the certainty of being all truth,"[55] is characterized by the fact that the master must be expelled. Only then can the question of human reciprocity, where consciousness opens up to the multiplicity of I's, begin.

While *Black Skin* laments the dependence of the Black slave "historically set free by the master" and therefore "content in thanking him for his freedom," *The Wretched* asserts that the colonized has been in constant, though not always apparent, revolt. It is true that in both books the specificity of the colonized slave adds a new dimension. In both, Fanon emphasizes the absence of reciprocity. Yet if in *Black Skin* this absence denotes the lack of something desirable, in *The Wretched* it becomes the grounds for an absolutely new beginning from which a new humanity is established. Genuine reciprocity, he now argues, can only be achieved by leaving Europe. In a turning of the tables on Hegel, Fanon argues that the dialectic has become motionless in Europe. Europe has reached the master's impasse and becomes the "unessential consciousness,"[56] whereas Africa, the site of the slave's revolt, best expresses the project of human reciprocity.

In marked contrast to the former slave who, Fanon complained, is bereft of even a "trace of the struggle for liberty," the colonized peasant, "embodying history," is endowed with a "mental picture of action" to "wreck the colonial world" (*WE*, 40). In the context of the Algerian revolution, Fanon does not address action in general terms but instead locates a specific revolutionary subject, willing to "risk" life and work for the cause of liberation. Yet before turning to Fanon's work in the Algerian revolution, we must go back to the "internal revolution" promoted in *Black Skin*, especially the dialectics of Black consciousness.

The addition of race to the master/slave dialectic first appears to take us outside of the dialectic itself toward a Manichean conception of the world, but consciousness is, in fact, forced back into self-certainty and the dialectic reappears in Black consciousness which becomes a basis for a new cognition. At the same time, the method of regression appears contradictory, especially in light of Fanon's quotation from Marx as the epigraph for his concluding chapter, "The social revolution . . . cannot draw its poetry from the past, but only from the future" (quoted *BS*, 223). However, Fanon's return to the problematic of "authentic disalienation," as a revolutionary reordering "in the most materialistic meaning of the word" (*BS*, 12), is in quite a different register when the "method of regression" is understood *not* as a return to or invention of the past but as critical self-reflection. In other words, the method of internalization, or inwardization, gives action its direction. Rather than a timeless human essence, Fanon's humanism emerges from the multilayered struggle for *self*-determination. So understood, an "authentic alienation" has to "find its own content" (Marx, quoted *BS*, 223). Rather than look to the Other, self-critical reflection understood socially rather than contemplatively necessitates a development out of itself. Fanon is not simply a man of action, he is also a critic of reactive action. The development of self-determining actional human beings, however, is central to his thinking and to the "method of regression," understood as part of an untidy, open-ended dialectic. Self-emancipation, a central tenet of the radical humanist project, is never automatic; for Fanon it requires a fundamental and continuous change in the nature of subjectivity, which in the colonial world means a fundamental shift in the situation of the dialectic.

2

Psychoanalysis and the Black's Inferiority Complex

Everything the Martinican does is done for The Other.

Fanon, *Black Skin, White Masks*

Black Skin is not simply about making sense of European representations of Blackness. Its thesis is to aid the disalienation of the Black, who has internalized the racial gaze of the White Other, which is expressed most commonly as "an inferiority complex." The book begins with an epigraph from Aimé Césaire's *Discourse on Colonialism*, "I am talking about millions of men in whom fear has been skillfully injected with fear, inferiority complexes, trepidations, servility, despair, abasement" (*BS*, 7). This chapter explores Fanon's discussion of the Black's inferiority complex in terms of psychoanalytic theory.

The diagnosis of the colonized suffering from an inferiority complex was not original to Césaire. Paulette Nardal praised the Harlem Renaissance poets Claude McKay and Langston Hughes for rejecting all inferiority complexes.[1] The complex had been advanced by colonial Africa experts like J. Colin Carothers and Diedrich Westermann, who found it among educated, "evolved" Blacks, as well as by Octave Mannoni, who located the source of the inferiority complex in the African personality prior to colonization. It is the dependency complex that makes them ripe for colonization, opines Mannoni. Suspicious of these terms as justifications for colonialism, Fanon nevertheless entertained them throughout *Black Skin*. For the colonized the problem with the inferiority complex is that there is no genuine way out: accept dependency, or try to become educated and face the inferiority complex by constantly looking to the White for recognition. Fanon entertained the belief that a psychoanalytical approach might point a way out by revealing "the anomalies of affect" responsible for the inferiority complex (*BS*, 10). But he adds,

> Freud insisted that the individual factor be taken into account through psychoanalysis. He substituted for a phylogenetic theory the ontogenetic perspective. It will be seen that the Black man's alienation is not an individual question. Beside phylogeny and ontogeny stands sociogeny . . . let us say that this is a question of a sociodiagnostic. (*BS*, 10)

From this perspective Fanon begins chapter 6 of *Black Skin*, "The Black and Psychopathology," with the question, what is the "extent to which the conclusions of Freud or of Adler can be applied to the effort to understand the man of color's view of the world"? The question, "can the White man behave healthily toward the Black man and the Black man behave healthily toward the White man" (*BS*, 169), requires a practical solution and Fanon turns to psychoanalytic theory to help understand the person of color's view of themselves and the world and to map out ways to undermine the inferiority complex and the world that makes it. Yet, while Fanon takes psychoanalytic theory seriously, every time he engages a psychoanalytic theorist there is an immediate qualification. When the question of race is introduced one has to move from the individual to the social and from the unconscious to the conscious: "The effective disalienation of the black man entails an immediate recognition of social and economic realities. If there is an inferiority complex, it is the outcome of a double process – primarily economic" (*BS*, 10). While the economic remains in the background, his concern with the internalization of the inferiority complex leads him to a psychoanalytic approach. But he argues that if there is an internalization – "or better epidermalization" – the process is not of an obsessive neurotic type but "*akin* to an obsessive neurotic type" (*BS*, 60), where the Black's attitude often *copies* delirium and frequently borders on the region of the pathological. For Fanon there is a difference between clinical neurosis and an internalization of the inferiority complex promoted by the socioeconomic reality, but this is not to say that one is more real than the other.

If, in its own terms, psychoanalysis is aware that it might not always produce the intended result (*BS*, 59), in a racist society more questions are raised about the usefulness of individual psychoanalysis. If in Europe trauma is repressed in the individual's unconscious, in the colonized countries there is a collective lack of objectivity: "The Black is phobogenic" (*BS*, 154) but, Fanon adds, "there is nothing psychotic in the Blacks who are discussed here." While it might be true that the Black suffers a weakening of the ego and stops acting as an actional person when the White Other is the goal of action, psychoanalytic language is useful more often as a metaphor. The disparity between psychoanalytic activity and Black reality leads Fanon to believe that a "dialectical substitution" operates when one goes from the analysis of the White to that of the Black. We are back to the social situation: "In every society, in every collective exists – must exist – a channel, an outlet through which the forces accumulated in the form of aggression can be released. . . . Each type of society, of course, requir[es] its own specific kind of catharsis" (*BS*, 145–6). In the colonized country this release is framed by the internalization of the authority of the European master. The authority of the White master is turned back onto the self or group. In the Antilles, the release from this dilemma is found in a substitution and an identification: "The young Black subjectively adopts a white man's attitude" (*BS*, 147).

Perhaps Fanon's biggest disagreement with psychoanalytic theory is the denial of the Oedipus complex. Every time Fanon invokes Lacan's name he denies the importance of the Oedipus complex.[2] Whatever other revision Lacan makes to Freud's conception, Fanon was not wrong to associate Lacan with the Oedipus complex, since Lacan's overhaul of Freudian doctrine was through transferring the Oedipus complex from the natural to the symbolic realm.

Freud had already suggested that the Oedipus complex was not reducible to an actual situation, so when confronted by the empirical evidence of the anthropologists, such as Malinowski, the Freudians simply shifted the level of abstraction by looking at which social roles expressed the prohibition against incest and which social modes expressed the triangular structure constituted by the child, the child's natural object, and the bearer of the law. Fanon notes the debate (*BS*, 152), but finds the arguments ethnocentric because the ethnologists often project the complexes of their own civilizations onto the people they study. "Putting aside the studies of the ethnologists," he contends that it would be hard to find one Oedipal neurosis in the Antilles (*BS*, 152). Neurosis is *not* a basic element of human reality, but like "every abnormal manifestation, every effective erethism in a Martinican is the product of his cultural situation" (*BS*, 151–2).

Neither neurosis nor the Oedipus complex are basic elements of human reality, but Fanon's departure from Freud and Lacan is not only based on cultural relativism. His phenomenological view of culture, as it reflects lived experience, underwrites his critique of the Oedipus complex. To speak of neurosis is to speak of a specific cultural condition that can be changed. By questioning the universality of the Oedipus complex, Fanon is not abandoning the utility of individual psychoanalysis, but to speak of neurosis in a colonized society while bracketing off the social context would be gravely misinformed. Fanon's critique of the Oedipus complex derives from "his determination to explain human psychology within its essential socio-historical coordinates,"[3] and thus ahistorical psychological perspectives have no place in the Fanonian conception of culture and personality.

The colonial White woman's neurosis, her attraction and repulsion to the native, seems to correspond with the importance that Lacan places on the decline of the image of the father. For example, in Doris Lessing's *The Grass is Singing* (1950), which is set in Southern Africa, Mary Turner's "madness" is fundamentally connected to her alcoholic father and her inept husband. Is her feeling of guilt not an expression of an infantile fantasy of aggressivity? Yet in the colonial situation, her sense of guilt and wrongdoing becomes entwined with the image of the native. The native that she strikes, the powerful, muscular man who becomes her house servant and who gets closer and closer to her as her husband becomes further removed, is the real Other and desired object. Again Fanon refuses the classic Freudian view:

> Here is my view of the matter ... At this stage (between five and nine), the father, who is now the pole of her libido, refuses in a way to take up the aggression that the little girl's unconscious demands of him. At this point, lacking support, this free floating aggression requires an investment. Since the girl is at the age in which the child begins to enter folklore and the culture along roads that we know, the Black becomes the predestined depository of this aggression. (*BS*, 179)

In a note on the Oedipus complex, Fanon adds, "psychoanalysts will be reluctant to share my view," especially "Dr Lacan [who] talks of the 'abundance' of the Oedipus complex." As with other references to Lacan, Fanon immediately adds a social and historical context, this time, to the problematic of nation and family: "The collapse of moral values in France after the war was perhaps the result of the defeat of that moral being which the nation represented. We know what such traumatism on the family level may produce" (*BS*, 152 n14). Fanon's sociodiagnostic analysis shifts from the family, the basic unit of psychoanalysis, to the wider social situation. The family is central to the socialization of the child into society. The parent is socially responsible for the child and is to blame, if you will, for the child's behavior. A "normal" child from a "normal" family will be a "normal" adult. Fanon adds a footnote to assuage the skeptics of his use of the word normal, but on contact with White society a splitting occurs. The Black who goes to Europe will have to choose, either family or society. One will have to be rejected: "in other words, the individual who *climbs up* into society – White and civilized – tends to reject his family – Black and savage – on the plane of imagination. . . . The family structure is *cast back* into the *id*" (*BS*, 149; emphasis added). In fact, "since the racial drama is played out in the open, the Black man has no time to 'make it unconscious' . . . The Black's inferiority or superiority complex or his feeling of equality is *conscious*" (*BS*, 150). If Fanon did think that psychoanalysis could help individual neurosis in a "normal" society, his clinical approach was sociotherapeutic, with an emphasis on the environment and interpersonal relations, and his radical criticism of society meant that the social context of human relations was a constant challenge to theory.

In the Martinican examples discussed in *Black Skin*, the dependency complex is a result of an inferiority that is felt historically. The reaction to it creates neurotic behavior, but its roots are social and cultural not individual. Consequently, Fanon found an affinity with Adler's emphasis on the social origin of neurosis and devoted a section of the chapter "The Black and Recognition" to it.[4] Adler had emphasized inferiority, compensation, and a striving for superiority, as well as social feeling and sibling constellation. Applying Adlerian individual psychology to the Antilles, Fanon's conclusions seem at first to concur with Adler's theory:

> The Blacks are comparison. There is the first truth. He is comparison . . . The Antillean have no inherent values of their own, they are always contingent on the presence of The Other . . . The Antillean is characterized by his desire to dominate the other . . . Everything that an Antillean does is done for The Other. (*BS*, 211–12)

However, once Fanon submits the Adlerian comparison and rivalry, "Ego greater than The Other," to racial domination, something else happens. Whiteness becomes transcendental. Like Sartre's Jew, the Black is dependent and not a *for itself*. The Black is a Black only in relation to the White. The Black is non-White but the White is not non-Black. For the Antillean the Adlerian formula becomes:

$$\frac{\text{White}}{\text{Ego different from The Other}}$$

In the Antillean situation, the Adlerian idea of comparison is overcome by a third. Because what is under discussion is not an Antillean individual but all Antilleans, the governing fiction is not personal but social. Thus "Antillean society is a neurotic society, a society of 'comparison.' Hence we are driven from the individual back to the social structure." Fanon's sociodiagnostic analysis comes to the fore. Adler had introduced social reality into his analysis of "overcompensation" but it was still grounded in the idea of separate and distinct egos. His mistake was to take the European individual as a model and present it as universal. In contrast, in the colonial situation, the colonized is utterly and unilaterally determined and objectified from the outside. In a colonized or racist society, individual neurosis has to be put in the specific social context.

Fanon's critique of divining the source of the inferiority complex in the unconscious is not simply a repetition of the view of some ethnopsychiatrists that the division between the conscious and unconscious does not exist for the African. Fanon's point relates to colonial society, anticipating the dialectic of the Black and the White, where the racial drama is played out like an open sore. In contrast to the European individual, the root of sickness for the "normal" Black child is a social one created by "contact with the white world" and played out in the open. Normalcy, in other words, does not exist. Thus psychoanalytic approaches which take colonialism as normal are not only mistaken but dangerous.

Critical of the importance of the unconscious in a study of the Antillean, Fanon was nevertheless willing to embrace Jung's conception of "collective unconscious," which for the Antillean was European. Embracing the Other's Manichean standpoint, the Antillean partakes in the same collective unconscious as the European. The Antillean does not simply mimic the European's collective unconscious, but embraces it as their own. The shameful desires projected onto the Black, which lie dormant in the remotest depths of the European unconscious, have to be doubly repressed.

Consequently the Antillean self-perception is White and their world conception is anti-Black (nègrophobe) (*BS*, 191).

The Martinican mirrors the unconscious internalization of the European at almost a conscious level. The idea of Blackness as evil, savage, bad, sexual organs, lascivious, promiscuous, etc., does not, in fact, need direct contact with European people, only with European culture. The identification of the Antillean with Frenchness (and consequently Whiteness) is culturally specific. However, this easy identification with Frenchness in the Antilles becomes problematic in France. In the Antilles the young Martinican identifies with Tarzan against the Africans. In the theater in Europe, the White audience identifies the Martinican with the savage on the screen. They are Black, what else is needed to be known.[5]

In a study of the European's collective unconscious through reactions to the word *Negro* (inserted among 20 other words) Fanon found that it was associated with penis, strength, athletic, boxer, Senegalese troops, biology, savage, animal, devil, and sin. For the European, the Black symbolizes "the dark side of the soul" where everything takes place on the genital level (*BS*, 190, 157). This hallucination is the result of the racial gaze, the pure projection by the Other. European society creates the Black and thus phobia becomes Blackphobia. Fanon is forced to state the obvious, "It is the attitude that seeks the context rather than the content that creates the attitude." The Black is genital and not wholly human (*BS*, 180): "If his psychic structure is weak, one observes a collapse of the ego. The Black man stops behaving like an *actional person*. The goal of his behavior will be The Other (in the guise of the White man), for The Other alone can give him worth" (*BS*, 154).

Black Skin is in part, like Octave Mannoni's *Prospero and Caliban* (published in 1950), a psychology of colonization: As Fanon puts it, "The Black enslaved by his inferiority, the White enslaved by his superiority alike behave in accordance with a neurotic orientation." But the problem is only "akin" to an obsessive neurotic type because it is completely situational. Whatever action the Black takes there is alienation. The Black is walled in, and thus the attitude of the Black to the White and to the Black "often duplicates almost completely a constellation of delirium, frequently bordering on the region of the pathological" (*BS*, 60). In the end all psychoanalytic theory comes up short. Neither Freud, Adler, nor Jung were thinking about Blacks in their research. "They were quite right not to have," Fanon adds. But they were wrong to have made universal arguments about culturally specific situations. In the center of Jung's "collective unconscious" of Europe's civilization was the heart of darkness, as Joseph Conrad most famously put it, the "uncivilized savage, the Black who slumbers in every White" (*BS*, 187).[6] Jung might not have thought about Blacks, but he had claimed to have found the archetype of bad instincts in uncivilized peoples. From the Manichean standpoint of good habits = civilization, Jung had deduced bad habits in the "savages." But there is really no such thing as an uncivilized psychic structure. Jung's idea of uncivilized is a product of a European Manichean standpoint. And Jung had deluded himself, confusing instinct and habit; for the so-called uncivilized people he had known had already had a traumatic contact with European civilization. Rather than a set of genes, the collective unconscious is "simply the prejudices, myths, collective attitudes of a given group" (*BS*, 188). In other words, it is cultural, and thus anyone – whatever color – who has breathed the racism of Europe and "assimilated the collective unconscious of that Europe, will be able, if he stands outside himself, to express only his hatred of the Black" (*BS*, 188).

Just as neurosis is not a basic element of human reality, the Oedipus complex is, then, the product of a specific cultural form, the European bourgeois family, which Fanon says produces 30 percent neurotics. By denying that the Oedipus complex operates in the Antilles, Fanon is maintaining that the family structure is not the prime source of neurosis. The source must be pre-Oedipal and social. The Martinican is and is not a neurotic. To understand the Antillean neurotic one must look at the social situation, which can be illuminated by an analysis of the neuroses. Antillean society is neurotic because it is a society of comparison (*BS*, 213). The basis of this neurosis is cultural not natural; in other words, the "basic personality" of the Antillean is variable not a constant, and the inferiority complex in the Antilles has to be constantly cultivated in a social context, of course.

Authentic Love

> Love, a gift of self, the ultimate stage of what by common accord is called the ethical orientation. (Fanon, *Black Skin*)

> You have nothing in common with real Blacks. You are not Black, you are "extremely brown." (Fanon, *Black Skin*)

The Antillean only exists in terms of the Other, for it is only through comparison with the Other that the Antillean is validated. Can the Antillean experience love, that is, an authentic love, that wishes for others what one wishes for oneself? Fanon views Sartre's formulation of love as "frustration" as one-sided and narcissistic. A love of the Other in order to see oneself in the Other. Fanon wants to consider the possibility of another situation where feelings of inferiority and inadequacy are purged. Reciprocity requires the meeting of equals where the beloved should not allow infantile fantasies to be turned into reality. What are a young woman's infantile fantasies? Marrying a rich man, living in a mansion, going to the ball, and so on. In the Antilles these fantasies are mediated by the quest for Whiteness.

Mayotte Capécia's *Je suis Martiniquaise* expresses this wish of turning White. The book, according to Fanon, is a neurotic expression of the inferiority complex that characterizes Antillean society.[7] Though Martinican society is neurotic, the Martinican is and is not neurotic, Mayotte Capécia is a Martinican neurotic. One cannot be sure whether her neurosis is simply a result of the social structure, but the social structure is certainly a necessary factor. Capécia perfectly expresses the economic Manicheanism of Antillean society. One becomes rich through Whiteness and one is White above a certain financial level.[8] The value Capécia puts on Whiteness – its beauty and intelligence – expresses the customary dream in Martinique of finding salvation by "magically turning White" (*BS*, 44). Whiteness means living on the hill that dominates the city and entering into high society. It means you've made it. Thus love is "beyond the reach of the Mayotte Capécias of all nations" who find Being only in having. They live not only on resentment but also self-loathing. Fanon quotes from Abdoulaye Sadji's "Nini" (set in Saint Louis, Senegal[9]) to the same effect: "The great dream that haunts every one of them is to be a bride of a White man from Europe" (quoted *BS*, 57).

Value is associated with a skin scrubbed and lightened. There is nothing beside phenotype. As a child, Capécia had tried to make Whites Black. That experiment failed. As an adult she attempted to bleach her body and her mind. It is not a coincidence that she becomes a laundress with a reputation for cleanliness and whiteness. Capécia articulates a social truth that every Antillean woman knows, to Whiten the race.

"I wish to be acknowledged not as Black but as White. Now – and this is a form of recognition that Hegel had not envisaged – who but a White woman can do this for me" (*BS*, 63). For the Black man who has internalized the inferiority complex there is an apparent way out, "marry White culture, White beauty, White Whiteness"

(*BS*, 63). By sleeping with a White woman, by caressing White breasts, the Black man has grasped White civilization, or so it seems. The product of the inferiority complex, alienated relations between a Black man and a White woman express another kind of neurosis produced by the racial gaze and its socioeconomic realities.

There is no such thing as a Black neurosis but that does not mean that there are not neurotics who are Black and who in the context of an anti-Black environment express that racism in an extreme anti-Black phobia. In reacting to racism the "reactional" Black becomes a racist.[10] Fanon analyzes this behavior in the work of the award-winning novelist, René Maran. Rather than Freud, Jung, Adler or Lacan, the psychoanalytic theory Fanon finds most helpful is Germaine Guex's pre-Oedipal "abandonment neurosis." Maran represents the évolué, the evolved and civilized Black. To become civilized, assimilated Blacks had to distance themselves from Blackness. But the Black is never completely assimilated. Maran contents himself with a kind of ersatz assimilation through litera-ture. He finds an intellectual way out. But unlike the Jew, intellec-tualization is not available to the Black.

Jean Veneuse fits Guex's idea of the abandonment neurosis per-fectly. The bitterness and resentment, the self-loathing, the devalu-ation and the uncertainty of self, are expressed in Veneuse's fear of being loved. Why? "Because once, very long ago, I attempted an object relation and I was abandoned" (*BS*, 75). Rejecting himself, he is ready to be rejected by the Other. The évolué looks for recogni-tion from the White. In Jean Veneuse's novel, which Fanon takes as autobiographical, a White woman loves him. He cannot believe it. He continually demands proofs of her love, a love which he cannot understand. How could she love a Black? Does she really love him? he asks, No, she only loves him because he is Black. "Tell me, Andrée darling," he says to her, "*in spite of my color*, would you agree to marry me if I asked you" (*BS*, 77, emphasis added). Fanon agrees with Guex that there is a dread of self: "Jean Veneuse is a neurotic, and his color is only an attempt to explain his psychic objective. If this objective difference had not existed, he would have manufactured it out of nothing" (*BS*, 78–9). Veneuse is a neurotic who happens to be Black. Using Germaine Guex's explanation, he is an abandonment neurotic. That Guex does not speak of Blacks in her analysis is absolutely appropriate. On the other hand, Jean Veneuse's "*Un Homme pareil aux autres* is a sham, an attempt to make the relations between two races dependent on an organic unhealthiness" (*BS*, 80). Jean Veneuse is a neurotic who symptomatically expresses Blackphobia and thereby indicates how the whole project of the évolué is a myth based on rising above the organic depravity of the Black. The myth is the internalization of the Manichean division imposed by the European that Blacks should pull themselves up toward the White man's level, or at least advance along the hierarchy of colors. To get beyond the myth means uncovering it, but this is not simply a mental action: it requires a struggle, "a restructuring of the world" (*BS*, 82).

Fanon's sociodiagnostic continues to use, and take insights from, psychoanalytic theories while shifting attention from the psychoanalytic concentration on the unconscious to the phenomenologically real, manifested in lived experience. The epidermalization of the inferiority complex is a process that is *akin* to neurosis in which Blacks do not make themselves inferior but are made inferior. In other words, the internalization of the inferiority complex acts like a neurosis but its causes are social, economic, and cultural. Fanon wanted to get under the skin.

Outside my Psychoanalytic Office:
Fanon and Mannoni

> This book sets out to describe colonial situations as primarily the results of misunderstanding, of mutual incomprehension. (Mannoni, *Prospero and Caliban*)

> Mannoni . . . leaves the Malagasy no choice save between inferiority and dependence. (Fanon, *Black Skin*)

"The So-Called Dependency Complex of Colonized Peoples," chapter 4 of *Black Skin*, is a critique of Octave Mannoni's recently published *Psychologie de la colonisation* – translated as *Prospero and Caliban: Psychology of Colonization*.[11] Mannoni rejected the possibility of independence for Africans, denouncing the 1947 anticolonial demonstrations in Madagascar as an irrational act of an abandoned psyche. *Prospero and Caliban*, in fact, has much to say about Mannoni's psyche. At the time of writing, Mannoni claimed that he was more interested in his own psychological makeup than in the "psychology of the subjects under observation" who, he said, "presented a less complex problem." It was his Madagascar experiences, he claimed, that cured his obsessional neurosis[12] and it was this self-understanding that was "an essential preliminary for all research in the sphere of colonial affairs."[13]

From 1925 to 1945 Mannoni worked in Madagascar as an ethnologist and director-general of the information service (the two trades often went together). Two years later in Paris he interrupted his psychoanalytic studies and his analysis with Jacques Lacan and returned to Madagascar. His return coincided with an anticolonial rebellion that resulted in the brutal massacre of 100,000 Malagasies by French troops. For Mannoni the rebellion tore aside a veil and, he said, "for a brief moment a burst of dazzling light enabled one to verify the series of intuitions one had not dared to believe in."[14] The series of intuitions were developed into a psychology of colonization that could explain Malagasy life and the dynamics of the rebellion. In short, his thesis was that the colonizer overcompensated for an inferiority complex that was the result of feelings of abandonment, and the colonized mired in a dependency complex was prone to feelings of abandonment by the colonial father figure.[15]

Fanon welcomed Mannoni's attempt to understand the colonial dynamic psychoanalytically. Here was a man working in the same area as himself, and the few essays had whetted Fanon's appetite. It was particularly arresting and new that the behavior of the colonizer and colonized was submitted to psychoanalytic inquiry, and that it was thought of in terms of an abandonment neurosis. However when the book was published Fanon was disappointed. Ideas that were apparently similar were based on very different notions of subjectivity, very different analyses of roots of colonialism and racism, and very different ideas about what constitutes being and existence.

Fanon argued that dependency was a *result* of colonial rule and not an ontology of human existence, whereas for Mannoni it was the Malagasy's very being to be colonized. According to Mannoni, the European quite easily became revered by the Malagasy as an ancestor and in fact took that place. The colonized are not made dependent because they are colonized, but are colonized because they are dependent. In fact the Malagasy "unconsciously expected – even desired" such a development, argued Mannoni: "Not all peoples can be colonized: only those who experience *this need*."[16] Fanon felt that Mannoni had turned everything upside down.

According to Mannoni, European colonialism unleashes rather than creates the different psychologies of the colonizer and the colonized. These archetypes find their true personalities in the colonies, where everyone amazingly falls into their allotted place. Fanon sarcastically adds, "it is obvious that the White man acts in obedience to an authority complex, a leadership complex, while the Malagasy obeys a dependency complex. Everyone is satisfied" (*BS*, 99). What Mannoni has forgotten, insists Fanon, is the lived reality of the Malagasy. Fanon repeats this over and over, even if he knows little about the details of everyday life and employs a Martinican negritude poet to describe reality. Lived experience is not detailed empirical knowledge and it is Césaire who provides Fanon with the most powerful expressions of lived experience of the racist dehumanization and the grinding poverty of the colonies.

For Fanon, lived experience is far from solipsistic, nor are the Malagasy "sealed" in their own customs. Culture is always in the process of being invented or reinvented. But it is the colonial regime that attempts to render them inert. Thus the Malagasy have ceased to be Malagasy since the time of General Gallieni's slaughter of innocents in 1905 (*BS*, 94). Gallieni's campaign interrupted Malagasy life and culture; sealed it; and then attempted to petrify it into forms of local rule and customs:

> What M. Mannoni has forgotten is that the Malagasy alone no longer exists; he has forgotten that the Malagasy exists *with the European*. The arrival of the white man in Madagascar shattered not only its horizons but its psychological mechanisms. As everyone has pointed out, alterity for the Black man is not the Black but the white man. (*BS*, 97)

Mannoni is unabashedly Eurocentric. Europe's development explains non-European cultures, and the Malagasy are understood to correspond to the feudal level of dependency, with lifelong pseudo-parents in the form of elders and ancestors. Faced with colonization, the Malagasy transfer their dependence onto the colonial master, who becomes a type of father figure. Abandoned by their own parents, the colonials, on the other hand, are dominated by an inferiority complex and need to dominate the natives. This dynamic is the "psychology of colonization."

Despite his use of scare quotes, Mannoni cannot find another word for *primitive* "because the alternatives, such as 'isolated,' 'unevolved,' 'archaic,' 'stationary,' and 'backward,' are in fact no better." All express the model of development from which he cannot escape. The linear development from primitive to civilized as a kind of recapitulation of an individual's development from dependency to independence absolutely determines his theoretical project. Thus ancestor worship was viewed as a "childish" act of protection against "persecution anxieties."[17]

Gallieni's pacification of the whole Island, which did not end until 1905, included the taking of "temporary wives" by French soldiers. Though aware of the charged atmosphere of sexual excitement and unconscious notions of the Black's sexual potency among Europeans,[18] Mannoni never asks why these unconscious tendencies were directed toward the Malagasy. Further, Mannoni claims that relations between soldiers and their "temporary wives" were "healthy" and unmarred by complexes. He adds, "this goes only to show that racial conflicts develop gradually and do not arise spontaneously."[19] In reality the pacification campaign, the murdering and domination of the Malagasy by the French, was a fruitful site for racial conflicts to develop quickly and "spontaneously." "Let us not exaggerate," writes Fanon in *Black Skin*, "when a soldier of the conquering army went to bed with a young Malagasy girl, there was undoubtedly no tendency on his part to respect her entity as another person. . . . The fact that Algerian colonists go to bed with fourteen-year-old housemaids in no way demonstrates a lack of racial conflicts in Algeria" (*BS*, 46 n5).

According to Mannoni, the Malagasy are sealed into their own customs and become Malagasy only in relation to the White man. In contrast, Fanon posited French colonialism as an absolute dividing line. An absolute shock to indigenous life. The loss of Malagasyhood is a result of French colonialism. "Robbed . . . of all worth, all individuality," the Malagasy are told that they are only human in as far as they are in step with the White world.

One Hundred Thousand Massacred

Mannoni explains the 1947 rebellion as a reaction to the dependent native's apparent abandonment by the colonial master, which resulted from a liberalization of colonial rule. Ignoring what Malagasy nationalists were saying, and ignoring rational causes for the revolt, Mannoni, as Maurice Bloch observed, "searched instead only for unconscious causes."[20] The feeling of abandonment apparently provided him with an answer to how thousands of Malagasy could face death in such unfavorable circumstances. For Mannoni feelings of abandonment were created by colonial policies that granted greater liberties and ended forced labor.[21] The weakening of the colonial father figure, exacerbated by World War Two and Allied rhetoric about self-determination and imminent independence,[22] aroused in the Malagasy "feelings of abandonment and guilt."[23] These feelings engendered a massive (childish) rage against the colonial system (father figure) and a massive over-reaction by the colonizers. Characterized by the inferiority/authority complex, the colonialists experienced the revolt as a threat exacerbating the complex.[24]

By ignoring the political activities of the nationalists, and by looking to the unconscious and the irrational for the "real" motives behind the rebellion, Mannoni also made the mistake of not retranslating these "unconscious feelings" back into a discourse of social and political grievance.

The roots of the rebellion can also be found in the changes effected by World War Two on the colonial system and on the character and goals of the nationalist movements. The local colonial administration aligned itself with the Vichy regime. The British invaded, occupied, and then handed the island over to the Free French. The Free French used the island as a war resource, creating disruptions in the local economies, rationing, scarcity, and a black market. But of enormous import, across the colonial world, were the hopes created at the end of the war, along with the victors' pronouncements about self-determination. In Madagascar, forced labor was abolished and laws forbidding political activities relaxed. Independence became the goal, with many of the returning veterans becoming hardened nationalist militants. The French response was to arrest the leaderships of the Mouvement de la Rénovation Malagache (MDRM). In Paris the Fourth Republic rejected calls for independence and Madagascar remained a colony. On March 29, 1947 armed groups of Malagasies attacked French government houses, French property, and French collaborators. The rebellion was not crushed until 18 months later, at which time the High Commissioner put the number of dead at over 100,000. Not until 1956 was the state of siege lifted from the country, but by then France was deeply embroiled in a far more serious conflict in Algeria, a conflict that could be dated to another French reaction to revolt, the slaughter of 45,000 people at Setif in 1945.

The 100,000 massacred, according to Mannoni, are a result not of colonial policy but of a latent inferiority complex made manifest by the colonial situation. The colonialists expressed an inferiority complex exhibited through domination and superiority. The few Europeans "unaffected by the contagion" understood that their power lay not with force alone but in exploiting "a certain 'weakness' of personality on the part of the Malagasies" which put Europeans in "roughly the same position as the dead ancestors."[25]

Therefore, the dependency complex meant that "what the immense majority of the Malagasies needed far more was to feel that they were not being abandoned," while the master wants psychological not economic domination. Economics, Mannoni argues, "has very little to say about a man who uses his economic superiority simply for the pleasure of enslaving another man."[26]

Fanon found this psychologizing problematic. Political and economic reasons were "behind" the systematic dehumanization of populations. What the White master wants from the Black slave, he insisted, is not recognition but work. While Fanon might agree with Mannoni that Blacks "are ill-treated because they are treated as *Blacks*,"[27] Mannoni ignores the types of labor that define "Blacks" *qua* "Blacks," and that this labor is a central characteristic of ill-treatment. For Mannoni the colonizer's "inferiority complex," with the attendant need to dominate on one hand and the fear of the native's sexuality on the other,[28] is the *realization* of a prototype, rather than a result of specific social relations. Fanon admits that the colonizer might derive pleasure from enslaving and dominating another man, but what keeps the *real* colonial tied to the colonial situation is getting rich as quickly as possible. All other motives are secondary or a result of the quest for profit. The inferiority complex does not antedate colonization.

Alterity is not absolute but situational, which is why "Bantu Philosophy" is not an adequate response (*BS*, 184–6). Fanon's critique of Alioune Diop's introduction to Placide Tempels' *La Philosophie bantoue* (the first book printed by *Présence Africaine* in 1949) illuminates situatedness in the *Présence Africaine* debates and indicates his refusal to bow to Manicheanism as method or goal of a philosophy of liberation, bringing us instead back to "the real": "Be careful! It is not a matter of finding Being in Bantu thought, when Bantu existence subsists on the level of non-being . . . Now we know that Bantu society no longer exists" (*BS*, 186). On the other hand, negritude had an important presence in Madagascar, as the title of Senghor's 1948 anthology attests. One of the most famous of the Malagasy poets was Jacques Rabémananjara, a cofounder of *Présence Africaine* and a leader of the nationalist movement, who had been sentenced to death for his part in the 1947 uprising.[29] He had earlier befriended Diop during the war, and from jail helped found *Présence Africaine*. He embraced negritude and *Présence Africaine* as vehicles to develop new values for the African and the "Black world," and viewed the Malagasy as part of that world.

Rabémananjara's involvement in the uprising of 1947 indicates that neither negritude nor Césaire's poetry were alien to the nationalist discourse in Madagascar. Negritude spoke to the meaning of the revolt even if it took an ambiguous form in Rabémananjara's "Song," which was both a declaration of national freedom and of his own innocence to the charge of being involved in the revolt. Provocatively he signed the poem 12 Juin, 1947, Prison Civile – Tananarive. Additionally, Mannoni was also no stranger to the Malagasy poetry included in Senghor's anthology, writing a preface to Flavien Ranaivo's 1947 *L'Ombre et le vent*. Thus Fanon's invocation of Césaire's negritude was not really out of place in a discussion of Malagasy subjectivity.

Dream and Reality

> Outside my psychoanalytic office, I have to incorporate my conclusions into the context of the world. (Fanon, *Black Skin*)

> The savage, as I have said, is identified in the unconscious with a certain image of the instinct – of the id. (Mannoni, *Prospero and Caliban*)

For Fanon it is not simply the arrival of the colonizer but the violent pacification campaign that creates Malagasy "dependency." It might seem that Fanon has taken the "shattering" of the Malagasy's "psychological mechanisms" too far. However, Fanon reminds us that something new had come into being on that island and it is necessary to understand the new relationships (*BS*, 97). When Mannoni sees the dependent character resulting from ancestor worship, Fanon argues that to be emptied and then refilled with the civilizing mission only to be "abandoned" might very well create complexes that have nevertheless been hitherto nonexistent.

Fanon's approach to criticizing Mannoni's analysis of Malagasy dreams[30] is to view dream interpretation sociodiagnostically. It is a mistake, Fanon believes, to begin an analysis from the individual's unconscious rather than from the individual's social situation. The social situation could easily weaken the disturbed individual. The disturbance produced by the social situation in turn requires an explanation outside the disturbed individual's everyday life. In a footnote Mannoni informs us that the dreams have come from different sources, though "in the main they have been collected in schools in the form of French homework." Mannoni is not bothered that the dream recollections were written in language foreign to the students, even though he attached a great importance to the choice of words.

Before he records Mannoni's dream analysis, Fanon questions Mannoni's use of the unconscious as the basis for answering why the Malagasy were prone to colonization. For Mannoni, it is the unconscious that accounts for why the Malagasy welcomed the shipwrecked Europeans and strangers. Why should the Malagasy assume the European was a being who would do them harm? Fanon answers that Mannoni could have easily given an answer in "terms of humanity, of good will, of courtesy," rather than free-floating unconscious desires. Thus, he says, "Outside my psycho-analytic office I have to incorporate my conclusions into the context of the world" (*BS*, 100). Dreams have multiple meanings and to understand them further we need to know who told them, and how, and under what circumstances. In Mannoni's world the informants knew nothing about the lived situation of the uprising and *thus* it was not the "uprising" that was fundamental but unconscious motivations lying deeper. For Mannoni this "real" was expressed in irrational terms and could only be read psychoanalytically. In con-trast, Fanon's argument clearly advocates a radical psychoanalysis: the Black should no longer be confronted by the predicament "turn White or disappear" but "should be able to take cognizance of a possibility of existence." In other words, if society makes it difficult to exist because of color, then the psychoanalyst, whose task is to help the analysand become conscious of their unconscious, should not encourage the analysand to adjust to a racist society but "put him in a position to *choose* action (or passivity) with respect to the real source of the conflict – that is, toward the social structures" (*BS*, 100).

Mannoni does not engage in a thorough analysis and gives very little background to each dream, seeming to be content with dream symbolism, which is dominated by notions of protection and danger associated with the mother and the more symbolically rich father. For example, the mother is equated with security and symbolized by a tree; the father is associated with a lack of security and sexual danger symbolized by bull's horns, the phallus, and Senegalese troops. Whereas Mannoni insists that even though the dreams "were recorded at the time of public disturbance . . . their authors had seen nothing of the disorders and knew nothing of them,"[31] for Fanon, the dreams had everything to do with the rebellion. Fanon's approach to criticizing Mannoni's dream interpretation is to view dreams socially. In other words, Fanon believes we should follow out the manifest surface meanings rather than seek meaning through an analysis of the unconscious: "what must be done is to restore this dream to its proper time, and this time is the period during which eighty thousand natives were killed" (*BS*, 104). What is central to Mannoni's dream analysis is the Malagasy's supposed reversion to routine, which Mannoni equates with the Malagasy's childish need for security. "To depart from routine," he argues, "is to wander in pathless woods; there you will meet the bull who will send you helter-skelter home again."[32] But routine is nothing other than that brought about by French pacification: "settle down Malagasies, and stay where you belong . . . You better keep your place" (*BS*, 107, 34), ventriloquizes Fanon, who responds, "Certainly not! . . . I will tell him, 'The environment, that is society is responsible for your delusion'" (*BS*, 216).

What then is the meaning of the dream imagery? For Fanon there is no ambiguity. The rifle of the Senegalese soldier is not a penis but a genuine rifle. The Black bull and the robber are not "reincarnated souls" but actually the irruption of real fantasies into sleep (*BS*, 106). In the circumstance of the massacre of 1947 the *socius* is more important than the individual or the symbolic. The Senegalese soldier is not the smiling consumer of *Banania*, but is part of the military intelligence terror machine, because it is the reality of torture, and the Senegalese torturers, that haunts the dreams. Fanon records a testimony at a trial where a witness spoke of torture at police headquarters. Prefiguring the French torture in Algeria, the Senegalese soldiers had been instructed in new methods: "When one reads such things," Fanon comments, "it certainly seems that M. Mannoni allowed one aspect of the phenomena that he analyzes to escape him: The Black bull and the Black men are neither more nor less than the Senegalese police torturers . . . The discoveries of Freud are of no use to us here" (*BS*, 106 n32, 104).

3

Negritude and the Descent into a "Real Hell"

A descent into hell . . . The poet seeks a new world: a world of truth and beauty. Where will he find it if not in the depths of his consciousness.

> Aristide Maugée, "Un Poète martiniquais, A. Césaire"

There is a zone of nonbeing . . . where an authentic upheaval can be born. In most cases, the Black man lacks the advantage of being able to accomplish this descent into a real hell.

> Fanon, *Black Skin, White Masks*

Independence is like negritude . . . it is a first negation, or more exactly, the affirmation of negation. It is the necessary moment of an historical movement: the refusal of the Other, the refusal to be assimilated, to lose oneself in the Other. But because this movement is historic, it is also dialectical. Refusal of the Other is an affirmation of self.

> Senghor, "Rapport sur la doctrine et le programme du parti"

The French policy of assimilating a small "evolved" and "civilized" Black elite, combined with the blatant discrimination against the rest of the population, created a conflict of loyalties that Fanon described as a Black skin with a White mask. The Black, René Ménil writes, "progressively rejects his race, his body . . . and finally ends up by living in an unreal world determined by the ideals and *abstract ideas of another people*."[1] It is this internalization of another's idea of yourself that is particularly important. The colonized Black elite develops a "split" consciousness – assimilating the values of the White community but it is never really socially accepted because, as Leopold Senghor put it, "we could never strip off our Black skins." Yet the Paris friendship of Césaire and Senghor, from two different continents, testifies to the apparent *success* of France's "civilizing mission." They had become "French," but with a fatal flaw – they were still Black. "Negritude,"[2] a product of that flaw, was coined in Paris in 1935 by Césaire, Senghor, and Léon Damas,[3] with the founding of the paper *L'Étudiant Noir*. Though it was a great privilege to leave their homelands, they found the "mother-land" closed to their aspirations. The three came to Paris seeking careers and instead developed a philosophic viewpoint loosely based on the idea of an essential quality of being African. Indeed, Césaire maintained that "in meeting Senghor, I met Africa," and it was Senghor as "Africa" that provided an important source for Césaire's negritude poetry.

Exile and the experience of "homelessness" were crucial in the education of these Black students. Leaving home, living at the center of French culture, and meeting men of color from diverse backgrounds were the contexts in which the Black poet wrote an "Orphic poetry." The poet, having deserted their native land, returns to it by descending into themselves.

Just as the poems of the founders expressed a process of self-discovery, they also conveyed a sense of the specificity of the Black middle class in the French colonies.[4] Negritude spoke of alienation and not exploitation; it spoke to the elite and not to the masses; to the literate and not to the illiterate. And though it represented itself as universal, it was, by and large, a movement which constituted a response by a section of the Black évolués in French society to their sense of alienation.

The young Paris-based intellectuals who championed negritude had three things in common:[5] the color of their skin, their language (French), and their colonial background. "In Paris," Césaire wrote, "I became conscious of the basic category of Negro. My poetry was born from that confrontation."[6]

Césaire's epic of negritude is a radical negation of White society and had a profound influence on Fanon; it was an expression of what he called a dive into the absolute. This chapter considers the problematic of Black consciousness in Césaire and briefly Senghor before considering Sartre's *Orphée Noir* and Fanon's response.

Césaire's Remembrance of Things Past and "Return" to the Future

As late as 1940 no Antillean found it possible to think of himself as a Black. It was only with the appearance of Aimé Césaire that the acceptance of negritude and the statement of its claims began to be perceptible. (Fanon, "West Indians and Africans," in *AR*)

We adopted the word nègres as a term of defiance. (Césaire, interview in *Discourse on Colonialism*)

Césaire's *Notebook of a Return to the Native Land* was published in a small magazine in 1939, but it was only during the war, with the help of the surrealist writer André Breton, a wartime refugee in Martinique, that the poem began to gain a wider, though still small, audience. There is no more revolutionary poem of negritude than Césaire's *Return* and his call to West Indians to rediscover their African roots was both radical and ambiguous.

The poem was a scandal, Fanon later noted, because Césaire was an educated, and therefore respected, man who said it was good to be Black. Up until the war, the West Indian intellectual mirrored the culture of the White world. Through constant repetition that Black was invested with value, Césaire brought into being the Black consciousness of a new generation of young West Indians.

When Césaire speaks of a native land, ambiguity abounds, given the Black slave's past in Africa. Written in Yugoslavia upon his "return" from France to Martinique, the poem discloses a memory of an earlier despondent return to the "inert" and "breathless" town of Fort-de-France. In contrast to this inert picture, there is the image of a return to Africa, and more importantly a return to a "true," or self-created self. To communicate this African heritage, or self-consciousness, Césaire creates a new language – "an Antillean French, a Black French."[7] This creativity of and through Black consciousness is the message of his assertion that "negritude is not a rock," not a primeval self-consciousness but the self-constructed one. For Césaire, the "return" to the self is a creative journey that both parallels and opposes the return to the hell of poor Martinique.

For Césaire, surrealism furnished a method of negativity.[8] He viewed it as a weapon that "exploded the French language" and shook everything up. Moreover, it represented for him a "liberating factor" and a "process of disalienation," which helped him summon up unconscious forces to "plumb the depths" and "reclaim Africa." During the war years, surrealism became synonymous in

Martinique with the revolutionary opposition to the war. "Poetry," Césaire argued, "equalled insurrection":

> Revolt against Western rationalism! Revolt against colonialism! Revolt against "browsing peacefulness" of the Martinican. A fundamental revolt against "a world torn by its own contradictions," the modern world.[9]

This spirit of resistance, which resulted in what Fanon called the West Indian's "first metaphysical experience," a prolonged encounter with French racism,[10] coincided with a violent reaction against French rationalism and assimilation, and called for "new paths" to enable "man to reach man" and "bypass the absurd zone of our false reasoning."[11]

The structure of the *Return* is itself important in expressing the sense of struggle and the development of negritude – the development, in other words, of Black self-awareness. The work is portrayed as the struggle to transcend racism and the effects of colonization, including the "colonization of the mind." Words are the weapons that will bring renewal. Argued in French, against the French, the language of the oppressor is used to convey the madness of slavery and the mad slaves.

Like the évolué, the *Return* is the story of a split subject: one is defensively introspective, looking inward from a distance, fearing the shock of reality; the other is retrospective, looking back for the means to narrate the "truth" of reality. The subject is split between moods of hope and despair: the grandiose dream of collective unity and the pettiness of life and death. Césaire saw his writing as "a poetry cursed because it was knowledge and no longer entertainment."[12] His vision engages a new world that claims equality with White men.

The *Return* begins with a description of the capital, Fort-de-France. Flat, soulless, and zombie-like, it nevertheless bubbles subterraneously with potential violence. It is not, though, the violence of liberation but the violence of survival: the "Black-on-Black" violence of the ghetto, cruel, brutal, vicious, and dehumanized. Along with hunger and grief, there is revolt and hatred, but such sentiments are atomistic, "strangely babbling and mute." "The Hungry West Indies, pitted with smallpox, dynamited with alcohol,[13] stranded in the mud of this bay, in the dirt of this city sinisterly stranded." Childhood is very different than that experienced by Senghor.[14] There is a vast separation between concept and reality – between, for example, the innocent child chewing a sugar cane root and the silent, famished voice of the "half-asleep nigger child . . . [being] sucked down into the marsh of hunger." The vision is of a desperate and immobile town where the Blacks treat each other as "dirty niggers." Martinique is an "Island ghetto," the bastard of Europe and Africa, dripping with self-hatred.

The Island is also a prison, a metaphor for the alienated self and the moment of self-evaluation. It is "cut off from the green oasis of fraternity . . . the archipelago bent like the anxious desire for self-negation."[15] This self-reflection is both an identity and a separation, it is, in other words, negritude:

> My unfenced island, its bold flesh upright at the stern of Polynesia; and right before it, Guadeloupe slit in two by a dorsal line, and quite as miserable as ourselves; Haiti where negritude stood up for the first time and swore its humanity; and the droll little tail of Florida where a Negro is being lynched, and Africa caterpillaring gigantically up to the Spanish foot of Europe . . . and I told myself of Bordeaux and Nantes and Liverpool . . .[16]

The drama of the African diaspora introduces resistance: "In Haiti negritude stood up for the first time." Yet the ambiguity of this claim is evidenced in Césaire's emphasis on the individual's alienation that passes into despair. Haiti represents the most heroic Antilles, "most African of the Antilles,"[17] and it also prepares the way for the suffering of an individual. Toussaint L'Ouverture, the leader and hero of the Haitian revolution, is a single and solitary man, "imprisoned in White." He is a Black island in a White jail, guarded by a White jailer and facing a "White death."

Césaire portrays West Indians as "suffering humanity," products of the weight of an "eternally renewed cross."[18] Cut off from their roots, the masses experience collective domination but no sense of collective resistance or memory. Crushed by poverty, they enjoy no solidarity, they do not mix but dodge and take flight. How can Toussaint, the first hero of negritude, be remembered when there is little memory of resistance? Eschewing the collective, the poet fixes his faith on his individual will and "invents" a history unavailable from the collective memory.

The figure of Toussaint also indicates an impossible return to the noble past in Africa and gives way to a description of the contemporary quotidian Black man. His is a condition of abject poverty.[19] Though the dialectic of negritude still expresses the alienated psyche of the Black elite, it here produces a moment of negation – the negation of the dominant White value system. And this negation is expressed surrealistically as a rant against "White reason" and a celebration of irrationality in the context of the Black slave's resistance:

> That 2 and 2 make five
> that the forest meows
> the tree plucks the maroons from the fire.[20]

Rationalism is subverted $(2 + 2 = 5)$ and the slaves taste liberty (the forest meowing the call of runaway slaves to one another) as they seek refuge among the trees. Césaire does not need to embrace madness like the European surrealists because the reality of slavery had already left its mark. Césaire's negritude no longer hails past glories, it assails present agonies – the Black's abjection and poverty, which have "without question" knocked the stuffing out of the human being both physically and mentally, have succeeded in gaining the complicity of the poet himself. A product of the French civilizing mission, the poet comes face to face with his race and is disgusted. This revulsion is an important moment of negativity in the poet's quest for self-definition. It leads to the realization of his cowardice and his elitism.

This moment of supposed irrationality is the turning point.[21] For it is, as Césaire puts it, a "madness that remembers" the pain of slavery; it is a madness that sees the brutality and lynchings. Césaire's madness signifies a refusal of accepted realities; it also means putting faith, against all odds, in a seemingly unrealizable future. But ultimately this "madness" bears the closest affinity to the mad inspiration of the poet – a madness which creates memory out of imagination. This remembering, which is a prerequisite to any consciousness raising, includes the "memory" of another life in Africa, nearly synonymous with "nature." Césaire flirts with the idea of this possible Africa: "I have become a tree and my long tree-feet have dug great hollows of poison in the earth / have dug huge cities of bones / by thinking of the Congo / I have become the Congo."[22] The irrational is pitted against a "Reason" that crowns the "wind of night" with its whips and authority when the "Reason" of the slave masters confronts the supposed irrationality of the slaves. Césaire reveals "Reason" to be schizophrenic and the slaves' "madness" to be an imaginative expression of anger: "Because we hate you, you and your Reason, we claim kinship with dementia praecox, with flaming madness, with tenacious cannibal-ism"[23] which both literally and figuratively "eradicates the distinc-tion between self and other."[24] It is with thoughts of Africa that the slave gains freedom: "thinking of the Congo I have become the Congo." It is through this Africanism that Reason is reappropriated: "I have become a Congo resounding with forests and rivers / where the whip cracks like a great banner." Reason, formerly equated with the crack of the White master's whip which scarred the Black slave's flesh (the reason of the slaver's account books), is now countered with "Black Reason" flourishing a soaring banner of freedom. It is an empowering act of mind to transform oneself into the Congo.[25] The reference supplies a genealogical origin and hence an identity, while the stereotype suggests that in one's imagination lies the force of a nation. At the same time, Césaire's negritude is not of African monarchs and African civilizations, it is of the African diaspora and the slave's Reason.[26]

Thus Césaire's "return" to Africa is an internal journey, exploring his own existential questionings and "dredging up the repressed contents of the psyche."[27] This dredging up of the past is like reentering the hell of slavery and the middle passage – the infamous journey across the Atlantic to the "New World," a crossing in which millions are estimated to have perished – acquiescing into its madness and horror. The apparent loss of the rationality splatters the text with bloodshed and death as he recalls those who have over the centuries been slaughtered by White men: "My memory is circled with blood. My remembrance is girdled with corpses."

What remains is work, sweat, death, and despondency – "the accumulated dung of our lies." If memory is to lead to freedom, then the memory Césaire supplies will necessarily be painful, it is a memory of the "good nigger," the "master's nigger." It is a memory of lies and cowardice. It is a memory of the master and the slave. In the dialectic of Black consciousness, negritude begins as a negative movement, an admission of nonachievement: "For those who never invented, or conquered, or explored." This anti-Promethean attitude is the antithesis of Senghor's observance of Africa's discoveries, kingdoms, and conquests. More importantly, Césaire's litany to non-events is intoned "tongue in cheek against the glorification of technology by the European, the bloody conquests and destruction of peoples by colonization."[28] Open to all the breaths of the world, Césaire accepts definition not by the representation of empires on maps, nor by biology, but only by "the compasses of suffering."

Through this self-knowledge, negritude is presented as creative, moving, developing, and in-the-making. It is opposed to a static object: "my negritude is not a stone"; it is opposed to the kind of memorials that are found in Europe: "my negritude is neither a tower nor a cathedral." It is an acceptance of race and a discovery of a new pride, an attitude that respects "my repellent ugliness" and even accepts the stocks, shackles, and slave ship. With this new sense of identity comes the power to imagine rebellion:

> The sitting-down nigger
> unexpectedly on her feet
> upright in the hold
> under the sun
> upright in blood
> upright
> and
> free.[29]

What Césaire expounds is the painful birth or transformation of the new Black out of the "old nigger."[30] The "great black hole," in which Césaire "wanted to drown," now becomes the fount of the new consciousness: "It is there I will now fish the malevolent tongue of the night in its motionless veerition" (true movement and recollection). It is a leap into "a new consciousness, to a new qualitative relationship with the natural community."[31]

Césaire's long "journey" toward a new Black consciousness ends with the acceptance of his race. He is "no longer miserably confined to a facial angle, to a type of hair, to a nose sufficiently flattened, to a pigmentation sufficiently melanose." Negritude is "no longer a cephalic index or plasma," it can be measured only by the "compass of suffering." Césaire urges mankind "to conquer . . . every rigid prohibition" and create a new humanism not based on race:

> No race holds a monopoly of beauty, intelligence and strength
> there is room for all at the rendezvous of victory.[32]

Senghor and Negritude Politics

> Negritude is the whole of the values of civilization – cultural, economic, social, political – which characterize the Black peoples, more exactly the Black-African world. It is essentially instinctive reason . . . the sense of communion, the gift of imagination, the gift of rhythm – these are the traits of negritude. (Senghor, *Liberté I. Négritude et humanisme*)

Though Césaire coined the term, Senghor systematized negritude into an ideology that later supported his political ascension and maintenance of power in Senegal. And though Césaire shared many of Senghor's views in the prewar period, he insisted later that Black culture was not a product of a Black "nature," as Senghor believed. Senghor's systematization can be seen in the schematic chart below.[33] Inspired by colonial ethnographers, as well as by racists like Arthur de Gobineau, Senghor came to the conclusion that Blacks were emotionally endowed with artistic genius.

Black Race	White Race
Energetically overtaken by emotion	*Reason is hellenic*
Emotion is negro	*Discursive reason*
Great emotional warmth	
Intuition: intuitive reason through participation	*Analytical reason through utilization*
Literature and arts	*Mathematics and science*
Dance and music	
Race of concrete conceptions	*An abstract race*
Tendency towards anthropomorphism	
Subjectivism	*Objectivity in thought*
Violence is part of its essence	
I feel therefore I am	*I think therefore I am*

Senghor's explication of the Black soul as intuitive and emotional rather than rational followed ethnologists of the time, who argued that the African had no separate unconscious, and that the divisions between dream and reality, between life and death, did not exist in traditional African life. As the chart indicates, Senghor characterizes the African as communal, as one who understands the world with sense, intuitive reason, and empathy. The European, in contrast, seeks to escape community and establish individual autonomy through a quest for material power. European society is one bound by formal law, force, and regulation, where each individual jostles for individual success; it is a society of great material and technical power but bereft of emotion and spiritual value. Although Senghor emphasized African sources of his philosophy, it would be possible to identify European sources for every one of his ideas, including Catholicism which he merged into negritude.[34]

Because Senghor defined negritude as "the sum total of the qualities possessed by all Black men everywhere," his thinking moved further away from individual experience into the realm of essentialism. By the time Senghor became a politician "he had the concept of negritude ready to serve as an ideology."[35] As President of Senegal, he used negritude in an increasingly instrumental way as an ideology that encouraged people to work harder for the "good of the nation." Despite Senghor's rhetoric about the "self-expression of the Black character," his particular fixation, after gaining power, was Senegal's technological backwardness. Progress became synonymous with "instrumental rationality and technology,"[36] and negritude became the ideological cover that deflected attention from the people's lack of involvement in the running of the country, and for the continuing influence of France in political affairs.[37] Before independence, Senghor preached unity with France. After he took over the presidency, negritude became the ideological support for his policies of development inside the French union. *"We are French"* meant total support for French efforts to hold onto the colonies against the wishes of the colonized. With regard to the war in Indochina, Senghor argued for peace but voted for war credits. He did the same over Algeria, where he even sent troops to fight against the Algerian National Liberation Front. Senghor's exaltation of Black culture, argues the Beninois philosopher, Paulin Hountondji, works as an alibi for evading the political problem of national liberation.

The Algerian revolution created an enormous crisis in French politics; De Gaulle claimed power in a virtual coup d'état and immediately called for referendums in all the French colonies. The choice was stark: either full integration or immediate independence. Only Sekou Touré's Guinea would say "Non" to De Gaulle. André Malraux, then a Gaullist minister, was sent to the Antilles to secure the relationship. He was met in Fort-de-France by the mayor, Aimé Césaire, who had supported French Union, with the greeting, "I salute in your person the great French nation to which we are passionately attached." David Caute reports that Fanon was disgusted by Césaire's reception of Malraux, who as Minister of Information had denied knowledge of any act of torture in Algeria: "In an article written in the immediate aftermath of the referendum, Fanon's reaction was one of stunned indignation." Implicating both Césaire and Senghor, "he concluded with the warning that no leader should trade on the respect which the masses have for him when the independence of the nation is at issue."[38]

An important philosophical difference between Césaire and Senghor, though both initially considered negritude as antithetical to Western rationalism, is the significance each attached to surrealism and subjectivity. Because Senghor viewed negritude as an objective fact that remained a *positive* "contribution to the universal civilization,"[39] he tended to downplay surrealism. For Césaire, negritude was conceptually different. He emphasized surrealism and the negative power of negritude. Because negritude was an attitude of mind, accepting the fact of Blackness was essentially a subjective experience. From its inception, negritude implicitly carried two different interpretations: Senghor's emphasis on an essence based on an "objective visible reality," and Césaire's on the individual's experience of color. This distinction between an "objective" and "subjective" negritude was recognized by Sartre in his *Orphée noir* (1948).[40] Written at the height of negritude's popularity *Orphée noir* became a major statement on negritude.

Sartre's *Orphée noir*

Poetry is necromantic. (Sartre, "What is Literature")

Sartre's introduction to Senghor's anthology of new Black and Malagasy poetry in the French language (1948), *Orphée noir*, or *Black Orpheus*, represents one of the most important attempts to understand negritude as an aesthetic and political movement. Showing a great appreciation for Césaire, not only as negritude's greatest representative but as a revolutionary poet, Sartre calls Césaire's negritude the "embodiment of negativity," encouraging "successive transformation which will lead the Black to coincidence with himself."[41] It is a process of discovery and knowledge, not a disposition but "an interior determination" and "conjuring of the world."[42] Sartre, who only a year earlier in "What is Literature?" had ranted against poetry in general and surrealism in particular, found Césaire's surrealistic poetry truly revolutionary. For Sartre, Césaire's surrealism was unlike the "European" variety because it was a "perpetual surpassing," a "forced coupling" rather than a "calm unity of opposites." In Césaire's hands, "surrealism . . . is stolen from the Europeans by a Black who turns it against them."[43]

Sartre distinguishes Césaire's "subjective" negritude from Senghor's "objective" negritude which seeks out and valorizes the existence of African civilization, values, myths, customs, etc. But he also holds that each leads to the same result, a generalization that undermines or even undoes his perceptive reading of Césaire. Consequently, rather than challenging he assimilates Senghor's essentialism, based on a "Black soul," into what he calls "the Being-in-the-world of the Black."[44] Additionally, the only "road" that can lead to the "abolition of differences of race," according to Sartre, is a "subjective" one – a moment of "separation or of negativity," something on the order of Black separatism.[45] But Sartre quickly passes over this moment, privileging an almost ontological division between White and Black. What is objective for the Black, in Sartre's view, is not the lived experience of colonialism but Black "nature," and he has a tendency to see the Black as synonymous with the peasant and with the "earth."[46] He maps out this objective negritude of "naturalness" in comparison with the objectivity of the White worker:

> The Black remains the great male of the earth, the sperm of the world. His existence – it is the great vegetal patience; his work – it is the repetition from year to year of the sacred coitus. He creates and is fertile because he creates. . . . To labor, to plant, to eat, is to make love with nature. It is thus that they rejoin the dances and the phallic rites of the African Blacks.[47]

Sartre's preoccupation with "objective" negritude – and the metaphors of natural Black male sexual potency – reflects his uncritical acceptance of Senghor's negritude. It results in the repetition of colonial anthropology's emphasis on "the phallic rites of the African Blacks," custom, and timeless African cultural forms, as well as the conventional image of the Black's sexual potency. Negritude celebrates *creation, perpetual coition, skin, flesh, sex, spermatic religion, rising phallus,* and the Black's consciousness, Sartre maintains, adopting Senghor's expression, "is primarily based upon a Black soul . . . on a certain quality common to the thoughts and to the behavior of Blacks which is called negritude."[48]

Sartre's consideration of negritude expresses an ambiguity in negritude itself. Despite its historical and geographic specificity, despite slavery, assimilation, and the diaspora and different experiences, the objective negritudists proclaimed a Black essence, an "innate solidarity" and "special reasoning process." On the other hand, there is subjective negritude, with its memory and "passion for liberty," expressed by Toussaint L'Ouverture and the Black heroes, through revolt and "the struggle for the definitive liberation." Revolutionary negritude, Césaire's negritude, is a "becoming," not a rhythm or a "cluster of primitive instincts"; it has its basis in a specific historic situation and, as Sartre declares, it is based in a "sense of revolt and love of liberty."[49] Nevertheless, Sartre continues, there is something much "more serious." The following is quoted by Fanon:

> The Black, as we have said, creates an anti-racist racism. He does not at all wish to dominate the world; he wishes the absolution of racial privileges wherever they are found; he affirms his solidarity with the oppressed of all colors. At a blow the subjective, existential, ethnic notion of negritude "passes" as Hegel would say, into the objective, positive, exact notion of the proletariat . . . Negritude appears as the weak stage of the dialectical progression: the theoretical and practical affirmation of white supremacy is the thesis; the position of negritude as the antithetical value is the moment of negativity. But this negative moment is not sufficient in itself . . .[50]

The negative moment, Sartre claims, only "prepares itself for a synthesis." Why should racism, countered by a racist antiracism, produce a synthesis of a society without color? Negritude, Sartre argues, is a dialectic that surpasses itself, "an absolute which knows itself to be transitory." It is dedicated to its own destruction and finds its victory in surpassing itself. In the end negritude is a tragedy because it is "not sufficient in itself."[51]

The Dialectics of Black Consciousness

Fanon's critique of Hegel appears at first sight to jibe with Sartre's denial of possible reciprocity in *Being and Nothingness*, where the slave's consciousness is incapable of transcending its objectification in the Other's look. Fanon's statement at the end of *Black Skin*, that the "French Black is doomed," also seems compatible with what Sartre called "ontological pessimism."[52] Furthermore, Fanon's analysis of an absolute and Manichean divide between White and Black appears consonant with Sartre's claim of an ontological separation, where "no universal knowledge can be derived from this relation of consciousness."[53] Yet, rather than making generalizations about the human condition, Fanon's observations are grounded by the gravity of the historical specificity of racism and colonialism. As Fanon put it in *Black Skin*, because "there is nothing ontological about segregation" . . . "what is to be done is to set man free" (*BS*, 186, 9):

> In the Weltanschauung of a colonized people there is an impurity, a
> flaw that outlaws any ontological explanation. Someone may object
> that this is the case of the individual, but such an objection merely
> conceals a basic problem. Ontology – once it is admitted as leaving
> existence by the wayside – does not permit us to understand the
> being of the Black man. For not only must the Black man be black;
> he must be black in relation to the White man . . . The Black man has
> no ontological resistance in the eyes of the White man. (*BS*, 109,
> emphasis added)

This "lack" of ontological resistance provides one basis for understanding Fanon's critique of Sartre's *Orphée noir*, and indicates a
markedly different conception of negativity. Paradoxically, Fanon
appears far more existentialist than Sartre, whose categories seem
fixed and where negation is absorbed into an a priori affirmation.
In the face of the impasses of reciprocity, Fanon's dialectic turns
toward Black consciousness. The methodology for such a move is
summed up in *The Wretched*, where self-consciousness is seen as the
guarantee for communication. (*WE*, 247)

In *Orphée noir*, Sartre insists that class is objective and negritude
is subjective, a "minor" stage in a pre-existing "historical" dialectic.
Yet something else happens, Fanon argues, when the Black dives
into the "night of the absolute," or experiences negritude's "psyche
of ascent." Fanon calls it a revolutionary leap in consciousness.
Black consciousness is not just a passing stage nor an antiracist
racism but a new mode of cognition, an "absolute intensity of beginning" (*BS*, 138). The White creates the Black, but it is the Black who
counters with negritude. This self-discovery is "remarkable" precisely because it is a dynamic movement, not a static condition.[54]

Fanon's critique of Sartre's contention that race is particular
and class universal also alludes to the methodological difference
between synthesis and negativity. While the structure of his argument might appear dialectical, in that negation is eventually subsumed into a higher synthesis, Sartre makes light of Hegel's insight
that all negation tends to see itself as absolute and lends momen-
tum to the dialectical process. Instead, Sartre imposed a mechanical schema – thesis = White / antithesis = Black / synthesis =
multiracialism. Because Black consciousness merely contributed to
an inevitable and preexisting goal, Fanon felt that Sartre was
curtailing possible futures. Fanon, on the other hand, posits Black
consciousness as an absolute because a dialectic of negativity
cannot close off in advance any possible development. "I didn't
need to know," says Fanon, who insists that the dialectic be worked

through without knowing the end. Thus the application of Sartre's conception of Other to Black consciousness "proves fallacious." Fanon returns to the master/slave dialectic now twisted with color:

> Though Sartre's speculations on the existence of the Other may be correct (to the extent, we must remember, to which *Being and Nothingness* describes an alienated consciousness), their application to a Black consciousness proves fallacious. That is because the White man is not only The Other but also the master, whether real or imaginary. (*BS*, 138n)

And Fanon reacts to Sartre's critique of negritude as if the proof of his very existence has been "snatched away."

> And so it is not I who make a meaning for myself, but it is the meaning that was already there, preexisting for me . . . Help had been sought from a friend of the colored peoples, and that friend had found no better response than to point out the relativity of what we were doing. (*BS*, 134, 133)

For Sartre, negritude represents the free existential choice of immediacy, but for Fanon there never was a choice (*BS*, 126). Black consciousness demands a "retreat" to a prior stage of the dialectic, "a stage preceding any invasion, any abolition of the ego by desire" (*BS*, 134) – a return to the certainty of self-conscious ego itself, before the resistance from the Other and "the experience of desire." Because the Other does not recognize the Black as a human being, Fanon insists that "the only solution was to make myself known" (*BS*, 115).

Fanon's position, which admittedly sounds solipsistic, expresses an aspect of his original engagement with Hegel and can be understood in similar terms to Hegel's contention in the *Phenomenology* that self-consciousness initially has only a pure I as its object.[55] Fanon wants Black consciousness to achieve this certainty from which the Black slave confronts limitations. As Hegel put it, the servile consciousness, "as a consciousness forced back into itself will withdraw into itself and be transformed into a truly independent consciousness."[56] In *Black Skin*, the "retreat" is a "quest of absoluteness" where one is recognized as a "primal value" and where subjective certainty is transformed into objective truth (*BS*, 134, 217–18). For this transformation to occur, consciousness must be forced back onto itself, into the "night of the absolute," argues Fanon, who locates Black consciousness at a stage he calls an "absolute density." In contradistinction to "historical becoming," he proclaims, "I needed to lose myself in negritude" and believe that it was the absolute concerned only with its independence and freedom.[57] He responds at a similar pitch to Sartre: "For once, that born Hegelian had forgotten that consciousness has to lose itself in the night of the absolute, the only condition to attain consciousness of self" (*BS*, 133). Where Sartre was trying to take a shortcut and skip over negation in his drive toward synthesis, Fanon is insisting that it is only through losing itself absolutely that consciousness becomes a being-for-self, a self-consciousness for itself. Fanon is also aware of the logical consequence of a desire for a world without the Other. Self-consciousness, through its negative relation to the object, is unable to supersede it. Instead the cycle is repeated and reproduces the desire for the object again. This is the problematic of the dialectic in *Black Skin*, but it is only from this standpoint that a new beginning can be made.

Paradoxically, Sartre forgot the specificity of the Black's lived experience, reducing it to a minor term which is sublated by a "pre-existing" meaning. Negritude is placed within the "evolution of Humanity": "Race is transmuted in historicity, the Black Present explodes and is temporalized, negritude – with its Past and its Future – is inserted in Universal History." "Universal history" and the "evolution of humanity" sound akin to Enlightenment thought, which had put Blacks at the bottom of the chain of being. Fanon's reaction is more radically dialectical and concretely historical. In Fanon's dialectic, the negation is not reduced to a mere moment but has to be fully embraced,

> The dialectic that brings necessity into the foundation of my freedom drives me out of myself. It shatters my unreflected position. Still in terms of consciousness, Black consciousness is immanent in its own eyes. I am not a potentiality of something, I am wholly what I am. I do not have to look for the universal. (*BS*, 135)

"I had to lose myself completely in negritude," Fanon argues, because Black consciousness is the only thing that can "shatter my unreflected position." In terms that seem to assume an a priori subject, Sartre has forgotten that "this negativity draws its worth from an almost substantive absoluteness" (*BS*, 135).

Though this negativity, namely Black consciousness, might create a deplorable confusion. Fanon demands a more situational view, insisting that the Black is not a given a priori but rather is a product of White society. Against the argument that negritude obliterates difference, Blacks in Europe – whether Antillean, Ethiopian, Senegalese or Malagasy – remain Black wherever they go. In a racist society, negritude must be taken as an absolute value, that can be a new point of departure for consciousness, the certainty that it is all of reality. The danger is that by positing itself as the only truth, this kind of certainty runs the risk of posing itself as a thesis against any equally valid antithesis, and remaining as an "unhappy consciousness which oscillates endlessly between two irreconcilable terms."[58]

Negritude expresses the ambivalence of an "unhappy consciousness" that has not yet gained concrete freedom (*BS*, 135). In terms of the master/slave dialectic, however, to attain a "mind of one's own" cannot help but seem to the slave a sufficient good, one that awakens a new consciousness and a new certainty, even if it has not transcended the reality of the slavish condition.[59]

While Fanon believes that the world outside is already embedded within the dialectic of Black self-consciousness, he might agree that Black consciousness is a "stage." But it is only by going deeper into the particular that one can reach a new beginning. The completion of this moment of negativity requires its own negation.

Fanon contends that the Black's existence must be defined from within, not from without. "This struggle," Fanon adds, "has to take on an aspect of completeness," but Sartre merely presents Black consciousness as an incomplete moment (*BS*, 134). It is ironic that Fanon responded in so pronounced an existential fashion to Sartre, who in this case was privileging a crude Marxism. It was not what my consciousness could possibly become, Fanon had shouted, but what it is. Sartre had "destroyed Black zeal" and ended with that commonplace: "I was like that too when I was young ... you'll see, it will pass." He sounded like the paternal White liberal. Fanon's response was to remind Sartre of lived experience: The negritude poets might have misread history if history is a tidy progression. But the immanence of Black consciousness is precisely its refusal to shirk the reality of the here and now. Fanon quoted Jacques Roumain (*BS*, 136), who founded the Communist Party of Haiti and whose "Dirty Niggers" later inspired the title, *The Wretched*:[60]

> we regroup our forces sundered
> by the deceits of the masters ...
> we proclaim the oneness of the suffering
> and the revolt
> of all the peoples on all the face of the earth.

Yet where Roumain had proclaimed the "age of brotherhood," Fanon emphasizes the specificity of negritude. He doesn't want to be told about "processes of history" but about an expression of existence, while echoing Merleau-Ponty that "expressing what exists is an endless task." If revolutionary negritude, Césaire's negritude, is a misreading of history, it at least faces reality, however wearing. But what is much worse, he adds, is that the man who presented himself as a friend "was reminding me that my Blackness was only a minor term" just at the moment he was trying to express his own negritude. "Sartre," Fanon concludes "remained the Other." He adds the now famous lines:

> In all truth, in all truth I tell you, my shoulders slipped out of the framework of the world, my feet could no longer feel the touch of the ground. Without a Black past, without a Black future, it was impossible for me to live my Blackhood [*négrerie*]. Not yet White, no longer wholly Black, I was damned. (*BS*, 138)

Fanon's reaction to Sartre's argument that negritude is a "minor" element of the dialectic cut Fanon to the quick. Here was a so-called "friend," who emerged as the White "Other" at the moment that Fanon had embraced Black consciousness. Sartre thus in a sense stripped Fanon of his newly won identity.

Fanon's Critique of Negritude

> It is a vigorous style, alive with rhythms, struck through and through with bursting life; it is full of color, too, bronzed, sun-baked and violent . . . it expresses above all a hand to hand struggle and reveals the need that man has to liberate himself from a part of his being which already contained the seed of decay. (Fanon, *Black Skin*)

Fanon's relationship to negritude is complicated. He embraces it, singing its praises, while emphasizing the brilliance of Césaire's dive into the depths to discover a "psyche of ascent." But he concedes that the Black's "intellectual alienation," the subject of his analysis in *Black Skin*, is a product of a middle-class society which is corrupt and has to be overturned (*BS*, 224–5). Consequently, Black consciousness doesn't seem to matter. However, Fanon is consistent in viewing negritude as a necessary negation of White values.

As a reaction to the évolués of Paris and Martinique who wanted to put on a White mask, Black self-awareness is not worthless. Despite the colonial liberal ideology that proclaimed that the Black évolué was really no different from the White and could "make it" in White society, it was pigment not "refined manners" or "knowledge" that remained the Black's defining feature. While not a blatant racist, the liberal White introduced himself as the best friend of the Black, still judging the évolué by pigmentation, the *Black* teacher, the *Black* doctor, or "my Black friend." The Black professional felt the judging and dissecting gaze of White eyes waiting for a mistake, waiting for the Black to be *just like a Black*. Fanon maintains that Blacks are always "walled in" by their appearance.

In terms of liberal thought that proclaims the equality of all, racism is illogical. The idea that one could be despised for the color of one's skin is unreasonable. Schooled in the Enlightenment, and reacting to its hypocrisy, the Black intellectual chooses the only path open, that is "toward unreason." Fanon remarks that "out of the necessities of my struggle I had chosen the method of regression" (*BS*, 123). Imbibing French culture and steadfastly learning its ways, its "moral laws" and its reason, Black middle-class intellectuals had convinced themselves that they were French (*BS*, 153n) but had found the White world not only impenetrable but oppressive. In reaction, Fanon proclaims, "I secreted a race. And that race staggered under the burden of a basic element. What was it? *Rhythm*" (*BS*, 122). Quoting Senghor, "emotion is completely Negro as reason is Greek," there is a moment when Fanon, the critical intellectual, embraces "objective" negritude virtually unconditionally, wading in its irrationality:

> So here we have the Black rehabilitated "standing before the bar," ruling the world with his intuition, the Black recognized, set on his feet again . . . "open to all breaths of the world" I embrace the world! I am the world . . . Somewhere beyond the objective world of farms . . . I had subtly brought the real world into being. (*BS*, 127–8)

The Black intellectual, who had "rationalized the world" but had been rejected on the basis of color prejudice, now finds pride in a "magical Black culture." Returning to the source, the intellectual embraces all sorts of cultural rituals that have been caricatured by colonialism: Black magic, primitive mentality, animism. "Going primitive" provides a psychological release.

Senghor's negritude is as much an appeal to Whites as it is to Blacks, hoping to enlighten the latter about the worth of Black civilization and the former about this civilization's very existence; but Fanon quickly insists on a more actional response and expresses how he is forced back into himself. "One had to distrust rhythm, earth mother love, this mystic, carnal marriage of the group and the cosmos" (*BS*, 125) because the affirmation of Blackness, the embrace of apparent unreason and the reclamation of the past, are all a *reaction* to the White world. The cards are stacked so that "every hand [is] a losing hand." Somehow the White world's "reason" has to be countered by another, more "real" reason, and for Fanon it was Césaire's negritude that helped him find himself.

Fanon's position in regard to negritude is far more contextual and historical than is recognized by critics who argue that it "runs parallel with his gradual appropriation of Sartre's dialectic."[61] In *The Wretched*, negritude is much more historicized and directly criticized from the standpoint of the Algerian revolution, with criticisms lodged explicitly against negritude's leaders (like Senghor) who continued to support the idea of Algeria as French. The critique of negritude in *The Wretched* as an oppositional culture is also more systematized. In *Black Skin*, violence expresses the negation of the internalized White man, a negation necessary for the development of Black consciousness; in *The Wretched*, violence refers to the external world, specifically to the absolute violence of French colonialism in Algeria and the counterviolence necessary for actual liberation.[62]

The problem of negritude poses a further complication. Alone, it cannot become a philosophy of freedom as Senghor proposed. Its power is as an inversion of colonial ideology. Though subjective negritude moves beyond this standpoint, it is not a philosophy of liberation. As a dialectic that brings necessity into the foundation of freedom, negritude is one fraught with contradictions. Inasmuch as negritude attempts to "recapture the self and scrutinize the self," and more importantly initiate the cycle of freedom (*BS*, 231), Fanon insists that it retains a positive value. Yet it was not an effective vehicle for social revolution. Negritude was useful in shaking everything up, but finally, its reliance on unconscious rather than conscious action, and the importance it placed on the irrational, meant that it was unable to articulate a *positive* conception of change. Nevertheless, negritude represented a new sensibility and Fanon wished instead that the Black intellectuals turn to Césaire for their inspiration and "take stock of the reality," of the "fires, the segregation, the repressions, the rapes" (*BS*, 187). To take stock of reality meant recognizing that being lost in negritude could be a prelude to action.

In *The Wretched*, Fanon considers negritude important, but concedes that it is not a sufficient condition for liberation from the shackles of an imposed essence of Blackness. He lashes out at the negritude politician's wish to separate culture from the struggle against colonialism, and he criticizes proposals for "cultural unity" from poets as different as Senghor and Rabémananjara because these men passively or actively supported the French against the Algerian liberation movement. What is important to keep in mind is a distinction between negritude's objective political failings and its subjective necessity, which lies in its power to transform or rebuild the character of the intellectual, who must "lose himself at whatever cost in his own barbarous people," and come face to face with his cowardice (*BS*, 218). Fanon describes the intellectual, dwelling in the shadow of colonial ideology, as a "living haunt of contradictions." Tearing away from it is difficult and "may prove deadly,"[63] but if it is not accomplished, "there will be serious psycho-affective injuries and the result will be individuals without an anchor, without a horizon, colorless, stateless, rootless – a race of angels (*WE*, 218). The price of Césaire's psyche of ascent could be the loss of sanity (*WE*, 218). But paradoxically, the defense of the "nation's legitimacy" is not motivated by any specifically national identification. The colonialist has regarded the Black not as a Ghanaian or Angolan but as a Black.[64] And just as the colonialist's condemnation is continental, the intellectual's defense is antithetical but "logically inscribed from the same point of view" (*WE*, 212). A politics based on race, then, is highly problematic.

At the same time, the intellectual's embrace of negritude is a sign to the colonialists that their civilizing project is tottering. In terms of the master/slave dialectic, in Hegel's words, the Black slave places "himself as the negative in the permanent order of things and thereby [becomes] for himself, someone existing on his own account."[65] This movement of becoming for self out of negativity is the type of movement that Fanon sees in the development of negritude as its "own foundation." Yet negritude can be progressive and reactionary, depending on the political situation. By placing such a "high value on custom, traditions and appearances," it can lead to "sterility." The objective negritudist's search for a Black soul could end in an empty celebration of "the exotic." By appealing to people of color solely on the basis of race, negritude ignores the specificity and distinguishing character of people's experiences. Like colonialism, it takes the whole continent (as well as the diaspora) as its frame of reference (*WE*, 216), and bypasses the demands of the present to revalorize the past. This is because it assumes that race always determines the individual's social identity, which in the context of the anticolonial movements is retrograde. "To believe that it is possible to create a Black culture," Fanon says of Senghor in *The Wretched*, "is to forget that niggers are disappearing" (*WE*, 234). To effectively challenge colonialism, culture must become national and specific. There is a dignity, glory, and solemnity in past African civilizations, like the "wonderful Songhai," but he adds, this does not alter "the fact that today the Songhais are underfed and illiterate, thrown between sky and water with empty eyes" (*WE*, 210). Vague and romantic images, an idealized Black mystique and nostalgia for an invented or real past, can at a certain point inhibit the drive toward freedom in the present. Negritude like Senghor's fails to confront, or even shrinks away from, the real struggle and history (*WE*, 234n) and thus his support for French union was an expression of his wish to remain a prisoner of "the confusion that reigns in his mind" (*DC*, 138). No one, Fanon argues, and here he includes Césaire, "can truly wish for the spread of African culture if he does not give practical support to the creation of the conditions necessary to the existence of that culture; in other words to the liberation of the whole continent" (*WE*, 235).

Nevertheless, a critical, actional negritude can claim for itself a "historical necessity" since it can lead to a genuine national culture *if* it abandons its elitism and reconnects with the people's struggle for freedom. The negritude intellectual has to shed his bourgeois individualism and become a social individual in contact with, and in the service of, the people. To remain progressive, negritude has to become a fighting culture. Nothing, Fanon argues, "can replace the reasoned irrevocable taking up of arms on the people's side . . . [and] join them in fluctuating movement." It demands that "the native poet . . . first realize the extent of his estrangement from [the people]" (*WE*, 226).

Because Black consciousness cannot look to the White world for recognition, and because "belonging" or not belonging to a particular race structures one's social position, Fanon's phenomenological speculations eventually yield to an imperative of praxis: "having taken thought, [consciousness] prepares to act" (*BS*, 222). Fanon's choice of epigraph from *The Eighteenth Brumaire* about the social revolution stripping itself of past superstitions should not be underestimated as an expression of Fanon's attitude to negritude. This turn to Marx is manifested in the assertion that there is ultimately only one solution – to restructure the world. He acknowledges that the existence of Black philosophy, architecture, and literature would be interesting, but, once again, how can it change the life of an eight-year-old child laborer in Martinique (*BS*, 230)? Fanon insists that he will not be a slave of the past, a slave of slavery. No longer concerned with fleshing out the ambiguities and nuances of race, he quite boldly says: "In no way should I derive my basic purpose from the people of color. In no way should I dedicate myself to the revival of an unjustly unrecognized Black civilization" (*BS*, 216).

Moreover, Fanon's interest in class reflects his own personal stake in clarifying the relationship between intellectual and worker: "the quest for disalienation by a doctor of medicine born in Guadeloupe, can be understood only by recognizing motivations basically different from those of the Black laborer" (*BS*, 223). However, even with his self-consciousness of class position, he asserts quite boldly that, on the basis of knowing a "few working class people" in Paris, he is "convinced . . . that without even knowing it they (the Black workers) share my views" (*BS*, 224). This vexed relationship between worker and intellectual will be reconsidered in the context of the Algerian revolution.

4

Becoming Algerian

The Algiers School

For Algeria, colonized by the French after 1830, the period 1871 to 1918 saw the most violent destruction of indigenous Algerian society. The long revolt was finally put down and "a holocaust" demanded. The settler's reaction to the insurrection was an "orgy of vengeance," writes John Ruedy, "compounded with a pell-mell rush for economic gain."[1] If it had taken the French nearly half a century to overcome Algerian resistance, the next 50 years saw the pauperization of the population, the massive expropriation of the best lands, forced labor, and the eradication of indigenous markets. Alongside the destruction of agricultural society, and the consequential ruin of old forms of property, cultural practices, and labor processes, was the idea of gradually "assimilating" Algeria, if not Algerians, into France. Algerians were considered French without citizenship, with a de facto inequality of the colonizers and colonized introduced in 1865. To gain citizenship Algerians had to renounce their Muslim civil status. Only a handful did. With the loss of land, the rural masses became landless peasants, many drifting to the edges of towns or abroad to France.[2] The material basis for Algerian cultural autonomy was broken.

It was in this context that theories of the "Algerian mind" were developed. The intrusion of Western medical practices went hand in hand with military penetration, and the physician became the missionary of the French civilizing project. Further conquest brought further classification, including the "scientific" designation of the Arabs (introduced in 1845)[3] as instinctively brutal, with innate abilities for thieving and raping. Central to this classification was the identification of Islam as a hostile, fanatical and violent religion. The Arabs, especially the nomadic people of Algeria, were viewed as not civilizable.

Lucien Lévy-Bruhl's *The Primitive Mind*, published in 1922, portrayed the African as wholly Other to the European. He proposed that the African had a "prelogical mentality." Consequently, "the African" did not have the power for individuation nor the capacity to separate myth and reality; in contrast to the European, the attitude of the mind of the primitive was very different.[4]

For Antoine Porot, the founder of the Algiers School, the North African was fatalistic, reminiscent of the feudal peasant of Europe: "a shapeless mass of primitive people, in most cases ignorant and gullible, very distant from our way of thinking and our reactions, never having grasped any of our moral attitudes or even the simplest of social, economic or political concerns."[5] In reality, the indigenous were of course quite logical. They understood the social, economic and political concerns of colonizers as a simple truth, the expropriation of their land and the exploitation of their labor. It is not surprising, therefore, that Porot deplored the stubbornness, laziness and inflexibility of the natives in contrast to "the flexible and polymorphous spirit of civilized Europeans."

The problem of African labor was a perennial issue for the colonists. As late as 1951, just a few years before Fanon's arrival at Blida-Joinville, John C. Carothers, the specialist psychiatrist in Mathari hospital in Nairobi, wrote a study of "African reliability." The examples, written up in the midst of the unmentioned "Mau Mau emergency," indicated various aspects of "primitive behavior" as pathologically lazy. For Carothers the colonial complaint that the African is a poor worker is a result of the African's limited mental capacity. For example, the cook who does not warn his master before the firewood runs out is "not used to looking far ahead," and the reason "the houseboys" cannot put furniture back level with the wall is because "spatial perception is foreign to the African." In his further discussion of the African staff at the mental hospital Carothers argues that "primitive custom" takes precedence over career advancement, that the African cannot coordinate tasks, that the African has no temporal urgency, that Africans fail to give attention and registration, that work appears as a series of memorized and meaningless acts, and that the African "takes advantage of" kindness, and can't be trusted.[6]

Just as Carothers's theory came to dominate in Britain's African colonies, Porot's theory was the doctrine according to which psychiatry was practiced in French North Africa. Porot's "North African Syndrome" (1952) was first discussed by Fanon in his article for the liberal magazine, *Esprit* (later collected in Fanon's *Pour la révolution africaine. Écrits politiques – Toward the African Revolution: Political Essays (AR)*). He describes it as an *idée fixe*, epitomizing the French doctor's attitude to the North African patient: "The North African today who goes to see a doctor bears the weight of all his compatriots . . . The man you thingify by calling him systematically Mohammed, whom you reconstruct, or rather whom you dissolve on the basis of an idea . . . don't you have the impression that you are emptying him of his substance?" (*AR*, 8, 14). In other words, from a therapeutic point of view reciprocity had been blocked by an a priori reduction of the North African not only to a body but the reification and dissolution of that body into a "repulsive idea." The patient is spoken to in the infantilizing language that "the hacks in the free clinic have mastered so well." Fanon maintained that "the North African Syndrome" was a form of the "inferiority complex," produced by the total social environment, and could be addressed only by totally changing it. Fanon's first goal at Blida was to humanize the environment of the hospital.

What was to Antoine Porot,[7] the founder of the militantly colonialist Algiers School,[8] a quick-tempered and violent thing was to Fanon a protagonist resisting colonial rule.[9] For Fanon, the degree of violence among the natives was in direct proportion to the degree of violence of colonial rule, and thus spontaneous outbreaks of "fanaticism" among the peasantry were really a logical response to the systematic expropriation. Porot's characterization of the Algerian as childish, impulsive, murderous, criminal and perverse, with inherent mental debility, suggestibility, and weakness of affective and moral life,[10] is rescribed by Fanon as the native's rationality and instinct for survival. In the Manichean world there are two truths, that of the settler and that of the native: "The settler paints the native as a quintessence of evil" and the native does the same to the settler (*WE*, 41). Rather than characterological, as colonial sociologists argue, the native's "fatalism" is a result of the colonial situation. For Fanon, the colonized lead a life resembling an "incomplete death": "an ever-menacing death is experienced as endemic famine, unemployment, a high death rate, an inferiority complex and the absence of hopes for the future" (*DC*, 123).

Fanon was appointed chef de service at Blida-Joinville Hospital in December 1953. Though he identified with anticolonial ideas and movements, and was on the radical wing of psychiatric practice, he had not gone to Algeria to join the revolution – which would not begin until a year later on November 1, 1954. Yet at Blida "the twin aspects of his activity cannot be separated: promoting the revolution and promoting his conception of *real* psychiatry are features of the same commitment."[11]

In the space of two months during his temporary appointment at Pontorson (Normandy, France) before Fanon left for Algeria, he had upset the authorities by trying to put into practice some of the principles of institutional psychotherapy he had learned under François Tosquelles. Dr Tosquelles, a revolutionary refugee from the Spanish civil war, had pioneered "institutional therapy" at Saint-Alban, where Fanon interned in 1952–3. The idea was to change the hospital environment by developing a therapeutic community within the hospital using a number of different techniques, including psychoanalysis, group therapy, and drugs and shock treatments.

At Blida, Fanon immediately put into place a number of reforms in an attempt to introduce a Tosquellean program. He introduced occupational therapy, group psychotherapy and other collective meetings in an effort to create a therapeutic community. Fanon shocked the staff by ordering the patients to be unchained and straitjackets to be removed. He started to unchain the inmates, creating an event remembered by staff years later. Fanon organized a soccer team, arranged weekly outings to the beach, the serving of traditional dishes, and a weekly publication, for patients and staff. Fanon desegregated the service, outlawing ethnic privileges. Not all the reforms were successful and it was the lack of success that proved a crucial turning point for him. Two separate groups, European women and Algerian men, were followed in the reform experiment. Whereas the European women participated in meetings and activities, the Algerian men failed to respond.

In his article "Sociotherapy in a ward of Muslim men,"[12] co-authored with Jacques Azoulay in 1954, Fanon refused to lay blame for the failure in terms of Algiers School reasoning: "It became clear that it could not be a question of laziness or poor will: we have taken the wrong road, it was necessary to re-examine the fundamental reasons for our failure so as to find a way out of the impasse." The failure resulted in a reassessment of the attempt to apply practices that had worked in France to a Muslim society. They were self-critical: "Under the guise of what poor judgement had we believed possible a sociotherapy of Western inspiration to serve Muslim men?"[13] Fanon's remarkable "leap" involved a critique of the

cultural biases not only of the prevailing but also emergent
psychiatric thought like institutional therapy, and therefore, also, a
critique of colonial claims of integration. "A revolutionary attitude
was indispensable." Quite honestly they summed up their experiment: "We were attempting to create certain institutions, but we
forgot that any attempt to do so has to be preceded by a tenacious
concrete and real investigation into the organic basis of native
society." Echoing his critique of Mannoni, Fanon returned to what
he called the "real," and that real had to do with the simple though
contested fact that the Algerian was not French.

Institutional therapy had taken it for granted that Algeria was
France and thus was adopting "an assimilationist policy." This
problem had to be radically reassessed. Self-critically, Fanon and
Azoulay admit that they had not attempted to get to know the
Muslim patient's situation. And they conclude that a "revolutionary attitude was indispensable to go from a position where the
supremacy of Western culture was evident to a cultural relativism."
To understand North African "reality" a change in perspective was
needed: "A leap had to be made, a conversion of values had to
be carried out. Let us admit it, it was necessary to go from the
biological to the institutional, from natural existence to cultural
existence."[14]

They asked themselves basic but profound questions. They
wanted to know the biological, moral, aesthetic, cognitive, and religious values of Muslim society as a "totality." Though the answers
are fairly rudimentary, there is a critical edge that is refreshing, indicating a new opening to the "real" lived experience of their patients:
"A sociotherapy could only be possible to the extent one accounted
for the social morphology and the forms of sociability."[15] A central
issue was language.[16] Fanon and Azoulay had used interpreters,
which further alienated the doctor/patient relationship, and noted
that in the hospital the communication between the French-
speaking doctor and Arabic-speaking patient had become impossible. The "need for an interpreter spontaneously produces a
mistrust,"[17] because the translator was part of the phenomenology
of the colonial machine, met in the police station, the law court, or
the government office. As Fanon would put it later, "the French language, the language of the occupier, was given the role of *Logos*,
with ontological implications within Algerian society" (*DC*, 91).[18]

Fanon's appreciation of his failed psychological experiment
indicates how quickly he was willing to change approaches. His
new program included field trips and further studies of Algerian

history and culture. If Fanon had paid little attention to the many-faceted Algerian culture on his arrival at Blida, he quickly changed his mind. Such empathy with the lived experience of his Algerian patients at Blida would lead him to identify with the Algerian war of liberation.

Fanon's work in psychiatry was not limited to a critique of the Algiers School; he was also developing a positive program for mental health, or the liberation from a pathology of liberty, as he put it. Fanon's critique of the Algiers School and the dehumanized reality of French colonialism went hand in hand with his work as a psychiatrist, which had the mark of an innovator. At first he had pursued principles learned with Tosquelles at Saint-Alban and adapted them to the social-cultural environment, but his trend toward a transcultural psychiatry was subjected to a dialectical self-criticism that led him in the direction of radical ethnopsychiatry.

Fanon was attempting to understand the social and cultural context of the people he was treating; he was not simply positing another ethnopsychiatry, but a radical psychiatry that got to the root, namely the human being, in a cultural context.[19] For Fanon, madness became a pathology of liberty, and so the practice of psychiatry had to be liberating. In small ways, his work at Blida and then later in Tunis put the practice of freedom into action – the destruction of the regime of incarceration, an end to the chaining of patients, and the creation of new institutional forms, day hospitalization for example, in the context of a new cultural understanding, were all attempts to break the walls between psychiatric treatment and social life. Fanon's was a work in progress, moving into uncharted waters. Razanajao and Postel speak of Fanon's method: "Fanon did find himself literally thrown into various fundamentally alienating situations which he tried to get through by getting thoroughly involved on each occasion so as to be able to overcome them without being taken in by them."[20]

In "The North African attitude to madness"[21] Fanon and Sanchez develop an ethnopsychiatric answer to the problem of the failure of psychiatric care. The North African conception of madness, they argue, produces a more humanistic and holistic way of treating the insane. Their study on indigenous ideas of the mad came at the same time as other colleagues at Blida were doing research on the social psychopathology of spirits and djinns, and taking field trips to the mountains of Kabylia.[22]

The notion of mutual incomprehensibility, of a blocked reciprocity, was also apparent in Fanon and Lacaton's 1955 presentation,

"Confession in North Africa,"[23] which confronted the Algiers School assumptions about the Arab. Here the mutual opposition of the two cultures is expressed in a failure of communication and interpretation. In a "normal" situation (that of reciprocal recognition), a confession of the accused is "the ransom for his reinsertion into the group." In other words what underwrites the meaning of a confession is a reciprocity between the individual confessor and the social group. In the colonial situation, the Manichean reality transforms the meaning of the confession. The accused denies the act and the confession. If he had confessed, it was under duress. The psychiatrist, faced with such apparently schizophrenic behavior, falls back into the Algiers School stereotypes: the North African is a liar, degenerate, and phylogenetically abnormal. To get beyond this mutual incomprehension and to judge the "truth," argue Fanon and Lacaton, there needs to be a change in standpoint. How to resolve the problem? It became increasingly clear that if there had ever been a purely therapeutic answer, it was fast dissipating. It was the abnormality of the colonial situation that produced the Algiers School notion of phylogenetic abnormality. As Fanon pushed psychotherapy further into the social milieu, breaking down the hospital walls, the war of liberation became more and more present inside the hospital, and in Fanon's psychiatric practice.

Beyond Ethnopsychiatry?

After he left Algeria Fanon and Asselah published a critique of institutional psychiatry that focused on the psychiatric institution itself as the cause of the destruction of the humanity of the patient. Exclusion and isolation, at the heart of the psychiatric hospital with its straitjackets, handcuffs, and punishments that "amputate and punish" the mentally ill, attack not "the illness" but the patient's very being. The exclusion and isolation of the patient is counterproductive, heightening the lived experience of hallucination and fantasy. Mirroring Fanon's description of colonialism in *The Wretched*, the psychiatric institution is seen as an organization of repression and punishment: "The lines of force which participate in the phenomenal field create a disastrous poverty." The patient experiences a double internment. In the mental illness and in the psychiatric hospital the social isolation of the patient is confirmed within a sadistic and antisocial system.[24]

Fanon's resignation from Blida did not stop his search for an answer to the problem. After leaving Algeria his next professional appointment was in the Tunis Hospital neuropsychiatry department, which, like Blida, had been created by Porot. Fanon ran the outpatients clinic from December 1957 to July 1959. Again, he introduced practices that originated in Europe, but this time their form and openness to the cultural context produced different results. In effect, this was a transcultural psychiatry rooted in the dialectic of individual and social environment. "Day hospitalization in psychiatry: value and limits,"[25] written with Charles Geronimi, is probably Fanon's most radical and original intervention into psychiatric practice, claiming that "our experience proves that it has been possible to establish this technique, which originated in economically developed countries, in a so-called underdeveloped country, without losing any of its value." They concluded that outpatient treatment allied to general hospitals should become a basis for psychiatric treatment and that treatment should "guarantee the patient's freedom as much as possible so that being a patient has no connotations of duress or being 'put away.'"[26] Though psychiatric day-care was beginning to be practiced, there were no such programs in Africa.[27] On the cutting edge of psychiatric hospitalization reform, day hospitalization was the form that Fanon pursued to work out a humanistic approach to mental illness, to get beyond the Manicheanism of the Algiers School and the jailer/jailed relationship of the traditional institution. The point was to bring a "sense of normalcy" to a relationship between human beings. To develop the relationship between doctor and patient so as "to free people which is necessary in all therapy and more so in psychiatry."[28] While Fanon recognized that day hospitalization would not be suitable in acute cases where the patient's entire being has been overwhelmed, it was absolutely essential that the creation of a traditional psychiatric hospital be avoided "at all costs." Instead the guiding principle should be a treatment directed toward strengthening the patient's self-image. As well as psychoanalysis,[29] psychotherapeutic treatment included group drama, or sociodrama sessions. Day hospitalization encouraged the feeling of freedom within a supportive environment, but the point was not to build an alternative "neo-society" in the hospital. The real environment was society itself. What was happening to the individual in society was absolutely crucial. Day hospitalization was thus not an end in itself but a way of "guaranteeing to the maximum the liberty of the patient in getting rid of every incarcerative and coercive aspect of internment."[30] Such treatment depended on a free society and not on creating a "neo-society" within the institution, as had been the case with Tosquelles:

> It must always be remembered that with institutional therapy we create frozen institutions, strict and rigid rules, schemes which rapidly become stereotypical. In the neo-society, there is no invention, no creative dynamism, no newness. There seem to be no veritable dislocation, no crises. The institution remains that "cadaveric foundation" of which Mauss speaks.[31]

In language that Fanon would again use to describe colonial society in *The Wretched*, Fanon and Geronimi continue:

> The inert character of the pseudo-society, its strict spatial limitation, the restricted number of movements and, why hide it, the actual experience of confinement-imprisonment, considerably limit the curative and rehabilitative value of its sociotherapy.[32]

We must turn to the social "reality."

The Collapse of the Division between Politics and Psychiatry: Torture(rs)

> Concerned about Man but strangely not about the Arab. (Fanon, "Letter to a Frenchman")

French colonialism in Algeria began in 1830, a year before Hegel's death, with the belief that the essence of French civilization was the noblest in existence. By virtue of its enlightenment it had a duty to disseminate liberty, equality, and fraternity to the world. In Algeria that essence was to be projected in a civilizing mission which meant that the indigenous culture was denigrated and considered barbaric. The "warlike and fanatic" Algerians, pronounced Thomas-Robert Bugeaud, who was the military leader of the 1830 invasion and French Algeria's first governor-general, had "to receive civilization even before its name can be pronounced."[33] Civilization and colonization went hand in hand. When Fanon said that violence confirms the supremacy of White values (*WE*, 34), he was simply repeating Bugeaud. "You subjected them by armed force," Bugeaud advised, and "you will not keep them subjugated except by armed force."[34] A civilizing mission meant training the native to "admit loudly and intelligibly the supremacy of the white man's values" (*WE*, 43); to become French meant speaking French and being Christian. Again, Bugeaud provides the clarity of colonial mission that Fanon would repeat in *The Wretched*. Bugeaud writes

> We have promised the Arabs to treat them as if they were children of France . . . In that way, we hope to make it possible for them to tolerate our domination, later to accustom them to it, and finally to identify them with us, so as to form one and only one people.[35]

The discourse of the civilizing mission, with its Manichean rhetoric, lasted until the French left. And it was not a long way from justifying the violence of colonization to justifying torture to save civilization. Even today, not much has changed.

A government report delivered in 1955 described the forms of violence used on Algerians, the beating, drowning, electrocution, and excessive imprisonment. It went as far as to describe the electrical method, "standing for four days and nights, unable to sit or lie down because [the victim] was attached to the ceiling by his fully extended arms,"[36] but the report did not call it torture. It insisted that "the methods used are old established; in normal times they are only employed on persons against whom there is a considerable weight of evidence of guilt and for whom there are therefore no great feelings of pity."[37] Justifying methods on the basis of a weight of evidence allows brutal methods to exact a confession in the first place, which then justified torture. In the midst of the rebellion, and as a signatory of the Universal Declaration of Human Rights in 1948, France publicly denied torture but wanted the ability to use the techniques under a different name: "the procedures of the water-pipe and electricity, when used with caution," continues the report, "would produce a shock with a much more psychological effect than physical" and are therefore not "excessively cruel."[38] In successive articles in *Moudjahid* and in *L'An V* Fanon, and others like Henri Alleg (*La Question*, 1958), attempted to enlighten the French public about the torture regime in Algeria.

Western medical science was introduced into Algeria at the same time as French colonialism (*DC*, 121). In a noncolonial society, that is a society in which reciprocal recognition takes place, the patient trusts the doctor, but in a colonial society the patient/doctor relation is irreconcilable, full of tension and distrust. While the Algiers School found the cause of such tension in the "primitive" practices of indigenous society, Fanon looked for the source in the

colonizer/colonized relationship: "Every time we do not understand a given problem . . . we must tell ourselves that we are at the
heart of the drama" (*DC*, 125). In other words, there is no disguise,
the source is the colonial situation. This might seem reductive, but
in the Manichean world of colonialism there is no need of nuance.
Every human relation is colored by it and the Algiers School is just
one aspect of the contradictory ideology of France's civilizing
mission[39] and its project of domination. In this context, medicine
introduced with colonialism increases the native's pain.

In a noncolonial society, Fanon contends, the doctor who works
with poorer patients tends to have a set of humanist values. This is
not so with the doctor who works with the natives in the colonial
situation. Humanist feelings are quickly turned into sadism and a
hateful brutality toward the indigent because the medical doctor is
an "objective" part of the brutal regime. From a self-interested point
of view, the doctor is interested in maintaining colonial oppression.
But something else happens. Because colonialism produces a
Manichean situation, the doctor cannot empathize with the Other.
The Other remains totally other. The doctor remains ignorant of
the country and its people, who are "transformed into the Saharan
stage set." The doctor's points of reference, of interest, are the occupier's world, having never mingled, shaken hands, drunk coffee or
exchanged commonplaces about the weather with an Arab (*AR*, 48).

The colonial situation creates "special realities," says Fanon. The
doctor becomes a torturer, or at least part of the torturing regime,
protecting the torturers. For Fanon this is standard colonial practice. To treat an Algerian humanly amounted to being a "race
traitor." The European doctors under Fanon's direction, who
remained true to their humanist principles, were a minority. The
normal action was to assist torture. Thus, in the colonies all the
liberal and humanistic values of bourgeois society become threadbare. Essence appears. Because Algeria must remain French by any
means, there is no middle ground:

> The European doctor assigned to examine the patient always
> concludes that there is no evidence to suggest that the accused has
> been tortured . . . On the strictly technical level, the European doctor
> actively collaborates with the colonial forces in their most frightful
> and degrading practices. (*DC*, 136)

Only ten years after the discovery that Nazi doctors were performing all kinds of gruesome experiments in the death camps, the

psychiatric services of the French army in Algeria were involved in studying the effects of experimental epileptic fits. The doctors performed the experiments under a "scientific pretext" just as the psychiatrists administered a "truth serum":

> Doctors attached to various torture centers intervene after every session to put the tortured back into condition for new sessions. Under the circumstances, the important thing is for the prisoner . . . to remain alive. Everything – heart stimulants, massive doses of vitamin – is used before, during, and after the sessions to keep the Algerian hovering between life and death. Ten times the doctor intervenes, ten times he gives the prisoner back to the pack of torturers. (*DC*, 138)

In this situation it obviously became more difficult to go to work as if nothing was happening. In fact the tortured and torturers were making their way into Fanon's care anyway. It is absolutely astounding that in these circumstances Fanon concludes the introduction to *L'An V* with the statement that "What we Algerians want is to discover the man behind the colonizer; this man who is both organizer and victim of a system that has choked him and reduced him to silence" (*DC*, 32). It is not the man behind the European anticolonialist but the one behind the torturer that Fanon is speaking of. Such a wish for human connection, such an ability for forgiveness, is reflected in Fanon's unwillingness not to turn away the torturer when he came to seek psychiatric help. Even the torturer was a victim of the dehumanization of colonialism. In "Colonial Wars and Mental Disorders" in *The Wretched*, Fanon reports on the pathology of the torturer as well as the tortured.

A European policeman seen by Fanon at Blida was in a depressed state hearing screaming at night. He plugged his ears and tried to tune out the nocturnal roar. It was "the real" that was troubling him:

> Sometimes we almost wanted to tell them that if they had a bit of consideration for us they'd speak out without forcing us to spend hours tearing information word by word out of them . . . So of course, we have to go through with it. But they scream too much. At the beginning that made me laugh. But afterward I was a bit shaken. Nowadays as soon as I hear someone shouting I can tell you exactly at what stage of the questioning we've got to. (*WE*, 265)

Whereas this policeman wanted to stop torturing, another patient, a European police inspector, was intent on continuing his job. He recounted to Fanon that he was frequently disturbed by nightmares. Not liking to be criticized, he hit out at anybody, including his children and 20-month-old baby. He met Fanon after tying up and beating his wife:

> Fanon: What happens to you when you are torturing?
> Inspector: You may not realize but it's a very tiring . . . It's a question of personal success. You see, you're competing with the others. In the end your fists are ruined. So you call the Senegalese. But either they hit too hard or else they don't hit hard enough and it's no good. In fact, you have to be intelligent to make a success of that sort of work. . . . You have to have a flair for it. (*WE*, 268–9)

Unlike the policeman, the inspector saw torturing as a necessary part of the job and wanted to remain in treatment for his action outside work while working full-time as a torturer. Fanon added in a note:

> With these observations we find ourselves in the presence of a coherent system which leaves nothing intact. The executioner who loves birds and enjoys the peace of listening to a symphony or a sonata is simply one stage in the process. Further on in it we may well find a whole existence which enters into complete and absolute sadism. (*WE*, 270n)

The year 1956 was a turning point in the war. The state of emergency declared in 1955 lifted all restrictions on police power. After the French military defeat at Dien Bien Phu in 1954, the Algerian revolt had to be broken by any means. Torture, refined by the psychological services, became the order of the day. Any "spirit of tolerance" had been spirited away so that the torturers themselves would become desensitized to their work. The intolerance toward the Algerian as a human being had become complete. By 1956 it had become impossible for Fanon to practice psychiatry. Violence in Algeria had reached new levels. If madness was the individual's loss of freedom, then it could not be treated in a sadistic society where torture and brutality had become normal.

Fanon had ended "The North African Syndrome" (1952) portentously: "psychoanalysis sees statelessness as a morbid condition, and it is absolutely right to do so" (*AR*, 15). This is why his call is to build not only houses but "the meaning of the home." In his letter of resignation from Blida in 1956 the connection of the depersonalization and homelessness takes concrete form. The Algerian in Algeria is declared a stranger:

If psychiatry is the medical technique that aims to enable man no longer to be a stranger to his environment, I owe it to myself to affirm that the Arab, permanently an alien in his own country, lives in a state of absolute depersonalization. What is the status of Algeria? A systematized dehumanization. (*AR*, 53)

In *The Wretched* he continued asking "in reality, who am I?" (*WE*, 250).

The Deepening Violence

There is no occupation of territory, on the one hand, and independence of persons on the other. It is the country as a whole, its history, its daily pulsation that are contested, disfigured, in the hope of final destruction. Under this condition, the individual's breathing is an observed, an occupied breathing. It is a combat breathing. (Fanon, "Algeria Face to Face with the French Torturers," in *AR*)

On May Day, 1945, a week before the Allied victory was declared in Europe, marches had been coordinated to demand freedom for Messali Hadj, the leader of banned Parti de Peuple Algérien, and independence for Algeria. Demonstrations had led to bloody confrontations, leaving many injured and three dead. The nationalist leadership decided that VE day would become an occasion to demand their own liberty. The result was bloody violence. At Sétif police charged the demonstrators, who fought back, attacking local Europeans and colonial offices. Ten thousand troops were brought in. Planes bombed and machine-gunned villages, a cruiser shelled the coast. Two weeks later 45,000 Algerians were dead.

Ten years later, as part of a general FLN offensive, guerrillas slaughtered the European inhabitants of a suburb of Philippeville. The French response was exponentially brutal, claiming the lives of 12,000 Algerians. The French continued to deny that a war existed in Algeria and called the war of liberation that had begun on November 1, 1954, "terrorist." As the insurrection expanded, the French responded with a tremendous show of force, criminalizing the peasantry through mass arrests, military sweeps, and collective punishment.

The Philippeville massacres were a major turning point in the war, hardening Algerian and European positions. It was in this context that Fanon made his first real communication with the

FLN.[40] The underground circles in Algiers and his field trips to Kabylia now put him in contact with some of the most radical elements in the FLN, including Abane Ramdane,[41] the mastermind of the Battle of Algiers and the ideological force behind the Soummam conference of 1956, which reorganized the FLN into a coherent political/military organization. Abane was "one of few leaders in the Front," writes Lou Turner, "not limited by a narrow nationalism of either religion or region and pivotal to Fanon's relationship to the radical intellectual leadership of the FLN."[42]

The French defeat at Dien Bien Phu in May 1954 had not only boosted Algerian confidence and French resolution not to be humiliated again, but meant that the lessons learnt by the French from the anticolonial war in Indochina, including psychological warfare, could be applied in Algeria – by the very same "red berets" and 11th Shock Battalion who were being transferred from Vietnam as an efficient counterinsurgency unit. By April 1956 the French had 400,000 troops committed to Algeria. The sheer numbers, made possible by military service, meant that saturation policing could be employed, including securing the countryside by "regrouping" about a million Algerians from their homes into camps. To revenge a French death, an entire village was held responsible. The Algerian war, which, like torture, did not exist in the French government's lexicon, became a total war. More and more young Algerians fled to the hills to become revolutionaries.

For the FLN the problem was how to continue the war. The FLN had become militarily bogged down and lacked a central strategy or ideology. In August the FLN leadership met for 20 days inside Algeria, in the Soummam Valley, to hammer out the next stage of the struggle. The Soummam platform expressed the need to provide a political structure for the emerging mass movement, and to establish the dominance of that social movement over military matters, as well as to organize the decentralized Wilayas (military districts) along national rather than local lines. The National Liberation Army (Armée de la Libération Nationale – ALN), the military wing of the FLN, was reorganized hierarchically, making the military subservient to the political, and the external wing subservient to a collective internal command. It was thought that collective leadership (influenced by the Kabyle democratic assembly called the Djemma) would guarantee against the "cult of personality" that had developed around Messali Hadj and destroyed the nationalist movement in the late 1940s.[43] Because the revolution was not simply about defeating the French but would involve a social transformation, the direction of the revolution would have to come internally, with the involvement of the masses through mass social/political movements, like general strikes, playing a central role.

The Soummam platform announced that the revolution was not a "religious war." In contrast to the FLN's fairly contradictory first declaration of goals in November 1954 for the "restoration of an Algerian state," and for democracy, liberty, and individual rights within "Islamic principles," Soummam declared that its goal was not an Islamic state but a democratic, socialist, secular, multicultural, and "national struggle to destroy the anarchist regime of colonization." The national project was articulated as "a struggle for the birth of an Algerian nation," not for "a restoration of a monarchy or a dead theocracy."

However, the Soummam platform was the FLN's secular highpoint. The criticism of "theocracy," and almost no positive statement about Islam, would later be used by Ben Bella in a gesture to "tradition" against Abane. Stuck on the border, Ben Bella never made it to Soummam, which helped Abane's political hegemony in the short run, but without Ben Bella's presence at Soummam its reversal was more easily accomplished. The Soummam platform condemned regionalism, but later the disproportionate numbers of leaders from Kabylia at the congress was used against it, as was its secularism, which pragmatists argued put it out of touch with the mass of Muslims.[44] Soummam was the FLN's most radical program, and for the moment the internal authority and Abane Ramdane were unchallenged.

Though Fanon was not at Soummam, its program as well as its conception of a radically democratic, multicultural, and secular Algeria of the future became Fanon's, and Abane Ramdane became his friend. All the issues raised by the Soummam platform remain central themes for Fanon and are taken up in *L'An V* and *The Wretched*.

One of Abane's first acts after Soummam was to bring the war of liberation into Algiers and onto the front pages of the world's newspapers.

The Battle of Algiers

Already active in the FLN, Fanon went to Paris in September 1956 to present his paper "Racism and Culture" at the first Congress of Black Writers and Poets. Fanon was part of the Martinican delegation, though his paper did reflect the current situation and a hopeful future for Algeria. He concludes: "A people that undertakes a struggle for liberation rarely legitimizes race prejudice. Even in the course of acute periods of insurrectional armed struggle one never witnesses the recourse to biological justifications." The struggle itself creates new human perspectives and reveals new realities, he proclaims: "The struggle of the inferiorized is situated on a markedly more human level. The perspectives are radically new. The opposition is the henceforth classical one of the struggles of conquest and of liberation." In this situation, racist arguments prove less effective. It is the liberation struggle that once and for all puts an end to the ideological power of the Algiers School and other theories of the African's innate inferiority: "There is talk of fanaticism, of primitive attitudes in the face of death, but once again the now crumbling mechanism no longer responds. Those who were once unbudgeable, the constitutional cowards, the timids, the eternally inferiorized, stiffen and emerge bristling." Rather than "assimilation" into French culture, it is only from this newly liberated culture of the oppressed, concludes Fanon, that a reciprocal recognition and relativism of different cultures can emerge (*AR*, 43–4).

During the summer, the war had moved into Algiers, spilling into Blida hospital. Violence increased. After Europeans blew up a house in the Kasbah killing 70 people, the cycle of violence deepened, with the FLN beginning its bombing campaign on September 30. The Battle of Algiers had officially begun. It was not only reactive. The idea was to bring the war to the city from the countryside, to undermine the colon's sense of security. The strategy reflected the decision of Abane (and the Soummam) to put the military under political control. Rather than a shadowy terror campaign, the Battle of Algiers had a mass character, with women playing a crucial role. It is important to keep this in mind when we discuss Fanon's theory of violence.

Popularly remembered as war between FLN operatives organized in small groups in a cell-like structure, and the anti-terror campaign of General Jacques Massu (who took over the responsibility for all police and security responsibilities from the Minister-Resident, Lacoste), the Battle of Algiers involved a significant section of the Algiers Muslim population. Even Edward Behr, a reporter for *Time*, had to acknowledge the mass character of the battle and gave a description of the revolutionary process that is quite at odds with what the designation "terrorist" conjures up in the popular imagination:

Despite French claims that at no time were there more than 4,500 Algerians directly concerned with terrorism (out of a total population of 450,000), it seems certain that the terrorists benefited from the complicity of a huge majority of the Moslem population, as well as from the aid of a small number of Europeans. Among those arrested and convicted for having taken part in terrorist activity during this period were employees of the Algiers gas and electricity services; postmen and post office clerks; students, doctors, tradesmen, custom officials, even Moslem police officers and a prominent "bachaga," [a functionary like a prefect] the Bachaga Boutaleb, whose nationalist sympathies overcame his basically pro-French sentiments. Practically no Moslem representative of Algiers society was lacking, from the most humble welders and dockers to the wealthy members of tiny Algiers Moslem "bourgeoisie" and including that well-known element of Kasbah society, the pimps and petty racketeers.

The number of people arrested and tortured also indicated the degree of support for the FLN:

It is estimated that out of the Kasbah's total population of 80,000, between 30 and 40 per cent of the active male population was, at one stage or another of the "battle," arrested for questioning. It is certain that without torture the FLN's terrorist networks would never have been overcome; it is equally certain that the degrading effect on those who used it and its hideous consequences on the thousands of innocent Algerians subjected to it outweighed in importance the "battle of Algiers" itself.[45]

Fanon's patients were increasingly the tortured and torturers. At the same time he was helping injured FLN operatives, and was part of the FLN underground. His colleagues were being arrested, but the police continued to send him officers with "nervous conditions." Geronimi was warned of a raid, Lacaton heard that he was going to be arrested. The situation became untenable. Perhaps on Abane's advice that revolutionaries don't needlessly leave themselves exposed, Fanon decided to leave, writing a letter of resignation to Lacoste in December 1956.

The letter is not simply a radical rejection of the status quo but also a letter in good faith, detailing his attempt, as the chef de service, to carry out a therapeutic mission, to remain true to his idea of human reciprocity. Instead he found the inhumanity toward the Algerians that he had witnessed in France magnified into a vicious system in Algeria. He had known this in 1953, and from the end of 1954 certainly believed that the system was not viable. Still, "it appeared to me that an effort should be made to attenuate the viciousness of a system whose doctrinal foundations are a daily defiance of an authentically human outlook" (*AR*, 52). One could work against the doctrinal foundations of the Algiers School but how could one retain humanist values in a context of torture and daily killings? In the context of the Battle of Algiers it had become impossible to continue work politically and medically.

The letter of resignation was the most direct political act that Fanon had taken in the sphere of medicine: an open letter of criticism of a racist and dehumanized society. In January 1957 he was officially expelled from Algeria. The Battle of Algiers still raged, and Prime Minister Guy Mollet continued to deny that torture existed: "France is the nation of the rights of man . . . I am sure that none of you commits the insult of thinking that the Government, the army or the administration could wish for and organize torture."[46] But the organized torture continued. In fact the civilizing mission found its logical conclusion in violence and torture, as Bugeaud had intimated over a hundred years before.

The Battle of Algiers seemed a disastrous defeat for the FLN but it was only a Pyrrhic victory for the French government, which had lost the initiative to Massu and the militant settlers. Abane and other FLN leaders were forced to leave the city. Like Fanon they ended up in Tunis, where Fanon and Abane became close during 1957 working on *El Moudjahid*. "Both men belonged, that is, to the 'hard-line' faction within the FLN," opines Macey, who adds that Abane was a dangerous man to be associated with, often bluntly criticizing other FLN leaders. Reported as a French act, Abane was murdered by forces inside the FLN in December 1957. Fanon still had his liquidation on his mind in the summer of 1961, when he said to Simone de Beauvoir in Rome that "I have two deaths on my conscience which I will not forgive myself for: that of Abane and that of Lumumba."[47] What Fanon thought he should have done, we don't know.

5

Violent Concerns

The Relativity at the Heart of the Absolute

We shall see that for a man who is in the thick of the fight it is an urgent matter to decide on the means and the tactics to employ: that is to say, how to conduct and organize the movement. If this coherence is not present there is only a blind will toward freedom, with terribly reactionary risks which it entails. (Fanon, *The Wretched of the Earth*)

Early in *The Wretched*, Fanon repeats the point that just as the Black is a product of White society, the native is a colonial product. And almost as inexorably as a law of physics, the colonial regime's action in creating the native gives rise to an opposing reaction – the native's violent response to it. The native is the truth of colonialism. The ideology of the native's character, a Manichean personality split between rage and stupor, is in fact a projection and truth of colonial narcissism.

Part of the political project of creating the native is to channel the violent reaction to colonial violence inward, to areas where this disruptive energy can be "released" without affecting the colonial setup or status quo. In short, the native's energy is directed or rather deflected toward the self. We learn, however, that it is at the moment when the native finds the *real* source of anguish that the process of decolonization can be said to begin.[1] If violence marks the appearance and essence of colonialism, does the emergence of counterviolence signal the appearance and essence of liberation? Is violence enough to constitute revolutionary agency? Is revolutionary agency, insofar as it is articulated as a reaction to colonial society, merely articulated in its terms? Is it, in other words, Manichean, only and completely determined by its reaction to the Other? Fanon's discontent at being defined by the Other raises the questions: What role does violence play in the transition from "reaction" to "action"? How can it create a "new" human being?

Fanon's opening chapter of *The Wretched*, "Concerning Violence," has been controversial ever since its publication. Its audacious claim that violence was a royal road to salvation was underlined by Sartre's introduction and his declaration that "violence, like Achilles' lance, can heal the wound that it has inflicted" (*WE*, 30).[2] The passages on the therapeutic power of violence, repeated countless times by critics and supporters throughout the 1960s and 1970s, have often meant that *The Wretched* has been reduced to a paean to violence written by a man "condemned to death."[3] While many readings have caricatured Fanon as a philosopher of violence, this exaggeration was perceptively recognized by Hannah Arendt, who nevertheless could not entirely escape its pull. She held that readers were generally familiar with only the first chapter of *The Wretched*, ignoring the rest of the book; but she darkly charged that Fanon "glorified violence for violence's sake."[4]

A re-evaluation of Fanon's idea of the importance of violence in the decolonization struggle is essential, yet we have to be careful. Critics following Albert Memmi have argued that for Fanon a new humanity emerges immediately through violence,[5] while others question whether violence is capable of fulfilling the psychological functions which he claimed.

Arendt is right to complain that the readings of *The Wretched* have been overshadowed by the first chapter. My own contention is that an adequate understanding of Fanon's idea of violence must take fully into account his critical analysis of spontaneity, national consciousness, and political organization. In other words, it should be noted that Fanon predicated the new society on a long struggle which prefigures a new humanism "in the objectives and methods of the conflict" (*WE*, 197). Obviously, the conflict closest to Fanon was the Algerian one, and the methods and objectives, as I have suggested, those discussed at the Soummam congress. When Fanon argues that the "conflict" produces social, psychological and cultural changes, he was in fact repeating from the Soummam contention that "It is an undeniable fact that the ALN has radically altered the political climate of Algeria. It has been the catalyst for the psychological shock which has liberated the people from their stupor, fear and skepticism."

Yet with Fanon, violence is a problematic, which conceptually has to do too much. For example, Fanon's categorization of the counter-violence of the native against the settler can be applied to Rwanda in a frightening way. There, the genocide of the Tutsi and moderate Hutu in 1994 was justified by Hutu Power activists as a struggle of "natives" against Tutsi "settlers."[6] The fact that Fanon's claim that violence – namely a zero-sum affair of native and settler locked in a death grip – can be applied to postcolonial Africa raises a problem at the heart of Fanon's project in *The Wretched*. That is, how to create, out of this violent encounter, a new *inclusive* nation no longer appealing to race or ethnicity?

We have to approach the question carefully because violence cannot be allowed to speak for itself. It does not have its own meaning but it has a context and a history and has to be approached nonreductively. To be made thinkable, violence has to be historicized. Additionally, Fanon's own concerns and qualifications about the efficacy of violent action to sustain a liberation movement indicate a problematization that has too often been skipped over.

In the following, I intend to bring to the forefront a nonreductive conception of violence in place of more literal and narrow-minded views – nonreductive because it is not reducible to individual acts of violence, but is diffused into, rather than opposed to, symbolic violence, which includes the indirect participation of broad masses of people in the revolutionary movement. How these people, not directly involved in the armed struggle, become included in the revolution will be considered in the next chapter, but it is worth remembering that though Fanon construes decolonization as a violent process, violence, whether symbolic or actual, is not sufficient for the development of a national consciousness: Fanon insists on a concomitant "enlightening of consciousness." How this enlightenment is established, and how it can be accompanied by an attendant new relationship between the intellectuals and the masses, will be developed more fully in following chapters. Nevertheless, the native's violence has to be understood not just as a reaction to colonial violence but as a conduit to a positive notion of subjectivity. The "enlightening of consciousness" is thus not defined in opposition to violence: Fanon's notion of "violence" has its own singular history and is based on many prior determinations; it is not exhausted in a Manichean "reaction" to colonial rule, but neither is it alone able to transcend Manicheanism. Another element is needed.

The myriad terms Fanon uses when writing about decolonization point to the many levels of his thinking about violence. In "Concerning Violence," he frequently uses the words *violence* and *force* synonymously, virtually assuming that violence and revolution are interlinked, even though the word violence is used over 70 times in chapter 1, and the word revolution not at all. Its overuse, for the reader and in reality, can lead to desensitization.

Anticolonial violence spells the end of the colonial regime, and thus is an indicator of decolonization. Any such revolution, which Fanon describes as a complete substitution of one "species" of human being for another, must be violent. Fanon's conception of violence is nonreductive in that he includes within it every single relationship between individuals. In the colonial context every relationship is strained. For example, naming a sports club after a famous French general is charged with meaning. To rename a club after an Algerian fighter requires a struggle and constitutes a significant action. Yet its meaning is not fixed. Changing the name alone does not constitute radical social transformation. In short, Fanon contends that the authenticity of decolonization, and thus the meaning of violence, depends on the degree of change in the social structure that is willed for, brought about, developed from the bottom up.

Manichean Realities

> The settler makes history; his life is an epoch, an Odyssey. He is the absolute beginning . . . (Fanon, *The Wretched of the Earth*)

A most telling shift between *Black Skin* and *The Wretched* is Fanon's understanding and description of hegemony. In *Black Skin*, he maintains that the Black "is a product of [the] cultural situation" which "slowly and subtly – with the help of books, newspapers, schools and their texts, advertisements, films, radio – work their way into one's mind" (*BS*, 152). In *The Wretched*, this "cultural situation" is based on sheer force: "Colonialism is not a thinking machine, nor a body endowed with reasoning faculties. It is violence in its natural state" (*WE*, 61).

Instead of legitimation through a whole system of "moral teachers, counselors, and 'bewilderers'" there is no such alleviating mediation in colonial society, where "the intermediary does not lighten the oppression, nor seek to hide the domination; he shows them up and puts them into practice" (*WE*, 38). In colonial society, the violence makes its way into the native's home and mind. The colonial project in Algeria, Fanon wrote in his letter of resignation from Blida Hospital, is one of systematically "decerebralizing" a people. The whole experience of colonialism, from start to finish and from without and within, is characterized by violence: "Their existence together, that is to say the exploitation of the native by the settler, is carried on by dint of a great array of bayonets and cannon" (*WE*, 36).[7]

French colonialism in Algeria was *totalitarian*, with an ideology based on the maintenance of the idea of the native as the "quintessence of evil" (*WE*, 41).[8] The colonial project, therefore, includes the destruction of the sense of selfhood; it has settled into "the very center of the Algerian individual and has undertaken a sustained work of cleanup, *of expulsion of self*" (*AR*, 65, emphasis added). Colonialism not only occupies the land but the native's entire life:

There is no occupation of territory, on the one hand, and independence of persons on the other. It is the country as a whole, its history, its daily pulsation that are contested, disfigured, in the hope of a definitive annihilation. Under this condition, the individual's breathing is an observed, an occupied breathing. It is a combat breathing. (*AR*, 65)

Colonial violence is not hidden. It follows the native everywhere, entering into every pore of life. It is drummed into the native's head, it is reinforced by its ideology that all the native's customs, religion, and culture are the products of "constitutional depravity." That is why, Fanon adds, the insecticide DDT operates on the same level as the Christian religion because both purge in the name of purification. The logical conclusion of colonial "cleansing" is the transformation of the native into an animal. It promotes dehumanization and speaks of the native in zoological terms: a piece of "laziness stretched out in the sun."

Colonial society appears as a Manichean one, whose superstructure is its substructure. It is a society of either–or, of radical polarities that baldly assert that simply belonging to one race determines your place in the society. Its reality and its ideology are reflections of an inverted world: the colonizer represents everything good, human, and alive; the colonized all that is bad, brutish, and inert.

Colonial society, of colonizer and colonized, is one of total separation which is "not in the service of a higher synthesis." Fanon's description of colonial Manicheanism is powerfully expressed in spatial terms because Manicheanism is atemporal. For the native, history has stopped. History is the settler's. For the colonized there is no history; only the taking over of space by the colonizer. History is the history of colonization and described as an epoch, and an "odyssey." "This land was created by us," say the colonizers, who see themselves as "the unceasing cause" (*WE*, 51). The native's "fundamental rebelliousness" is represented by the bush, mosquitoes, and fever, and colonization by the taming of this nature, the building of railways, and the draining of swamps (*WE*, 250). The absolute opposition of two zones is expressed in the physical dividing lines of colonialism – the frontiers and police barracks – and, in general, in its geographical layout. Fanon contrasts the modern "developed" colonial town to the premodern "underdeveloped" colonized living quarters. The colonial town is well lit, well fed, easygoing, a place where people walk along wide streets in strong shoes. It is a town without violence. The other zone – the natives' quarters – reminds one of the opening lines of Césaire's *Return*. It is "a hungry town, starved of meat, of shoes, of coal, of light . . . wallowing in mire" (*WE*, 39). These zones are totally separate.[9] The colonizer surrounds the natives' quarter and lays siege to it: "Every exit from the Casbah of Algiers opens on enemy territory" (*AR*, 51–2). In settler colonialism – Algeria was not only considered a model colony but was viewed as part of France, with a European population of more than 1 million – the urban area was monitored by the modern techniques of policing, and the geographical space was divided to protect the European from infection. Fanon's description of colonial urban Africa, which finds its logical conclusion in apartheid, is presented as practical medical policy for "indirect rule" by the British administrator, Lord Lugard. Because there are "malarial germs" organic to the native, it is a "moral" duty to segregate the native from the European as long as it doesn't interfere with work.[10] The area between the reservations is not only a "fireguard," according to Lugard, but a parade ground which displays not only the pomp and ceremony of colonial rule but also power, expressing exactly Fanon's idea of a "line of force."

Violence, the essence of settler colonialism, appears to the native with daily regularity. Its absolute expression, in a relentless "chain of reasoning," is expulsion, ultimately demanding the total disappearance of the colonized people. In other words, under threat, the colonialists begin to lay down "precise methods" for the eradication of the colonized. When Fanon writes that "the settler asks each member of the oppressing minority to shoot down 30 or 100 or 200 natives" (*WE*, 66), he is reporting on the real wishes of a significant section of the European settlers.[11] Yet because this temptation to destroy the colonized would spell the end of colonialism, this "logical option" is not really open to the colonizer, though it is a recourse open to the colonized. It is the colonized who can take the proposition of a world without the colonizer to its logical conclusion. The destruction of the colonial world is nothing other than the "abolition of one zone, its burial in the depths of the earth, or the expulsion from the country."

Violence Interiorized

> The war of liberation is . . . the grandiose effort of a people, which has been mummified, to rediscover its own genius, to reassume its own history and assert its sovereignty. (Fanon, *The Wretched of the Earth*)

The totalitarian character of settler colonialism destroys the *living element* of the indigenous forms of organization and culture and creates the native. But the native has not so acquiescently accepted the colonialist portrayal: "He is overpowered but not tamed; he is treated as an inferior but he is not convinced of his inferiority" (*WE*, 53). Indeed, the constant exhibition of force by the colonial regime is ironically the telltale sign of colonialism's lack of hegemony and confidence. In such an atmosphere of violence, the permanent tension of colonial relations, the pent-up aggression and anger, must be allowed outlets. Fanon's argument, based in the phenomenology of "the real," evokes Freudian ideas of energy; the native's agency "is on watch constantly for an opportunity to make itself known" and often reappears in "disguise" (Freud quoted in Fanon, *BS*, 144).[12] In every society, Fanon writes in *Black Skin*, a channel must exist for aggression to be released (*BS*, 145). Colonialism maintains its hegemony by directing and focusing the pent-up energy, making sure it is expressed and released in the native's own zone.[13] There a knife will be pulled on another: "for the last resort of the native is to defend his personality vis-à-vis his brother" (*WE*, 54). The native, who kowtows under daily indignities and violence at the hands of the colonial authorities (especially the police), will react to the least provocation. This state of affairs has euphemistically been called "Black on Black violence" when "niggers beat each

other up" (*WE*, 52). This period, a product of colonial totalitarianism, is described powerfully early in Césaire's *The Return*: people
do not mix, they are individualized but are not individuals; they are
massified.

Fanon maps out the areas in which colonialism allows the
native's pent-up anger to be expressed. Even though its work is to
"make even the dreams of liberty impossible" (*WE*, 93), the totalitarian colonial structure inhabits but cannot control dreams. Always
near to the surface of conscious life, there is nothing nuanced about
the native's dreams. Wish-fulfillment dreams of liberation are the
exact opposite of waking reality. Pent-up aggression is released in
dreams of action and vigor:

> the dreams of the native are always of muscular prowess; his dreams
> are of action and of aggression. I dream I am jumping, swimming,
> running, climbing; I dream that I burst out laughing, that I span a
> river in one stride ... During the period of colonization, the native
> never stops achieving his freedom from nine in the evening until six
> in the morning. (*WE*, 52)

Fanon is not content to have freedom limited to dreams. In fact, he
is very critical of the dream-like "magical superstructure which per-
meates native society [and which] fulfills certain well-defined functions in the dynamism of the libido" (*WE*, 55). For liberation to be
realized, he insists, this superstructure must be replaced. What
also needs replacing is the structure of "consent" derived from
"tradition" or the "customary" which keeps the native in place.
Encouraged by colonialism, the customary feuds reflect a sublimation of "the real" into "the unreal" because in it the native tries to
"persuade himself that colonialism does not exist." There are "tribal
feuds," disagreements and fights but there is no room for resistance.

Just as it cynically and opportunistically values ethnic or regional
identity as "custom," colonialism also sanctions magical and religious outlets for they channel and exhaust the native's aggression
in flights from reality. This working of aggression turned inward,
already described in *Black Skin* as a classic schema of masochism,
remained important for Fanon's model (*BS*, 176). Magic and myth
in the colonial context take on a frightening reality "more terrifying
than the settlers." Indeed, in the face of the terrible power of possession, the settlers' powers are seemingly feeble (*WE*, 57).[14] It is a
topsy-turvy world where the settler doesn't have to be fought
because the real struggle takes place on the "phantasmic plane"

(*WE*, 56). In place of an organized resistance to colonialism, religious fatalism produces a stoical and "stony calm" and a kind of "interior restabilization," the internalization of defeat which leads to fatalistic inactivity "ordained by God" (*WE*, 55).[15]

As in his analysis of the dream world, Fanon interprets the social character of dance,[16] which exhibits a certain permissiveness under the watchful eye of the "customary" authority, as a "huge effort of a community to exorcise itself, to liberate itself, to explain itself" (*WE*, 58). In contrast to the zonal limits of colonialism, the dance offers no apparent limits. Like the unconscious, it transgresses boundaries and allows for complete possession and disintegration of the personality. This apparent self-liberation is really just another symptom of colonialism, because it is, in fact, only a symbolic and controlled release that returns peace and calm to the village and changes nothing. Thus, Fanon concludes, violence is controlled and sublimated:

> We have seen that this same violence, though kept very much on the surface all through the colonial period, yet turns in the void. We have also seen that it is canalized by the emotional outlets of dance and possession by spirits; we have seen how it is exhausted in fratricidal combats. (*WE*, 58)

However, in the period immediately preceding decolonization the direction of violence begins to change. The native finds an expression for revenge in the memory of anticolonial resistance and reconfiguring the inert and sclerosed precolonial traditions: "When formerly it was appeased by myths and exercised its talents in finding fresh ways of committing mass suicide, now new conditions will make possible a completely new line of action" (*WE*, 58).

For Fanon, the stage preceding decolonization is manifestly Manichean. The liberation movement seeks to divide the collaborators from the people, attempting to isolate those who work for or support "native institutions." This means liquidating collaborators as publicly as possible "to encourage the others."[17] While colonialism paints the militant as a terrorist, violence is also used by the militants as an object lesson to the leaders of the movement who still seek a compromise with colonialism. Once that movement goes over to violence, there is no turning back. The middle ground shrinks and those seeking a compromise with colonialism are painted into the corner: "From now on the demagogues, the opportunists and the magicians have a difficult task. The action which has thrown them into a hand-to-hand struggle confers upon the masses a voracious taste for the concrete. The attempt at mystification becomes, in the long run, practically impossible" (*WE*, 94–5). What is also at stake is not only violence as the response to colonialism but violence as a strategy that divides the masses from "those enfranchised slaves," that is, those who have got something or believe they can get something out of colonialism. The latter include those who believe the colonial moralizing system and have internalized the idea of the backwardness of the people, and those who identify – if not with the civilizing mission itself – with the colonial reformers as the best bet. They include among them bourgeois nationalists.

What develops from Fanon's analysis in *Black Skin* is his critique of the "enfranchised slaves" who think that liberation can be granted by the White Master. In *The Wretched*, the master/slave dialectic is reflected in the struggle between a dominant colonialism and an emergent nation. Freedom has to be fought for, and independence without a struggle essentially achieves only "a fancy dress parade," a doomed *pseudo*-liberation. A transfer of power to a new elite brings no real change in the lives of the people, who lament that independence wasn't worthwhile (*WE*, 46).

The beginning period of decolonization brings emergent contradictions. It is the reformist parties and the new classes they represent that set great barriers to full decolonization. Instead of promoting real social change, violent speeches and symbols operate as a new type of sublimation, masking accommodationist politics which put a brake on mass activity. In place of a precise political or social program, they offer "dreams," often couched in xenophobic or racial language. These leaders perceive the disorder that mass action brings as the greatest threat to their goal of taking the place of the colonial masters and conducting business as usual. They attempt to appease the people while appealing to the colonialists, warning them that the masses are beginning to get out of control. "Violent in their words and reformist in their attitudes" (*WE*, 47), they introduce into the political discourse, at a decisive moment, the language of nonviolence which "signifies to the intellectual and economic elite of the colonized country that the bourgeoisie has the same interests as them and that it is therefore urgent and indispensable to come to terms for the public good" (*WE*, 48–9). The type of independence resulting from such negotiations would be a hollow one. An implicit class division is indicated by the attitudes of these parties to violence. Though anticolonial rage naturally produces the fantasy of replacing the master, it becomes clear that middle-class nationalists will never get beyond this elemental negativity of "having." Freedom is only the issue insofar as they can kick out the old rulers and take their place. The bourgeois nationalists realize Mayotte Capécia's dream of living in high society, not by magically turning White, but by taking over the White's mansion (*BS*, 44). Through becoming a conduit in the exchange of commodities, the nationalist bourgeoisie attains the (pseudo) equality it has striven for, and this consumes its hostility toward the settler. It is a pseudo equality because for Fanon the nationalist bourgeoisie cannot be "real," that is, it cannot be a productive bourgeoisie but only a poor copy, a huckstering caste. Thus Fanon intimates the limitation inherent in reactive violence. On the other hand, because anticolonial violence leads to a period of negotiations with colonialism, the reformers can reappear and the mass movements that brought the negotiations are likely to be sidelined. Violence, then, cannot substitute for a political program.

Exploding Manicheanism

At the very point in *The Wretched* when Fanon speaks of decolonization as a "program of complete disorder," he adds: "Decolonization, as we know, is a historical process: that is to say that it cannot be understood, it cannot become intelligible nor clear to itself except in the exact measure that we can discern the movements which give it historical form and content" (*WE*, 36). The radical mutation of consciousness that takes place during the decolonization movement expresses its "historical form and content," declares Fanon. This transformation is a result of a critique of politics based on violence alone. Specifically, it is the negation of the earlier Manichean view and the articulation of a positive one which can, without reference to colonialism, create new ways of life. To trace the evolution of this historical process, we must first begin with the reaction to colonial violence as expressed by and within an incipient anticolonial movement. We must, then, consider how decolonization becomes "clear to itself."

At first the anticolonial project is stated in terms identical to those of colonialism: the colonized will strive to take over and claim "that same violence" (*WE*, 41). The settler's phrase "it's them or us" does not "constitute a paradox," but is a concise expression of the Manichean reality. The native has always known this, Fanon contends, "has always known that his duel with the settler would take place in the arena." Despite the rhetoric, equality is not found in colonial legal institutions but in the readiness to fight the settler, to "discover" the reality of violence and "transform it into the pattern of action" (*WE*, 46). The native's mimicry of colonial action, which represents a reaction to colonialism, is expressed in the wish to take the master's place. The native reacts to exclusion from colonial society with dreams of possession:

> The look that the native turns on the settler town is a look of lust, a look of envy; it expresses his dreams of possession. And this the settler knows very well; when their glances meet he ascertains bitterly, always on the defensive, "They want to take our place." It is true, for there is no native who does not dream at least once a day of setting himself up in the settler's place. (*WE*, 39)

This relationship of equal exchange – to make oneself the equal and equivalent of the settler – is an act of resistance that includes the dream of self-possession, even though it reveals a self mediated through things. The terms, just like the reality, have been provided by the settler. Envy is a product of colonial deprivation. Colonialism reduces the native to a "thing" who dreams of self-subsumption within thinghood, that is through taking over the colonialist's belongings to acquire the feeling of belonging. Moreover, this movement is carried out by violence, which has been the only point of contact in the Manichean world of native and settler:

> The settler has shown him the way he should take if he is to become free. The argument the native chooses has been furnished by the settler, and by an ironic turning of the tables it is the native who now affirms that the colonialist understands nothing but force. (*WE*, 65)

Manicheanism is the form colonial relations take. It allows no perspective beyond the zones delimited by colonialism. The settler creates the native but also creates the Black skin in a White mask, representing a pseudo-synthesis of colonized and colonizer which Fanon believes only serves to reinforce the colonial world. The only authentic way out of this bipartite world is not through synthesis but by negation expressed in the colonialist's own form – that is, through violence. Decolonization is first an inversion of colonial Manicheanism: "Obedient to the rules of pure Aristotelian logic, they both follow the principle of reciprocal exclusivity" (*WE*, 38–9). What is at issue are the "two trains of reasoning" (*WE*, 93): what

Fanon calls the Aristotelian logic that characterizes colonial Manicheanism and the dialectical logic that emerges from the liberation movement. It is a logic which is proved not by theory but by revolutionary action and experience (*WE*, 175). Counterviolence, namely anticolonial violence, is different from colonial violence because, Fanon maintains, it transforms the colonized and the colonizer. The formerly invincible settler and the dehumanized colonized become equals. Colonial violence is the violence of the master, it can create no new system; anticolonial violence, the violence of the colonized, is dialectical, it establishes, Fanon argues, the basis for reciprocal recognition.

Just as the native is a product of colonialism, and just as colonialism begins in and continues through violence, self-consciousness begins in anticolonial violence. Colonial violence, then, is negated not by nonviolence but by counterviolence. Fanon expresses this turning of the tables of the settler/native relationship as "an extraordinary reciprocal homogeneity." In contrast to nonviolent propositions, he maintains that colonial violence, which is a central element of colonial rule, can only be broken by a violent resistance to the colonial regime. This is why he credits the act of violence by the colonized as an act of emancipation, because it aims at *removing the existing structure of violence*. It is a simple fact which "every Algerian felt at heart" (*WE*, 61).

Contrary to the colonialist's truth that the native is a lazy, dishonest, greedy, good-for-nothing, Fanon asserts that the unemployed and starving peasants "do not lay claim to the truth but are the truth" because they understand most clearly how things really are in the world of colonial Manicheanism. It is not a relativist idea of truth but a "certainty of being and the whole of truth," as Hegel put it, lived in the historical context and believed absolutely. "In every age, among the people," Fanon proclaims, "truth is the property of the national cause": "The native replies to the living lie of the colonial situation by an equal falsehood. . . . In this colonialist context there is no truthful behavior: and the good is quite simply that which is evil for 'them'" (*WE*, 50). Fanon's perspective is quite clear. The truth the peasant espouses is based on the simple, inclusive and obstinate self-interested fact, "Bread and Land." The peasantry is revolutionary because it has no investment in the colonial system at all, and this realization represents an elemental consciousness that only violence pays. The peasants' rudimentary, and in Fanon's view correct, apprehension that colonialism is based on nothing but pure force and will respond to nothing but force is evidence of their sound revolutionary intuition. Colonialism can be made vulnerable by the direct threat of violence, which is not limited to armed struggle. Passive demonstrations and strikes quickly turn to violence in the context of the colonial reaction.

In the Fanonian schema, the question becomes how to lay hold of this violence which up to now has been "canalized" through dance and daemonic possession, in fratricide, and in dreams? How to catalyze its implicit force into direct activity? Fanon follows this question with far more daunting ones: "When can one affirm that the situation is ripe for a movement of national liberation? In what form should it first be manifested?" (*WE*, 59). In other words, to understand the form and timing, violence has to become reasoned action. Decolonization is historical insofar as it becomes clear to itself, but it is only through reflexive activity of the decolonization movement that its real content becomes clear.[18]

The historical period of decolonization is filled with international and regional struggles. The international exchange of ideas produces a "veritable panic" among the colonialists, who now wish to decolonize as quickly as possible. On the colonized side, success breeds new confidence. The outlets that had appeased the native's pent-up aggression are no longer placating. The colonists are increasingly trigger-happy, but the increasing repressions begin to have diminishing effects. In fact, Fanon argues, they give credence to the native's belief that everything can be solved by force. A local incident can start a machine-gunning, which overnight becomes an international event. Thus there is available an immediately recognizable historical context where the increase in violence by the colonialists has a diminishing return. Whereas the 45,000 killed at Sétif in 1945 went virtually unnoticed, in 1960, Fanon points out, the shooting at Sharpeville and the repercussions in Algeria, take on an international significance:

> Far from calling a halt to the forward rush of national consciousness, [the repercussions] urge it on. Mass slaughter at a certain stage of the *embryonic development of consciousness* increases that consciousness, for the hecatombs are an indication that between oppressor and oppressed everything can be solved by force. (*WE*, 72, emphasis added)

The colonialists do not seriously entertain the option of leaving, but there is a turning point, a climactic moment marked by a huge repression where the rubicon is crossed. This increase in repression does not alone cause decolonization, but it is a sign of the weakening hold of the colonizer on the mind of the colonized.

At this time, Fanon notes, the "slave's sense" reads in the hieroglyphics on the brow of the colonizer "the increasing bankruptcy of colonialism" (*AR*, 75). The timing of the anticolonial explosion is also an effect of the new awareness of the colonialist's *fear*. It is a moment when everyone realizes that things cannot go back to the way they were before. All of a sudden the native becomes part of the world (*WE*, 43). Once the claim of equality with the settler is made, it becomes realized. At this moment, the whole material and moral universe, all the ways of thinking that had been permeated by colonialism, begin to break up.

It is not violence *per se* but the process of liberation that is central to the "embodiment of history" and the creation of a revolutionary agency that begins to strip away colonial reification. Fanon calls it the creation of humanity "by revolutionary beginnings." The native transcends nativehood only insofar as subjectivity is intimately connected to self-determination and is intrinsic to revolution. What now is crucial are not the traditions which initially sustained an elemental resistance, but rather the new sense of the possibility of freedom. This is the seam in colonialism's totalitarian fabric, for it is this idea of freedom which the native makes historical. The argument that the form that national liberation assumes is based on its process may seem circular, but it is profoundly dialectical:

> Decolonization . . . influences individuals and modifies them fundamentally . . . It brings a natural rhythm into existence . . . with a new language and new humanity. Decolonization is the veritable creation of a new humanity. But this creation owes nothing of its legitimacy to any supernatural power: the "thing" which has been colonized becomes human during the same process by which it frees itself. (*WE*, 36–7)

The "process" might be violent, but violence does not exhaust the process. Fanon posits that in place of the earlier pseudo-reciprocity with the master which had taught the slave that each individual should be shut up in their own subjectivity (*WE*, 47), the revolutionary movement fosters a new social consciousness arising from a reciprocal life expressed in the new language of "brother, sister, friend." Very much like Rosa Luxemburg's conception of spontaneity which proclaims that revolution irradiates the genius of the masses, Fanon sees the same elemental creativity taking place during the struggle for national liberation.

The Qualifications of Violence:
Descent from an Absolute

Though violence is the crucial variable that marks the beginning,
the depth, and even to some extent the success of national liberation, national liberation itself is not solely determined and defined
by it. There are places in *The Wretched* that have been commonly
cited to prove that Fanon was simply calling physical violence the
be-all and end-all of national liberation. For example, Fanon is
notoriously known for construing violence as "cleansing" the
individual. The following is frequently quoted:

> At the level of individuals, violence is a cleansing force [*la violence
> desintoxique*]. It frees the native from his inferiority complex and from
> his despair and inaction; it makes him fearless and restores his self-
> respect. (*WE*, 94)

Some critics have translated "cleansing" into religious terms,[19]
others maintain that Fanon is justifying violence as catharsis.[20] His
point may be a little simpler. If one translates *desintoxique* as detox-
ifying or disintoxifying, it carries the sense of getting rid of a poison
rather than the more loaded idea of a mind-washing. At most, one
might say that detoxification clears a mental fog, dispelling ideological obfuscation and helping the mind redirect internalized pent-
up aggression toward its proper source – in this case colonial
violence. Confronting the object of one's fears does not mean rec-
ommending wanton violence.[21] The process must be understood as
just that, a process, as much internal as external. Anticolonial violence properly directed is psychologically liberating for the native;
that is, it liberates the native from despair and inaction. The formerly all-powerful colonial master is cut down to size. Because the
colonizer can be killed, he becomes contingent, and because he is
no longer absolute he can be killed. The defeat of the colonial forces
helps restore self-respect and is a psychological blow for the colonizers, who had also believed in their invincibility. For though it
uses the mask of liberty, colonialism only understands violence.

Second, it is frequently argued that Fanon posits violence as a
necessary condition for the creation of a unified nation:

> The native's violence unifies the people. By its very structure, colo-
> nialism is separatist and regionalist. Colonialism does not simply
> state the existence of tribes; it reinforces it and separates it. The

colonial system encourages chieftaincies and keeps alive the old
Marabout confraternities. Violence is in action all inclusive and
national. (*WE*, 94)

Again, the historical context is important. The divide-and-rule violence of colonialism reinforces certain tribal, regional, religious, and
local identities as channels for aggression. Turned against the colonialists, violence can become creative and positive, breaking up
colonial forms of rule, alliances, and patronage. It can help build a
new social consciousness and "unify a people" if it operates under
a national and inclusive banner: "the armed struggle mobilizes the
people," Fanon adds, "it throws them *one way and in one direction.*"
That is to say, the success of violent action can only be judged by
the extent to which it mobilizes the people along national lines. But
being thrown in one direction forecloses democracy and discussion.
Violence is a dividing line indicating not only a change away from
the politics of patronage, but also the exhaustion of politics.

Third, we need to give equal weight to both the "atmosphere of
violence" in which Fanon's pronouncements were made, and the
specific concerns Fanon voiced. Counterviolence is not wanton
violence but an organized and controlled means to a worthy end,
decolonization. Though I have emphasized that the central element
in Fanon's conception of violence is self-activity, there can be no
doubt that Fanon is claiming that real violence is usually necessary.
Where self-conscious activity has been realized without violence, it
is because the threat of violence has been sufficient or something
else has united the people and undermined colonialism, such as
political agitation made more ominous by violent activity in surrounding areas. By formulating such a loose conception of violence,
ranging from the symbolic to the actual, what remains absolute,
whether the violence is directed toward the destruction of an "internal" or "external" oppressor, is the imperative to become a self-
determining being, not determined by an Other. This imperative
provides the positive element of the struggle.

Fourth, and perhaps more importantly, though more problematically, Fanon maintains that anticolonial violence liberates the
native from the inferiority complex created by the destruction of
indigenous ways of being. The question is how far can anticolonial
violence be psychologically liberating for the colonized? Fanon says
that this depends on directing the native's consciousness to the "real
source" of the complex, namely the violent colonial relationship. Organized violence committed against a colonial regime that

appears to have totalitarian control does have a liberating effect psychologically. Nevertheless this is a mere beginning. Much criticism of Fanon turns on the negative effects of violence. Empirically those who take part in violence can experience posttraumatic stress and other disorders, rather than liberation.[22] Certainly Fanon was aware of this issue, having treated FLN combatants, and the success of a Fanonian day hospitalization in a newly independent society would depend on fundamental social change. In other words, for Fanon, the issue of violence cannot be viewed outside the context of social change. Without it, violence is simply destructive.

Despite these qualifications Fanon's claims for the restorative, cleansing power of violence leave many questions. For Fanon, violence is the solution. It can break the native's inferiority complex and the colonial machine that produces it. Yet what is the cost? Did he really believe that the native was liberated by violence? Certainly the tragedy of violence did not escape him. *L'An V* is prefaced with the warning:

> Because we want a democratic and renovated Algeria, we believe we cannot rise and liberate ourselves in one area and sink in another. We condemn with pain in our hearts, those brothers who have flung themselves into revolutionary action with the almost psychological brutality that centuries of oppression give rise to and feed. (*DC*, 25)

Fanon has a zero-sum model of violence. The reaction to the violence produced by colonialism and directed toward the colonized must be released somewhere. It is much healthier in his eyes to direct it to its source rather than sublimate it internally. Whether violence can resolve the inferiority complex[23] in one fell swoop is another question, but from Fanon's point of view, the channeling of violence toward the colonial regime is at least getting to the source of the problem. But Fanon warns that the colonized, so starved of recognition, can be disarmed by scraps of charity and within a Manichean frame violent action can be easily exhausted. While violence is necessary for the destruction of colonialism and inferiority complexes, it is not a sufficient condition for the development of a new humanity.

Dizzy on Violence

> The very forms of organization of the struggle will suggest to him a different vocabulary. Brother, sister, friend – these are words outlawed by the colonialist bourgeoisie. (Fanon, *The Wretched of the Earth*)

The following passage from *The Wretched* which has been identified as expressing key philosophical issues about violence also indicates the political and practical levels at which the idea of violence works in Fanon's theory:

> For the native, this violence represents the absolute line of action. The militant is also a man who works . . . To work means to work for the death of the settler . . . Violence is thus seen as comparable to a royal pardon. The colonized man finds his freedom in and through violence. This rule of conduct enlightens the agent because it indicates to him the means and the end. (*WE*, 85–6)

Let us take these pronouncements sentence by sentence: "For the native, this violence represents the absolute line of action." In other words, the colonized understands that violence is the only strategy that gets concrete results. The point is valid for settler colonialism in Africa (Kenya, Algeria, Mozambique, Angola, Rhodesia and South Africa) and is proved in the history of the anticolonial movement in Algeria. Up until 1954 all kinds of political actions and requests had been made of the colonial government. Reforms had not been forthcoming. It was coordinated violence that forced the colonizers to think about decolonization.

"The militant is also a man who works." This has been understood in terms of Hegel's master/slave dialectic read through Kojève.[24] The militant's work is to kill the settler, but Fanon's point is also political, related directly to the experience in the Battle of Algiers.[25] "The questions that the organization asks the militant bear the mark of this way of looking at things: 'Where have you worked? With whom? What have you accomplished?' The group requires that each individual perform an irrevocable action." This is dangerous work. The group is dependent on the loyalty of each member. "In Algeria, for example, where almost all the men who called on the people to join in the national struggle were condemned to death or searched for by the French police, confidence was proportional to the hopelessness of each case. You could be sure of a new recruit when he could no longer go back into the colonial system."

Violence corresponds to action by a people who were previously politically inactive. It is a kind of action which makes sure that one cannot "go back" to the way things were. One cannot become politically passive again. Violence becomes the dividing line. Fanon relates this to the revolt in Kenya: "This mechanism, it seems, had existed in Kenya among the Mau-Mau, who required that each member of the group should strike a blow at the victim. Each one was thus personally responsible for the death of that victim. To work means to work for the death of the settler."

The willingness to partake in acts of violence against the colonial regime is the glue that holds the group together. Fanon calls it "comparable to a royal pardon," which means that individuals who have been members of other organizations, like the followers of Messali in Algeria for example, have the ability, through an act of violence, to gain admission or readmission to the revolutionary movement. The following two sentences are among Fanon's most controversial:

> The colonized man finds his freedom in and through violence. This rule of conduct enlightens the agent because it indicates to him the means and the end. (*WE*, 86)

Taken narrowly they mean that violent action is the means and end, but Fanon later criticizes this position. Nonreductively, violence "indicates" the means and the end, in other words violence is the way in which colonial rule, a rule by violence, is brought to an end. In the colonial situation, violence frees the native from the violence of the old regime. Anticolonial violence is contradictory, it is both Manichean and dialectical. It indicates the end of colonial rule but does not, in itself, constitute a program. In other words, rather than an answer violence becomes a problematic that needs to be worked out.

The foregoing, which almost certainly underlies Sartre's account of violence as self healing and self curative (*WE*, 21), has been cited as proof of Fanon as a "prophet of violence." Yet the passage also continues to indicate the mark of the declaration of the Soummam platform against a cult of leadership: "Even if the armed struggle has been symbolic and the nation is demobilized through a rapid movement of decolonization, the people have the time to see that the liberation has been the business of each and all and that the leader has no special merit" (*WE*, 93). The reduction of armed struggle to symbolism elevates the importance of the revolutionary process itself (that the people see that liberation has been their own work and not based on the charisma of any particular leader or party). Liberation is a process rather than a "trial of strength," a series of battles rather than a frontal assault.

There is a possibility that liberation could occur from a "symbolic" armed struggle. For example, when one reads "violence unifies; it illuminates the consciousness of the people and directs them against any pacification" (*WE*, 94), Fanon is not simply saying that a new humanity is a product of violence, but rather that anti-colonial violence demystifies politics. Additionally, that life for the colonized "can arise only from the rotting corpse of the colonized" (*WE*, 93) does not mean that a new humanity is literally born from the colonizer's cadaver, but that just as colonialism means the living death of colonized life, the death of colonialism marks the birth time of the formerly colonized.

Only after the oppressors are removed can the healing process and the project of creating a new nation and a new citizen become practical. Because humans are feeling, thinking, and actional beings, a new humanism cannot develop out of violent acts alone but requires the nurturing of creative, inventive, and thoughtful activity. Prefigured in the struggle for freedom, it must also be nurtured in the period after liberation. Thus, to the extent that violence becomes the program of a political party, national liberation is doomed to failure and barbarism. Violence alone cannot win the revolution. It is not enough to move the protagonist from reaction to becoming a thinking, actional being. Action is, of course, the key to reaction, but reaction is still an action determined by the Other. Only "enlightened action" (which cannot be furnished by violence alone) proves once and for all the native no longer exists within the Manichean world developed by colonialism.

Finally, many of Fanon's conclusions about the importance of violence in the development of a revolutionary consciousness emerge from the experience of the Algerian revolution. Though he construes the Algerian revolution as paradigmatic, it actually represents an extreme case, having "lived under police and military domination never equalled in a colonial country." The colonial system in Algeria had an unusually heavy impact upon the rural denizens, who were subjected to a "pacification" campaign that lasted two generations. This prolonged assault was necessary because the Algerian had never been completely disarmed.

The "uniqueness" of the Algerian situation leads Fanon to remind us that, "[if] we have taken the example of Algeria to illustrate our subject, it is . . . to show the important part played by the war in leading them [the people] toward consciousness of themselves. It is clear that other peoples have come to the same conclusion in different ways" (*WE*, 193). The "different ways" toward self-consciousness include other forms of political and social pressure to get rid of colonialism. Each would have to be judged by its success, not just by becoming independent but by the degree to which the mind of the colonized is liberated from "inferiority" and gains real independence. Furthermore, intercontinental liberation movements may have an impact on the necessity or degree of violence. Fanon maintains that the new nation will be the result "either of a violent struggle of the people in their own right, or of action on the part of surrounding colonized peoples which acts as a brake on the colonial regime in question" (*WE*, 70). He also concedes that the nation could emerge from a compromise with colonialism if principles are not relinquished and concessions are the result of choice rather than the colonialist's imposition (*WE*, 143). Fanon's observations and qualifications in *The Wretched* about "absolute violence" are not unique. Reporting in *El Moudjahid* on the African People's Conference in Accra, where he had been a delegate, he wrote of various "possible types of struggle." He noted that nonviolent decolonization had been made possible by "successive setbacks to French colonialism in the other territories," but in settler colonialism "only armed struggle will bring about defeat" (*DC*, 155–6). In other words, it was the intransigence and violence of colonialism itself that dictated the degree and type of response.

Based on his study and experience of the Algerian revolution, Fanon develops two propositions that indicate an inherent relativism in the relationship between violence and decolonization. First that the larger the *settler* population the more violent, and second that "violence among the colonized people will be proportionate to the violence exercised by the threatened colonial regime." He adds that it is virtually impossible for the colonized to retaliate with the same degree of violence as the oppressor. The colonizer's brutality, often abetted by sophisticated weapons, far outreaches the resources of the native. Yet he warns, "was freedom worth the consequences of penetrating into that enormous circuit of terrorism and counter-terrorism?" (*DC*, 57). He prefaces *L'An V* with another important qualification: the colonized people must win "cleanly, without barbarity." To create a nation demands a "most lucid, most self-controlled people" (*DC*, 24). In other words, Fanon is painfully aware that violence alone can lead to both "terribly reactionary results" and neurosis.

Fanon presents the possibility of a much more developed consciousness than dependency affords and an opportunity for developing a new humanism. When Fanon argues that "antiracist racism"[26] cannot sustain a war of liberation or constitute a program (*WE*, 139), he seems to be embracing Sartre's critique of negritude as an antiracist racism that Fanon had rejected in *Black Skin*. But while Fanon continues to engage Sartre's critique, his dialectic and

conclusions remain quite different. Fanon's notion of a new humanism and his concern about the future after colonialism find little
valence with Sartre, who finds the dialectic ends with the colonizers (*WE*, 31). While Fanon leaves us with doubts about the nature
of violence framed in reaction to the Other, the destruction of the
colonial world, because it is a Manichean one, logically entails the
abolition of the colonial zone. It cannot be reformed. It is not in
the service of a higher synthesis, but obeys the "principle of reciprocal exclusivity." It is only through the abolition of that Manichean
structure that one can transcend the reciprocity of terror and build
a new society on its own foundation. However, as we shall see in
the next section, Fanon warns that if the native's consciousness and
the political program remain reactions to the settler, then the result
will be barbarity. Violence is left to feed on itself, which is exactly
the critique often made of Fanon. Fanon writes:

> Those lightning flashes of consciousness which fling the body into
> stormy paths or which throw it into an almost pathological trance
> where the face of the other beckons me on to giddiness, where my
> blood calls for the blood of the other, where the sheer inertia of my
> death calls for the death of the other – that intense emotion of the
> first few hours falls to pieces if it is left to feed on its own substance.
> (*WE*, 139)

By including the section on mental health and colonial wars in
The Wretched, Fanon was aware of a double bind. Can we escape
from becoming dizzy from all this blood and violence? (*WE*, 253).
In the case studies included in *The Wretched*, he writes of a young
ALN soldier who was depressed and suicidal. The soldier dreamed
of his blood being sucked by a vampire. His mother had been shot
point-blank by a French soldier. One day he went to the estate of a
leading colonist. Only the colonist's wife was there. She begged him
not to kill her, but he killed her with a knife. Fanon analyzed the
young man as suffering from an unconscious guilt complex following the death of his mother, whom he felt he could not protect.
He had attempted to master the feeling associated with the trauma
by doing the same thing (*WE*, 261–4). The atmosphere of violence
is plain to see. His actions are the product of a Manichean reality –
blood for blood: a circularity of violence in which he tries to master
his feeling of guilt. Clearly this is neurotic behavior not fitting for
the development of a new society. The blood of the colonist's wife
was not disintoxicating but drove him further into psychosis. The

fact that the liberation movement brought charges against him indicates that violent actions were not treated lightly.

Later Fanon writes of neuroses created by the "atmosphere of total war." War creates tragic acts such as the case of the two Algerian boys who killed their European friend but "weren't a bit cross with him." "One day we decided to kill him," they said, "because the Europeans want to kill Arabs." The 14-year-old boy justifying his action added: "had there ever been a European arrested and sent to prison after the murder of an Algerian?" (*WE*, 270–1). "Man's tragedy" is that he was once a child, Fanon's quote in *Black Skin* from Rousseau by way of Nietzsche (*BS*, 10) had become painfully real. For the colonized, childhood had disappeared. Decolonization is a violent phenomenon, stresses Fanon on the first page of *The Wretched*, but taking the life of an innocent boy is tragic. At a military level, Fanon recognizes how acts of terror can lead to brutality, and he is far from arguing that killing a European friend is a "healthy" act.

Fanon charts a very tricky terrain by arguing that violence is therapeutic. Colonialism creates a native who is envious and hurtful, and the war of liberation gave expression to some of these feelings. By problematizing the notion of violence we can see that Fanon knows it will not lead to establishing total liberation, "that which concerns all sectors of the personality" (*WE*, 310). I think he understands the problematic more than has been thought.

6

Radical Mutations: Toward a Fighting Culture

In the midst of the gravest dangers the Algerian adopts modern forms of existence and confers on the human person maximum independence.

Fanon, *L'An V de la révolution algérienne*

Fanon claims that participation in violent action provides the foundation for national consciousness because it mobilizes the people as a group and throws them in one direction, but in the preface to *L'An V* he notes that "our forces do not exceed five thousand poorly armed men." What role can the other 10 million Algerians play? How can they be mobilized by the armed struggle and develop a national consciousness if only a few can play a direct role?

One immediate, though still partial, solution to this problem is provided in Fanon's Mali logbook written in 1960. There he writes of the commando's role to rouse the population, "to reassure them as to the future, to show the armament of the ALN, to *detach them psychologically and mentally* from enemy ascendancy" (*AR*, 189, emphasis added). Military success is secondary to the battle of ideas.

Is the involvement of the mass of people in violence purely a strategic problem? Would Fanon be in favor of everyone being directly involved in physically violent engagements as part of the revolutionary process? And if so, should more removed and mediated cultural forms of resistance be created? As to the desirability of everyone's involvement in violence, the answer is, on one level, yes. After all, real violence is the most immediate way to cast off the old servile consciousness and become part of a national movement. But we must remember Fanon's critique of the native's reactive mindless violence, as well as the "mirage of his muscles' own immediacy." Although "inventing" a national consciousness aims at involving people in the struggle, it cannot be produced by violence alone. What Fanon calls a "fighting culture" mediates between organization and mass activity and, at the same time, suggests how subjectivity might be constructed positively. What truly matters is not the fact of violent action but the cultural context in which it occurs, for the context of a fighting culture sets the stage for a "radical mutation of consciousness" and the subsequent development of a genuine national consciousness.

Fanon insists that forging links with the people means subordinating the military to the political. Only a small proportion of the people has direct links with the military; thus how to develop political links with the masses becomes a fundamental concern. The problematic of involving the masses in the struggle was addressed strategically at the Soummam conference. As we have seen, the Battle of Algiers included a large part of the city's population, affecting the imaginations of those not directly involved. Because the struggle for the liberation of the nation is real, not imagined, there is a powerful relationship between the real anticolonial violence, symbolic anticolonial violence, and imaginary anticolonial violence. The power of the imagination is seen in Fanon's essay "This is the Voice of Algeria," where those listening to the radio do not create a nation out of thin air, nor simply from the airwaves, but in the forums of discussion and debate that emanate from the sounds of the radio. Battles are imagined and victories won. A new nation comes into being, Fanon proclaims, willed by the consciousness of the Algerian people.

In Fanon's schematic mapping of anticolonial activity – which in effect imitates the two modes of logic, the Manichean and the dialectical – the organization of the first resistance is *determined* by the colonizer. That is to say, the actions of the occupier "determine the centers around which a people's will to survive becomes organized" (*DC*, 47). From various cultural constellations of discontents, a "whole universe of resistances" develops "to justify the rejection of the occupier's presence" (*DC*, 93). These protests represent an obstinate allegiance to tradition, not because of any inherent value in tradition, but because tradition had offered a refuge from colonial predations. Fanon calls this negativity a "defense mechanism." For example, the performance of certain rituals might serve not so much as a devout observance of tradition, but rather as a form of resistance against or repudiation of the colonizer who has been bent on destroying those traditions. "The fighting phase" sloughs off the moribund, giving new life to formerly inert elements, reevaluating the Algerian cultural symbols and practices, and moreover introducing new cultures born of the struggle.

Under constant attack, the colonized cultural life during colonialism has been a subjugated one, steadily shrinking and drying up. It is only during the period of decolonization that culture, and with it subjectivity, is reinvigorated as it becomes a *fighting culture* where the struggle for the new way of life and the native's daily "ways of life" become one and the same.

Antibiotic Attitudes

The Algerian's hostile reaction to everything French is characteristic of this Manichean stance, at first glance reminiscent of a skeptical consciousness which enjoys being contentious for its own sake, saying B to the other's A and A to the other's B. The colonized rejects values, "even if they might be objectively worth choosing" (*DC*, 62), because they are the values of the occupier. This tendency to stand against anything colonialism introduces simply because it is colonial, and to appraise all the colonizer's contributions in a pejorative way, is in fact an expression of the native's absolutism described by Fanon in his essay on "Medicine and Colonialism" in *L'An V* (*DC*, 121–46).

We would think that any society would unreservedly welcome knowledge or discovery of methods to ease pain and promote health. But rather than recognizing advanced medical technology as an improvement, the colonized view such technology as "proof of the extension of the occupier's hold on the country." The native's reaction, like a skeptic's, might seem childish but it is rooted very much in reality. In the colonial world, argues Fanon, with the Algerian example at the front of his mind, the colonial doctor is very often associated with the army, and is thus *correctly* p⁄ of a system that functions as a policeman. In this a⸃ is real difficulty in being "objective," for there is nc

Medicine in the West is characterized by trust a⸃ Hippocratic oath is taken seriously, and there i⸃ of checks to enforce medical ethics. In the col objectively expressed is constantly vitiated by the lie of the colonial situation" (*BS*, 128) and the attitude to Western medicine (the medicine of the settler) is entirely different. Because "the doctor and the patient belong to two irreconcilable species"[2] the discussion between them is completely at odds. The patient entering the doctor's office is tense and rigid. "The doctors say: 'Those people are rough and unmannerly.' The patients say: 'I don't trust them ... I know how to get into your hospital, but I don't know how I'll get out – *if* I get out'" (*DC*, 127). Because everything is modified by the colonial system, there can be no neutral standpoint to distinguish the objective from the attitudinal. In the colonial set-up, the idea of what is true is constructed through a Manichean interpretation. For the native, saying "no" to the French "yes" can be the only truth. It is an absolutely intransigent attitude that provides no room for any qualification. The absolute here is Manichean, with any qualification or compromise constituting error, a concession to the colonial world; "every qualification is perceived by the occupier as an invitation to perpetuate the oppression, as a confession of congenital impotence"; any agreement with the colonizing society signals an acceptance, a signal of willingness to integrate.

In the colonial situation, where the subjugation of the colonized body is particularly marked, medicine takes on additional import. The native reacts in an "undifferentiated, categorical way" (*DC*, 122) because swallowing the pill constitutes a feeling of infection by the colonial power. In short, colonialism has entered the body, has invaded the internal organs, has compromised the native's natural immunity, making the pill nothing but an extension of colonial power.

The fatalism exhibited by a "father's apparent refusal, for example, to admit that he owes his life to the colonizer's operation must be studied in two lights," argues Fanon:

> the colonized person ... in underdeveloped countries, or the disinherited in all parts of the world, perceives life not as a flowering or development of essential productiveness, but as a permanent struggle against an omnipresent death. This ever-menacing death is experienced as endemic famine, underemployment, a high death rate, an inferiority complex, and the absence of any hope for the future. All this gnawing at the existence of the colonized tends to make of life something resembling an incomplete death.

In the context of a living death the "raison d'être" of colonial Manicheanism is complete: "acts of refusal or rejection of the medical treatment are not refusal of life, but a greater passivity before that close and contagious death" (*DC*, 128).

It is not surprising that the French medical service could not be separated from French colonialism. Doctors, schoolteachers, and engineers are literally little different from policemen, parachutists, and army commandos, and they are all to be dismissed in "one lump." Because colonialism is a total system it must be totally rejected. There is no need for nuance. As we have seen, medicine is part of the disciplinary system, introduced into Algeria at the same time as "racism and humiliation," and finds its most dehumanized character in monitoring the pain of the tortured. This is an extreme example of the colonial medical enterprise whose project is the dehumanization of the native. Degraded, polluted, and diseased, the native is the object of medical classifications, and colonial regimes look to medical practice as a means of political domination and control. The practical concern of hygiene is part of the project of disciplining the body, taming the native workforce, and segmenting the population, which is seen as a source of great wealth and great danger. The native's attitude to sanitary improvements "as fresh proof of the extension of the occupier's hold on the country" expressed the reality.[3] Yet we also face an ambiguity. What to do in the face of a medical crisis when traditional medicines won't do but the treatment by the European doctor is an insult? The patient becomes a "battleground for different and opposed forces" (*DC*, 131).

In *The Wretched* Fanon argues that the colonial system is also in the business of interpolating the native within certain traditions. In the medical context we find the understanding that the "traditional" healer expresses not only custom, or even a remedy, but also a social truth. Though defined by this Manichean world, the native is not simply a victim and does not thoughtlessly embrace traditions. Because relations with the traditional healer have immediate psychological and political ramifications, even if the colonized understands the advantages of a modern drug like penicillin, they will have to continue to pay tribute to traditional remedies (*DC*, 130–1). To shun the traditional healer would be to risk ostracism from the social group. In fact, any qualification is a sign of disloyalty because the Manichean attitude reflects the way things really are. There is no room for discussion or choice. Despite its rhetoric about "individualism," colonialism always dismisses the colonized as a homogenized mass. The native's distrust of the rhetoric about the "individual" follows suit: it is us and them. This is

why treating the "individual" case of meningitis with Western medicine, for example, has to be immediately remedied socially by a
visit to the traditional healer.

This defensive, intransigent, and clandestine resistance to colonial society is characteristic of the dominant period of colonial rule,
a period which attempts to break up the economy and cultural life
of the people and reproduces a Manichean culture and distorted
and disfigured traditions: "Colonialism is not satisfied merely with
holding a people in its grip and emptying the native's brain of all
form and content. By a kind of perverted logic, it turns to the past
of the oppressed people, and distorts, disfigures and destroys it"
(*WE*, 210). Culture under colonial domination is contested, condemned to secrecy and extinction. Always shrinking, becoming
more and more "shrivelled up, inert, and empty," the culture of
the colonized reflects poverty and oppression. As the native
moves from "desperate refusal" to active revolt, the habits of
Manicheanism are challenged. With decolonization there is an
opportunity for radically new behavior in both public and private
life, a chance for cultural regeneration where positive concepts of
self-determination, not contingent upon the colonial status quo, are
generated. "The shock that broke the chains of colonialism," Fanon
claims, "has moderated exclusive attitudes, reduced extreme positions, made certain arbitrary views obsolete" (*DC*, 139).

Whereas the first stage of anticolonial resistance expresses the
contradictory interrelation of tradition and resistance, this second
stage expresses the breaking up of this affinity. Rather than valorize
tradition, a fighting culture seeks to forge totally new relations
between people. The fight for liberation, Fanon declares, "sets
culture moving and opens to it the doors of creation." This
struggle is dialectical because it "does not give back to the national
culture its former values and shapes" but "aims at a fundamentally
different set of relations between men that cannot leave intact either
the form or content of the people's culture" (*WE*, 245–6). Fanon's
dialectical conception of national culture separates him from
nationalist thinkers who see culture as a stock of symbols, traditions, customs, etc.; instead techniques formerly shunned by the
Algerian people are adopted during the "course of the fight" and
the "mechanical sense of detachment and mistrust" of everything
associated with the colonial regime begins to weaken (*DC*, 126).
Such change marks a dialectical development where something
eschewed as part of the colonial system becomes consciously appro-

priated and used in the struggle. In a fighting culture "everything becomes possible" (*DC*, 145).

What kind of open-ended dialectic are we talking about here, where everything seems possible? Indeed, the notion of appropriating and "taking over" modern techniques does not mean that the movement is indebted to the colonial system. Fanon's earlier description of the absolute divide of colonial Manicheanism is not vitiated. The fact that techniques can be "taken over" as an element of how "everything becomes possible" is an internal dialectic of decolonization. The mental and real strategies of the native are no longer hemmed in by Manichean logic, and the rapid assimilation of "modern forms of technology" (*DC*, 145) does not warrant a newly uncritical attitude toward them. Rather than focusing on how the technique is part of the oppressive system, Fanon is at pains to describe the mutation of attitudes among the colonized. The change is a result of how techniques (such as Western medicine) are put into the "service" of the people. The resulting embargo on antibiotics and tetanus vaccination, ether, and alcohol, which created a terrible health problem for the ALN, brought about an important reaction. Doctors who had previously been considered ambassadors for the colonizing system became "reintegrated into the group," and the restriction on the availability of drugs brought sympathetic Europeans, who could acquire medicines, into the struggle. In the utopian atmosphere, Fanon argues, the Algerian doctor "sleeping on the ground with the men and women of the *mechatas*, living the drama of the people . . . became part of the Algerian body" (*DC*, 142). The antibiotic was stripped of its negative associations and the "most modern forms of technology" were assimilated "at an extraordinary rate" (*DC*, 145). It was a remarkably creative and dynamic atmosphere, in which Fanon shared, that approached the prevention of disease in new ways.

Thus, in contrast to the powerful descriptions of colonial Manicheanism in "Concerning Violence," where the native is described in zoological terms, Frantz Fanon's *L'An V* expresses a type of postcoloniality where the subjugated come alive. The lived experience described in *L'An V* is a social phenomenon which liberates and transgresses the restrictive physical and mental boundaries of the colonial spatial order. Such a conceptualization is attained by thinking of lived experience not only as a social construct reflecting reality, but as dialectically embodying tensions and contradictions that give rise to the struggle to shape new actualities.

In the almost utopian atmosphere of *L'An V*, the previously sub-altern is no longer the dehumanized object of the colonial regime, nor a ventriloquization or mimic of the colonial civilizing regime. Instead, the subaltern speaks.[4] For the social individual that Fanon describes, lived experience is a world of new social relations, dis-rupting family, work, and community. This national liberation struggle, opines Fanon, is not a return to the past but a reaching for the future.

Fanon had concluded *Black Skin* with a quote from Marx, "the social revolution . . . cannot draw its poetry from the past, but only from the future." Though critics have maintained that he under-estimated how much the Algerian revolution also had to "strip itself of all its superstitions concerning the past" (quoted in *BS*, 223), one of Fanon's strengths as a theorist is his capacity to embrace an idea as an absolute and follow it dialectically to its conclusion. *L'An V* expresses an anticolonial absolute (Algerian self-determination) not simply as an inversion of the colonial order, but as a creative moment reaching untidily for a new beginning. In the essays Fanon argues that the veil, an object of "tradition," and antibiotics and the radio, objects of "modernity," detached from their original cultural contexts, lose their symbolic power during the revolution.

L'An V de la révolution algérienne (Year five of the Algerian revo-lution) was, as the title suggests, published in the revolution's fifth year, 1959. Fanon wrote and collected the essays in a three-week period in the spring, imbibing the oxygen of the revolution and basing them on fieldwork as he traveled the Algerian countryside for the FLN. But he had in fact been thinking about writing a book which would reflect the radical changes in Algerian society ever since his resignation from Blida-Joinville hospital and his public identification with the Algerian revolution in 1956. *L'An V* reflects the fluidity of a revolutionary period.[5]

Fanon hoped that *L'An V* would provoke debate about what was happening in Algeria among left-leaning French intellectuals. As an editor of the FLN paper, *El Moudjahid*,[6] and later as a member of the Ministry of Information, Fanon was concerned about the represen-tation of the Algerian revolution in France. He not only battled the misinformation perpetrated by the local colonial and metropolitan press, but used the pages of the paper to polemicize and harangue the French liberal left.[7] To broaden the discussion about the Algerian revolution among French radicals (that is, outside of the small group of radicals who supported the revolution, like Sartre, de Beauvoir and Jeanson[8]) he published "Algeria's European

Minority" in *Les Temps Modernes* in June 1959. The article would become the final chapter of the book and addressed the importance of a minority struggling against a dominant power. It spoke directly to the French left, which, though a minority, could still influence events. The article, which reflected Fanon's own situation as part not only of an ethnic minority but of a political minority, also engaged the "Jewish question." Rather than a colonizing minority like the Europeans in Algeria, or the Afrikaners and British in South Africa, the Algerian Jew, who had been in Algeria for over 2,000 years, occupied a wholly different historical space and future:

> One of the most pernicious manoeuvres of colonialism in Algeria was and remains the division between Jews and Moslems. Jews have been in Algeria for more than two thousand years; they are thus an integral part of the Algerian people. . . . Moslems and Jews, children of the same earth, must not fall into the trap of provocation. Rather, they must make a common front against it, not letting themselves be duped by those who, not long ago, were offhandedly contemplating the total extermination of the Jews as a salutary step in the evolution of humanity. (*DC*, 155)

During Fanon's time at Blida-Joinville Hospital it had become known as a place friendly for the FLN. Though raided often by the police, nothing was ever discovered. The appendix to "Algeria's European Minority" included two testimonies of Europeans who had joined the movement. The first was his colleague, Charles Geronimi; the second was a policeman, Bresson Yvon, who had become disgusted with colonial torture and begun working as a double agent for the FLN. Going behind the reciprocity of violence, Fanon challenged both the French liberals and the FLN to rethink, and claimed that the Algerian revolution was not about "one barbarism replacing another barbarism, of one crushing of man with another crushing of man" (*DC*, 32).

L'An V was marginalized by the establishment press. More than an antipropaganda book, *L'An V* became ominous. It literally got under the French skin. It details what Fanon called the "reality of the nation," his first title, describing the changes in social relations which that reality entailed. Behind its didactic and programmatic character lurks a deeper dialectic, expressing the state of emergence in consciousness and reality. The future society was already in evidence, he claimed, and the point was to discern it and help it evolve in relations between women and men, relations in the family, in attitudes to modern medicine, or in the radio, or in the place of minorities. The old Manichean attitudes were crumbling under the pressure of the revolutionary movement. The old was dying and the new was emerging.

At the same time, in mapping the contours of the revolution, showing that its power resided not in military hardware but in the very consciousness of the Algerian people, *L'An V* contained an implicit critique of ALN militarists. In *The Wretched*, against the legal nationalists who were overly concerned with the military superiority of the enemy, he took on no less an authority than Frederick Engels, noting how the outnumbered and outgunned Spaniards had defeated Bonaparte (*WE*, 63–4). In *L'An V*, with the defeat of the French forces at Dien Bien Phu just recent history, he challenges the half million-strong French colonial military machine in Algeria:

> Colonialism shuts its eyes to the *real facts* of the problem. It imagines that our power is measured by the number of our heavy machine guns. This was true in the first months of 1955. It is no longer true today . . . The power of the Algerian Revolution *henceforth resides* [not in the military but] in the radical mutation that the Algerian has undergone. (*DC*, 31–2, emphasis added)

He concluded the work with the words, "The essence of the revolution, the true revolution which changes mankind and renews a society is . . . the oxygen which brings about and sustains a new kind of human being – that too is the Algerian revolution" (*DC*, 180–1). It is not guns, not leaders, but the very organism of the revolution – thinking, breathing, living Algeria (to mimic Marx speaking of the Paris Commune) – that sustains its self-creation.

The lived experience of revolution is so radical that being Algerian includes all who are willing to fight for new human relations in a multicultural Algeria. The revolution summoned the "new reality of the nation," sloughing off the old Manichean myth of French Algeria. Multiculturalism is grounded in revolutionary beginnings, which is to say the peoples of Algeria are judged by what they do and how they act, not by ontological abstractions. The reconfiguration of Algeria is based on the reconstruction of the self, what Fanon calls "an inner mutation" (*DC*, 179), stripped of the "mental sedimentation of the emotional and intellectual handicaps which resulted from 130 years of oppression." Here Fanon's writing is similar to his proclamations in *Black Skin*, where he speaks of a dialectic of consciousness that is "immanent in its own eyes" and does not "look to the universal" (*BS*, 135). But where that dialectic reached into negritude poetry for its substance, the new persona of *L'An V* is a product of the new narrative of Africa in motion, where "the rusty chains" are breaking their moorings. In a dialectic reminiscent of Hegel's *Phenomenology*, *L'An V* underlined the power of consciousness, specifically an African consciousness, to change world reality. *L'An V* powerfully expresses Fanon's commitment to the Algerian revolution and the new humanity prefigured in the struggle; in this sense, it is quite different from the racial contours of *Black Skin*. It is a practical rather than metaphysical consciousness (*WE*, 247). This does not mean Fanon is not painfully aware of the racism at the heart of the colonial project, but his goal shifts from the vision of *Black Skin* of the Black and the White hand in hand (*BS*, 222) to a new humanity emerging in the practice of the Algerian revolution. In the preface to *L'An V* he declares: "The form and the content of national existence *already exist* in Algeria . . . there can be no turning back . . . in Algeria *it is the national consciousness . . . that makes it inevitable that the people must take its destiny into its own hands*" (*DC*, 28, emphasis added).

"Concerning Violence," in *The Wretched*, has often been criticized for two reasons. First, because violence is described as liberating, it is argued that Fanon simply condones the shedding of blood. Second, it was observed that the native is always a man – the colonized, the native, the peasant, the unemployed, the starving man, the rebel, the militant, the guerrilla, the protagonist – and thus, woman is absent; or when she does appear it is only as helpmate, caretaker, and repository of memory.

The radical mutations that Fanon charts in *L'An V* go to the root of the "nation" by transgressing its borders in a continental offensive with a reach which is both external and internal. It challenges the foundational notion of nation in the gendered hierarchy of the family. If in *The Wretched* it is the peasant who is the fault line in national consciousness, then in *L'An V* it is woman. Together, woman and peasant, "outside the class system,"[9] have nothing to lose and everything to gain from a permanent revolution (*WE*, 61, 175). Though Fanon's Manichean descriptions of the colonial situation are indeed essential to an understanding of his project, so too is the necessity to get beyond Manicheanism. *L'An V*, especially its chapter 1, "Algeria Unveiled," is integral to understanding *The Wretched*, bearing in mind that *L'An V* is a work limited to the Algerian situation whereas *The Wretched* is a more generalized critical analysis of Africa's decolonization. As much as *The Wretched*'s

"Concerning Violence" and the painful case studies in "Colonial War and Mental Disorders" problematize a too simplistic understanding of violence, in "Algeria Unveiled" Fanon is clearly sensitive to the fact that terrorist acts, even in the context of an ongoing war of liberation, are not by nature disintoxicating. In fact the opposite might be true. Fanon's ethical humanism comes through in the question: "Was freedom worth the consequences of penetrating that enormous circuit of terrorism and counter-terrorism?" Additionally, it is when women engage in revolutionary action, and use the veil as a technique, that they not only invent new dimensions of their body (*DC*, 59), but also create new dimensions for Algerian society. Fanon's notion of women's liberation,[10] however unfinished and problematic it was (and it should be remembered that he wrote this in the late 1950s),[11] was a feature of his unfolding view of humanism. That women's liberation is only temporary and partial makes many of Fanon's views problematic, but does not undermine them. On the contrary, the fact that the idea of woman's liberation remained a crucial issue for postcolonial Algeria[12] underlines the unfinished nature of decolonization, which is of paramount concern in "The Pitfalls of National Consciousness."

Nevertheless, there is a tension in Fanon's writing between his concern for individual freedom and his critique of the liberal individualism promoted by the colonizing regime. Individual freedom is found in national liberation, but is it guaranteed by it? This question is particularly important when considering women's freedom. In the Manichean period of colonial resistance (before 1954) the individual is subsumed by the collective which becomes caricatured by colonial sociology and its idea of the Arab hordes and veiled women as formless masses without individuality. It is only in the active period (after 1954), Fanon argues, that a new individual, very different from the colonial mimic, or the masked colonial, arises. It is this period that is scrutinized in *L'An V*.

We turn first to a discussion of these themes in arguably the most controversial and problematic of Fanon's articulations in *L'An V*, that of the creation of a new woman and altered gender relations. It is in these writings that we get the clearest idea of a subaltern speaking and acting without precedent, through no institution and with no help from outside. In Fanon's eyes what was a central feature of the uprising was the unique and unmistakable role played by women in it, both in terms of their physical presence and also through their grasp of its meaning:

The woman does not merely knit for or mourn the soldier. The Algerian woman is at the heart of the combat. Arrested, tortured, raped, shot down, she testifies to the violence of the occupier and his inhumanity. As a nurse, a liaison agent, fighter, she bears witness to the depth and the density of the struggle. (*DC*, 66)

The "Absolute Originality" of Women's Actions

Fanon's imagination of the future society is nowhere more apparent than in his writing on women's liberation in *L'An V*. He maintains that the Algerian revolution has liberated women from a double dependency which results from "feudal traditions" on one hand and colonialism on the other. The colonialists force women to be free of the veil, but it is anticolonial action against the colonialists that allows women to break out of the vicious circle and demand equality with the male militant. The action of the revolutionary woman has an effect on the whole of Algerian society and, Fanon claims, "even the Algerian father, the founder of every value" underwent a radical change. Thus, just as hearing the news of battle on the radio brings the listener into a lived experience with the revolution, the militant woman becomes a point of reference "around which the imagination of Algerian feminine society is stirred to a boiling point" (*DC*, 108). The war of independence became a total war. For the French, everybody became a potential enemy and their policy was indiscriminately violent and bloody. For the Algerians the war touched everybody and resulted in a vast opening up of society. For Fanon, this loosening of social hierarchies and the tapping of new creative energies prefigured the socialist humanist Algeria, which he "identified with women's liberation" (*DC*, 107).

Perhaps the most sustained and profound critique of Fanon over the past decade has been launched by feminist and postcolonialist theorists focusing on "Algeria Unveiled".[13] The essay has been criticized for equating women with the family and with "nation," consequently normalizing gender inequality.[14] Most agree with Fanon's claim that the release of the imagination makes it impossible for revolutionary woman to turn back. Yet the transformation of imagination in the face of future repression needs to be understood in terms of what was happening and what ought to happen. If radical shifts took place, why was there not the kind of permanent revolution in these women's situations that he envisioned? In one sense, Fanon is talking about what *should* happen and thus is giving a normative meaning to national liberation. In another sense, his understanding of the fluidity of national liberation and culture indicates what was happening.

Contradicting the "Islamicists" who described Algeria as a "womanless society," Fanon declares that the revolutionary war is not a war of men but of women. In this "woman's war" Fanon finds "a new dialectic." Yet in emphasizing women's involvement he also describes how they had become depersonalized by the anticolonial politics of the veil. The woman is not only hidden behind the veil but intentionally made permanently invisible (*DC*, 44). This intention was reproduced, not challenged, by the nationalist leadership. The dialectic of "Algeria Unveiled" at first sounds akin to the assertion that the revolt is determined by the form of rule.[15] It is the colonialists who create a cult and fetish of the veil and the will to unveil, and thus "determine the centers of resistance" (*DC*, 47). Yet Fanon goes one step further, arguing that the colonized attitude to the veil undergoes a radical change during the struggle for liberation. It is this shift in identity and construction of personality that is truly remarkable. The alienating gaze of the White of *Black Skin* is not only reproduced but it is also undermined. It no longer carries ontological resistance.

In this new situation, the veil hides danger. It hides a bomb and a protagonist who, looking out at the heart of the European sector of the city, threatens it, and transgresses its boundaries. Veiled or Europeanized, revolutionary woman is given, in the context of Algiers, the ability to disappear into the European sector. This new context for the veil transcends the absolute division of the previous period and introduces us to the birth of the revolutionary woman. To understand this historic rupture we need to return to Fanon's understanding of the dynamics of the colonial period.

Before 1954, the colonial strategists viewed the woman as a battleground for the body and soul of Algeria. Judging Algeria as essentially matrilineal (beneath the patrilineal pattern (*DC*, 37)), they concluded, ventriloquizes Fanon, that "if we want to destroy the structure of Algerian society, its capacity to resist, we must first of all conquer the women" (*DC*, 37–8). It was in the urban areas, where colonialism had been investing in its civilizing mission, that the battleground for "saving" the woman from "tradition" was most extreme.

French colonialism in Algeria reinforced what it considered to be the "traditional system" both in its policy and in the reaction to it. The native was deemed male and the co-option of local rulers in the rural areas reinforced hierarchical and patriarchal relations. On the other hand, the impoverishment of the rural population, as a result of the expropriation of the best lands and the introduction of the money economy, eroded the socioeconomic base of the extended family, which had been the site of women's influence.[16] As Assia Djebar has argued, alongside the "progressive enclosing of outside space," which began with the colonial intrusion, came "a progressively silent freezing of internal communication . . . between the sexes."[17] In the twentieth century, as indigenous peoples were dispossessed of land, its tribal structure began to turn inward, closing in on itself. Women were "doubly imprisoned." The constriction of space was manifested in the tightening of relations within the family. Often it meant disinheriting women in favor of men.

Hemmed in, the Algerian woman became the victim of colonialism and the family, which was "the only real arena in which men, deprived of most external sources of self-esteem, power, and achievement, could act as sovereigns and masters."[18] Yet the colonial intrusion was uneven in many parts of the countryside where the "natives" were less directly subjected to the "modernizing" civilizing mission; many women often went about their business unveiled in the rural and especially Berber-speaking areas. In the urban areas the tenacity of the colonialists to unveil deepened the loss of the woman's autonomy, and in the zero-sum atmosphere meant that colonialist modernizing plans were countered by strengthening the "traditional patterns."

The colonialist's passion to unveil the Algerian woman – to strip her – had the intention not of finding the person behind the mask, but of making her available for "adventure." Psychologically, the history of the French conquest is "an evocation of freedom given to the sadism of the conqueror, to his eroticism" (*DC*, 45): behind the violence and the aura of rape, there was a will to dominate that mirrors both the pillage of the country and its civilizing mission. As a product of this history, the nationalist movement first responds in a crude way, with the leaders of the resistance discovering unexpected power in the revalorization of "tradition." By eliding women's specific areas of control and power in the precolonial period, their views were remarkably similar to those of the colonizers. The rationale that "tradition" demanded veiling provided an answer to the occupier's will to unveil. The dream world of the European to brutally dominate Algerian women is countered by the Algerian man's attempts to seclude the women. Couched in the rhetoric of Islamic "orthodoxy," the Algerian women, the metaphor for the nation, became the "revered objects of the collective act of national redemption and the role models for the new national patriarchal family."[19]

Refusing to unveil became a symbol of general dissent;[20] the woman took no conspicuously active role, nor did she find a meaningful voice through a gesture that could be construed as insidiously self-negating. This negation of the individual is characteristic of the Manichean period of anticolonial resistance in general, but it is especially apparent when gendered. Protected from the gaze, the veiled woman, in fact, doesn't exist. It was the Algerian male who responded to the pressure of colonial society to unveil "their women" by insisting that women remain veiled. This resistance to unveiling, with its connotations of sexual power and control over women's bodies and minds, forcefully expressed the refusal of Algerian society to accept colonialism and neatly delineated the gendered characteristic of nationalist politics. In reality, the conflict over the propriety of exposing the woman's body was a particular expression of the more general Manichean struggle between the colonizer and colonized male over the elementally gendered nation: "Every new Algerian woman unveiled announced to the occupier an Algerian society whose systems of defense were in the process of dislocation, open and breached . . . that Algeria was beginning to *deny herself and was accepting the rape of the colonizer*" (*DC*, 42, emphasis added). The husband's fear of his wife's violation is repeated at the national level. The woman is merely the vessel – the representation of the nation – but there is another twist. The male also feared his wife or daughter would either succumb and consent to the colonial rapist or, even worse, encourage it. In this situation the woman was vulnerable and had to be monitored, controlled, and covered up.

In Fanon's view, the radical shift that takes place in attitudes toward the veil corresponds to the development of the liberation struggle. It is when the reactive resistance to and defiance of the colonial system passes into an active and explicit resistance, becoming a fighting culture, that the veil loses its sacred power. However, these changes in attitude toward the veil were not included in the FLN's program but brought about by women's action. Women joined the movement often against the will of nationalist leaders, and by doing so also challenged the idea of what was being fought for. By joining the movement, women contested the nationalists' perception of women as "passive," and men's monopoly over what constituted nationalist militancy.[21]

For Fanon, the women's actions outside the revolutionary organization represented a new type of creativity and consciousness, which forced the FLN to recognize them. Viewed as unstable and as a security risk before 1955, women were kept in "absolute ignorance" by the FLN. But as the war spread into every area of life, women were first given domestic roles in the movement and then, by their own activity and despite the leaders' reluctance, a more direct involvement in the liberation movement that was never anticipated in the doctrine of the revolution or the strategy of combat (*DC*, 47). Women became historical protagonists.

Whether carrying bombs or messages, traveling unaccompanied, staying with unknown comrades, giving refuge in their homes to militants while their husbands were away, or particularly by partaking in discussions and activities on their own initiative, "the tight, hermetic, and hierarchical structure of the family was now exploded."[22] This created a totally new experience without any precedent: "What we have here is not the bringing to light of a character known and frequented a thousand times in imagination or in stories. It is an *authentic birth in a pure state, without preliminary instruction* (*DC*, 50 emphasis added). This birth is not bereft of historical motivation, but is a disruptive making of history. Women's entry into the public sphere – "an intense dramatization, a continuity between woman and revolutionary" (*DC*, 50) – upsets the tight supervision preferred by the FLN.

The idea of an authentic birth without any previous instruction has resonance throughout Fanon's work. In "This is the Voice of Algeria" he claims that radio broadcasts bring the "nation to life . . . out of nothing" (*DC*, 96); in the opening pages of *The Wretched* he declares that decolonization is achieved without transition; and finally, in the philosophic language of *Black Skin*, he formulates Black self-consciousness as an "absolute intensity of beginning" from itself (*BS*, 135, 138). It is Fanon's notion of the self-construction of the self. But rather than simply an individual's will to liberty, Fanon's conception of self-construction, in the Algerian context, is the coming to be of a new *social* individual.

Tactically, the removal of the veil meant that women could move about freely in the colonizer's zone: "Removed and reassumed again and again, the veil has been manipulated, transformed into a technique of camouflage, into a means of struggle" (*DC*, 61). The process of taking off and putting on the veil, stripped it *"once and for all* . . . of its exclusively traditional dimension" and enabled it to become an "instrument" of liberation (*DC*, 63 emphasis added). It is this repetition that distinguishes Fanon's position from those who concentrate on the opposition to the French unveiling as *the* "mark of resistance," rather than what Fanon calls the "absolutely original aspect" of the women's action (*DC*, 36). In this "woman's war" Fanon finds "a new dialectic." He explains that the young Algerian woman who takes off the veil experiences a phenomenological dissolution. The breakdown of her body's integrity is expressed spatially. Crossing the street she "commits errors of judgement." The young woman has to invent new dimensions for her body in the world, overcome awkwardness and "relearn her body . . . in a totally revolutionary fashion" (*DC*, 59). This new dialectic of body in the world thus not only challenges the woman but also "traditional society."

During the Battle of Algiers in 1956, the European sector, unknown to all except the cleaning women, became the space for a new persona to emerge from behind the veil. We witness a double process. To move undetected through the European sector, to be veiled in the invisibility it conferred, at once present and absent, to become Europeanized and thus depersonalized from a nationalist standpoint, the Algerian woman had to overcome a number of taboos. She experienced a "double deflowering," as Fanon puts it. On one hand, nationalist patriarchs caught in a politics of Manicheanism viewed her as dangerous and loose, transgressing the borders of order and morality and thus also the gendered space of the nation. On the other hand, being discovered, in other words, unmasked as a gunrunner by the paratroopers or police, the woman ran the risk of certain torture and rape, and possible death, at the hands of the colonial forces. This is the tragedy of her new self-constructed identity, an identity for which there was no model to fall back on. Unveiled in the context of the revolutionary movement she has pledged herself to be part of, she forces herself to (re)learn her own body, asserts Fanon, to appear at ease unveiled on the European streets and to invent new dimensions of sublimation and of muscular control (*DC*, 59). Where the veil had given a feeling of protection, without it there was a sense of incompleteness. This mind/body distortion could only be addressed by the birth of revolutionary woman "out of nothing," solely from her lived experience.

No longer an inert object but a link in the revolutionary machine, the veil is removed and reassumed again and again, becoming manipulated and thus losing its sacred character. But what is really at stake is not the veil but the woman as a protagonist who, qua subject of revolution, has come "out of nothing."[23] That is to say, she has arrived not as a result of material conditions but out of her own will to liberty firmly embedded in the social and historical context.

It is not accidental, then, that *L'An V* begins with a discussion of the Algerian woman as revolutionary, considering the fact that she was fighting a double oppression (colonial and indigenous). It is in the battle over cultural domination that the question of violence emerges, first through attempts to unveil Algerian women and the anticolonial reaction to it, and second, through women's direct involvement in the Battle of Algiers. For Fanon, women's activity creates fundamental changes in the social relations of the Algerian family, which are not exempt from the far-reaching disruptions of revolutionary change. In every sphere, Fanon enthusiastically maintains, all settled expectations concerning such matters as marriage, death, and sexuality (for instance, a father's uncomfortable position vis-à-vis the sexuality of a daughter) were "knocked over and challenged by the national liberation struggle" (*DC*, 107). The division of labor in the household was upset, and new and "unanticipated types of behavior were introduced." For women the "organic solidarity" with the liberation struggle created a totally new attitude toward self and an "inner renewal."

Change was also a result of the "unheard-of violence" with which "the adversary cuts into the Algerian flesh" (*DC*, 116). One grim instance of this violence was the forced removal of more than 1 million Algerians to "regroupment centers" (disease-ridden detention camps). Tens of thousands of families, many headed by women, were forcibly removed from their villages into these camps, completely undermining and disrupting their way of life. "Under these conditions," Fanon writes, *"no gesture is kept intact.* No previous rhythm is to be found unaltered. Caught in the meshes of barbed wires, the members of regrouped Algerian families neither eat nor sleep as they did before" (*DC*, 117, emphasis added). It is not only counterviolence but the social experience of colonial violence that creates revolutionaries. Set up to subvert the revolutionary movement, these camps became schools of revolution.

The ambiguous birth of woman as revolutionary is expressed in two events aimed at "destructuring" Algerian society. Because a prominent place was given to women by colonial strategists, De Gaulle's referendum on the new Algerian constitution in 1958 included women in the franchise for the first time. The FLN organized a boycott. Like donning the veil in solidarity with the revolution, this might well be dismissed as a tactic; yet when coupled with the FLN response to the introduction of French family law as a "Koranic" rather than political issue, it emphasized the fragile birth of women's autonomy. In this context, putting the veil back on as an expression of solidarity against the French was also oppressive. How could the veil suddenly be viewed as a technique when it was powerfully described earlier by Fanon as a uniform that allowed no modification, and was presented by the FLN in terms of women's modesty? In *L'An V* Fanon avoids this problem, concentrating on the originality of the women's actions, and pinpointing May 13, 1958 as the date that colonialism "obliged Algerian society to go back to methods of struggle already outmoded." But by donning the veil women took a step back and Fanon speaks of it as "a turning back, a regression" (*DC*, 63). Yet he does not regard this regression as problematic to his idea of radical mutation. Instead, he claims that "after the 13th of May, the veil was resumed, but stripped once and for all of its exclusively traditional dimension" (*DC*, 63). After noting the regression, the optimistic liberation seems hollow. Whereas the idea of regression in the revolution would be developed in *The Wretched*, here we see the limits of *L'An V* in its erasure of untidiness – the revolution's *internal* contradictions – arguing that the veil had been "stripped once and for all of its exclusively traditional dimension." Thus the critical insight into the problematic of reveiling as a regression is undeveloped alongside his main thesis that the old ideas have been destroyed in the utopic vision: "militant man discovers the militant women, and jointly they create new dimensions for Algerian society" (*DC*, 60 n14). Just as he had identified freedom for the Algerian people with women's liberation, he might have gone on to identify the "regression" of reveiling with a deep contradiction in the Algerian revolution.

Fanon's optimism about changes brought by the revolution were not as misplaced as the accusations of his critics make out. The post-independence constitution guaranteed equality between the sexes and women's right to vote. Women were elected deputies and, veiled and unveiled, they voted in the National Assembly. But women's political power was fleeting.[24] The memory, the actions, the language of women's actions were soon muted and silenced. Alongside the new euphoria of women's equality there was a reaction against "cosmopolitanism," manifested by attacks on women. Men and women walking down the street hand in hand were ordered to be married immediately; a woman walking alone was perceived to be "loose" and vulnerable to vigilantism. And between the euphoria of women's liberation and the puritanism of the vigilantes was the formation of the Union Nationale des Femmes Algériennes. Its original constitution spoke of equality and rights, but it did so while emphasizing woman's role as mother, wife, and guarantor of Arab-Islamic values.

Perhaps Fanon understood the defeat of what he had earlier considered irreversible when he spoke of revolutionary woman as so new and so unique a phenomenon that her birth was premature, reaching "the level of tragedy" (*DC*, 51). Ato Sekyi-Otu has argued that women's historical actions were indeed unheralded, unauthorized by the patriarchal tradition, and contrary to the normative expectations of woman's moral capacities: "The disclosure of woman's agency, her decloistering is, in this view, an event every bit as subversive of the order of things as, indeed arguably more cataclysmic than, the program of national liberation."[25] It is the conspicuous place Fanon gives to the "creation of new forms of being a woman" that keeps his work at the heart of an anti-imperialist feminism. It is that cultural creativity reported in *L'An V* and theorized in *The Wretched*'s "On National Culture" that offers a nonessentialist and nuanced framework for understanding the functioning of the veil during the Algerian war of liberation that does not give in to European projections of the "Third World" woman as a passive victim or fetishistic object.

The tragedy of postcolonial Algeria, the inability to institutionalize radical change, did subvert the optimistic thesis of *L'An V*. What is left is the underlying polemic of the work, with the dominant factions in the FLN, who were a "surrogate patriarchal authority"[26] working to reverse the changes he records. Thrown into the whirlpool of revolution, young liberation army recruits made a radical break with previous values. Yet political education was quickly reduced to the mouthing of slogans, bolstered by an elective affinity of FLN leaders and Ulama clerics.[27] *L'An V* does not speak directly of the problem that Fanon alluded later to as the great threat to the revolution: "the lack of ideology" (*AR*, 186). Perhaps an equally great tragedy was lack of time: the rapid degeneration of the revolution and the acceleration of Fanon's own leukemia occurring simultaneously.

Nevertheless, *L'An V* does intimate areas of concern that were touched on at the Soummam conference of the FLN inside the country in 1956. That platform purposefully announced that the revolution was not a "religious war" and the goal was not an Islamic state. Instead that goal was a democratic, secular, socialist, and multicultural nation. Though Soummam was overturned and its principal leadership liquidated by 1958, its goals remained the perspective of *L'An V*, which was grounded in the Marxian idea that people change as they change the world (*DC*, 30). Yet the problem remained: how to institutionalize such change, how to realize the goal of a continual revolution, not as a permanent dislocation, but as a basis on which to allow a voice to those silenced by colonialism?

Wiring Participatory Democracy

The identification of *The Voice of the Revolution* with the fundamental truth of the nation has opened up limitless horizons. (Fanon, *L'An V*)

Though Fanon also charts the development of new subjectivities in *The Wretched*, its critical focus remains the analysis of the nationalist leaders, the intellectuals, and the middle class. In *L'An V* the examples of a fighting culture explicate how an organization "inside the people" is not synonymous with the FLN. Just as "Algeria Unveiled" illuminates the development of historical protagonists and gender disruptions outside the formal organization of nationalism, Fanon's essay "This is the Voice of Algeria" (in *DC*) intimates the form that might be taken by the dialectic of spontaneity and organization. Fanon's writing on the radio also provides an indicator of radical changes that have occurred and how far Manichean thinking has been transcended. The radio has a direct utility in forming the new reality of the nation and the development of a new social consciousness.

During the war of independence, the radio assumed a vital role, especially as a means of mediation between the liberation army and the people: the radio could reach everybody. Through listening to radio broadcasts, those not directly involved in the armed struggle could identify with the liberation movement, and feel they were part of the emerging nation. Radio, however, was an alien Western commodity and had been stubbornly resisted by the Algerian people. For it to become an important medium in the revolutionary struggle a dramatic change in attitudes was required; and it provides a fascinating example of a dialectic of revolution and the transition from Manicheanism.

A colonial import, the radio had previously functioned as a link to "civilization" and "culture" for the settlers and helped them achieve a sense of community; it was an invention, Fanon argues, that strengthened their certainty in the "historic continuity of the conquest." Until 1945, the radio represented the French in Algeria – the news of France, the music of Paris; radio was a reminder of the reality of colonial power. As a technical instrument of the dominant society, it protected the Europeans against "Arabization."

The radio as a "technique in the hands of the occupier . . . [was] a symbol of French presence . . ." (*DC*, 72–3), and as a "bearer of [the French] language," the radio existed in colonial society in "accordance with a well-defined statute":

> Before 1954 . . . the radiophonic technique of long-distance communication of thought was not a neutral object . . . switching on the radio meant giving asylum to the occupier's words; it meant allowing the colonizer's language to filter into the heart of the house . . . Having a radio meant accepting being besieged *from within* by the colonizer. (*DC*, 92, emphasis added)

Fanon notes that from the colonialist's point of view, the native's resistance to the radio was a reactionary reflex based on feudal traditions and religious and patriarchal hierarchies which perceived in such technology a threat to their stability, and the "traditional types of sociability." Discounting this interpretation, Fanon argues that the initial resistance can only be understood from the point of view of the anticolonial movement.

The rejection of the radio expressed the resistance among the colonized to the extension of the colonialists' "sensorial powers." Moreover, there was no reason for the colonized to listen to the French broadcasts because, under colonialism, Algerian society "never participate[d] in this world of signs" (*DC*, 73). The fact that Radio Alger was "Frenchmen speaking to Frenchmen" about things French should sufficiently explain the native's indifference or hostility. How Fanon accounts for the change that came about involves his theory of radical mutation taking place among those who were not directly involved in the fighting. Can the transformation be simply explained by its utility in the radio's reporting of day-to-day events of the liberation struggle?

Because the mass of people couldn't read the press, they had been "relatively uninvolved in the struggle" (*DC*, 82); consequently, there was a tendency during the early period of the anticolonial war to overestimate the movement's successes. The Voice provided a new objectivity and "in less than twenty days the entire stock of radio sets was bought up" (*DC*, 82–3). It brought into being the historical protagonist living with the revolution in a sensuous way, "Since 1956 the purchase of a radio in Algeria has meant, not the adoption of a modern technique for getting news, but the obtaining of access to the only means of *entering into communication with the Revolution, of living with it*" (*DC*, 83, emphasis added). A technology formerly accounted as totally alien was now arrested from the "occupier's arsenal" and served as the "primary means of resisting" the psychological and military pressures of the colonialists. As a means of communicating with the revolution, the radio acted as an organizer, unifying the nation. It brought together all the "fragments and splinters," fitting together the "scattered acts" of rebellion "into a vast epic." The radio helped organize the resistance into a national and political idea as "Algerian society made an autonomous decision to embrace the new technique and tune itself in on the new signalling systems brought into being by the Revolution" (*DC*, 84). The radio became a power for sedition: "Establishing contact with the official voice of the Revolution became *as important* for the people as acquiring weapons or munitions for the National Army" (*DC*, 85n). Listening to The Voice attained a status comparable to helping the armed militants, offering a way of partaking indirectly in armed fight, of "experiencing" liberation. When the French jammed The Voice, it responded by rebroadcasting from a second station. A new form of struggle, the battle of the airwaves, began: "The listener involved in the battle of the waves had to figure out the tactics of the enemy, and in an almost *physical way* circumvent the strategy of the enemy" (*DC*, 85). Rather than listeners being merely passive, the radio drew them into a collective battle: turning the dial, searching for The Voice, brought the listener closer to the real fight of the revolution and to the feeling of being part of it.

The radio, as an organizer, became an important medium for the expression of a new democratic society. Fanon describes a room full of people, with one person glued to the radio and shifting along the dial in the search for news; everyone is listening to the static and trying to comprehend what is being said. At the end of the broadcast, the audience asks about a specific battle that had been mentioned in the French press which the "interpreter" had not heard The Voice mention:

> But by common consent, after an exchange of views, it would be decided that the Voice had in fact spoken of these events . . . A real task of reconstruction would then begin. Everyone would participate,

and the real battles of yesterday and the day before would be re-fought in accordance with the deep aspirations and unshakable faith of the group. The listener would compensate for the fragmentary nature of the news by an *autonomous creation of information*. (DC, 86, emphasis added)

Here we have an example of the subaltern becoming a protagonist, not only entering history but becoming its author. Everyone could participate in the reconstruction and invention of the nation creating a social collective, where truth becomes subjective and subjectivity acquires a dimension of objectivity.

Those who had listened to static all day, through the jamming by the French, would insist, after some debate, that they had heard The Voice speak of certain engagements. The idea of truth now took on a different character as it was invented in a social and revolutionally democratic context: in this collectivity, truth becomes subjective and subjectivity acquires a dimension of truth. Fanon saw it as the "practice of freedom" taking place in "the structure of the people," not merely truth in reaction to colonialism. Thus it is not the actual sounds of The Voice, but the people's collective interpretation that represents the turning point and the creative moment. The listeners' invention involves a productive dialogue, imparting meaning both to the fragments of information and to the nascent national consciousness; this dialogue is an engagement that prefigures a possible democratic form for the new society.

The meanings attached to the static are interpretations, perhaps akin to an interpretation of dream fragments. Just as for Freud the dream is a window into the unconscious, calling forth the creative activity of dream interpretation, for Fanon the collective interpretation of static is an illumination of another world, the form of an Algeria "no longer in future heaven." These interpretations are products of a social dialogue, which imparts meaning both to the fragments of information and to the nascent social and national consciousness, challenging "antique social arrangements." As Fanon puts it, "Traditional resistances broke down and one could see in a *douar* groups of families in which fathers, mothers, daughters, elbow to elbow, would scrutinize the radio dial waiting for the *Voice of Algeria*" (DC, 83).

Through the static, the very act of listening to the radio denoted new relationships not only within the family, but also between the FLN, epitomized by the "choppy, broken voice" of The Voice and the people. The militant's authority, just like the announcer's, shifted: instead of telling the listener what was going on and what it meant, the militant now had to listen to the people (the subaltern who had become audible) and accept "by common consent [and] ... after an exchange of views" the "reconstruction" of events (*DC*, 86). This local and decentralized discussion group represented a new, direct and democratic organizational context, which did not stifle creative energies but encouraged them. The "imagining" of concrete battles, together with an *"inner perception"* of the nation which now "materialized in an irrefutable way," fostered the development of historical protagonists and social individuals who took the creation of the nation into their own hands, realizing that the future lay with them, not with some "authority" telling them what to think. This was the "true lie" of the nation. That is, not "the nation" as an a priori nor as an echo of Plato's elite "noble lie" nor Nietzsche's perspectivism, but the truth of the nation built on the creative imagination of the people. In this case the "lie" was the creation by the social group of something out of the nothing, that is the static. The truth of the static became the construction of national consciousness.

The shift from the hysteric's *hearing voices* to the revolutionary subject's hearing The Voice represented part of the real, not hallucinated, disintegration of colonialism. Fanon declares almost too triumphantly that, under these conditions, "claiming to have heard the Voice of Fighting Algeria was, in a certain sense, distorting the truth." But it meant making a choice between two lies, the "enemy's congenital lie and the people's own lie, which suddenly acquired a *dimension of truth*" (*DC*, 87, emphasis added). Such a choice expresses a transcendence of Manicheanism insofar as it proves to itself that it can grasp and manipulate its own ends against colonialism; but it is still an expression of alienated consciousness. Moreover, the process of interpreting static and reconstructing fragments emphasized the importance of the group's "own working existence." The people take the creation of the nation into their own hands, realizing that the future lies with them, not with some "authority" telling them what to think. Further, the French radio jamming inadvertently mobilized the people's energies by demanding a more active imagination; it abetted a dialectical progression which helped liberate the people from The Voice as a "directive" and transformed its role into one of mediation in the democratic process.

Additionally, the search for The Voice across the wavelengths introduced the colonized to other voices and "other prospects." In place of the Manichean monologue of the colonial radio, having a radio gave access to a whole range of views (not only those of The Voice) communicated in different languages and expressing the multicultural richness of the anticolonial absolute. The colonial world was "destructured" (to use Fanon's term) and in its place The Voice helped create a "fundamental change in the people," a change that "out of nothing brought the nation to life and endowed every citizen with a new status" (*DC*, 96). Thus it is not the radio nor the static but self-organization detected in the social dialogue involved in interpreting the static that creates national consciousness.

The "radical mutation" of consciousness was "not a back and forth" nor "an ambivalence" but rather, Fanon argues, "a dialectical progression" that brought about a "radical change in valence," and a "transformation into opposite" (*DC*, 89n). Furthermore, the attitude to the French language underwent such a significant change that it also became "an instrument of liberation."

While one might challenge the "mutation" vis-à-vis the radio as little more than a pragmatic adaptation to a rather "neutral" technology, the changed experience of language is harder to dismiss as it involves a structure fundamental to consciousness and experience. As we have seen in *Black Skin*, Fanon viewed language as integral to a dialectic of recognition. Language and recognition presuppose each other. But in the colonial situation language is intimately connected with nonrecognition. "Civilization" is expressed as the language of orders and as the means of advancement within the *White* world.

Paradoxically, The Voice represented a liberation from the French through the French language in that broadcasts in French "liberate[d] the enemy language from its historic meanings" (*DC*, 89). The language of order, threat, and insult was transformed into its "antithesis" and thus "lost its accursed character, revealing itself to be capable also of transmitting, for the benefit of the nation, the messages of truth that the latter awaited." Before 1954, French was a sign of the influence of the occupier, with "ontological implications within Algerian society" (*DC*, 91). French was the language of oppression, Arabic the language of choice in the nationalist movement. But the revolution "stripped the Arabic language of its sacred character," while it removed the negative connotations associated with everyday French language.

Just as Fanon rejects the sociologist's interpretation of the native's initial resistance to the radio, so too he rejects a cultural politics narrowly based on language. In contrast to the native's silent resistance to the "master's orders" conveyed in French (*BS*, 19), French, now a language of The Voice, becomes the language of discussion. The Voice's new universalism and ability to unite the nation's "fragments" were further manifested in its multilingual transmission (broadcast in Arabic, Kabyle, and French) and attested to the "multiracial reality of the Algerian nation" (*DC*, 157). French became one among many languages liberated from their historic meanings, argues Fanon: "The same message transmitted in three languages unified the experience and gave it a universal dimension" (*DC*, 89). More than the veil, the radio becomes an empty medium. It is not the radio, nor even the broadcast, but the creative subjective response to the French jamming of the broadcast – its organization seen in the dialogue involved in interpreting the static – that creates a "radical change in valence." Listening to the radio reflected and assisted the people's desire to be involved in a dialogue: "Every Algerian felt himself to be called upon and wanted to become a reverberating element of the vast network of meanings born of the liberating combat" (*DC*, 94). To include "everyone" meant transmitting in various languages, and the radio, reporting on the scattered struggles across the nation, fit them into a tapestry no longer in reaction to colonialism: the Kabyle were no longer the "backward" people from the mountains but heroes of resistance against enemy troops, French Algerians were not all to be condemned as colonialists, and not all Algerian Arabs were friends.[28] At a fundamental level, the radio broadcasting helped bring to an end the physical and cerebral "destructuration" that had characterized colonial rule. As Fanon put it, "the fragmentation and splinters of acts gleaned by the correspondent of a newspaper . . . lost their anarchic character and became organized."

No doubt the fragments and splinters, as a kind of uncertainty and ambivalence inherent in spontaneity, would appeal to a reading of Fanon which might see in this spontaneity a liberatory moment insofar as it is not articulated. But I think that in an implicit way Fanon's writing on the radio in the context of a mass anticolonial movement offers another type of organization which does not necessarily utilize the structures of the system.

The existence of The Voice helped liberate the masses from the Manichean viewpoint and challenged the "sclerosis" of the FLN leadership (see *DC*, 66). Resonating beyond the FLN program, it provided a much richer organizational context in which a new democratic society was prefigured. In this, the radio is not identical to attitudes toward medicine. Whereas medicine, or attitudes to

it, is a sociological *indicator* of the radical mutation of Algerian consciousness – the transformation of national into social consciousness
– the radio had a direct utility in forming the new reality of the
nation. With the radio, the division between "Western" and "traditional" is transcended and the broadcast provides the basis for a
reinvigoration of the type of democracy found in village assemblies
where decisions are arrived at by "common consent."

In structural terms, listening to the radio contributed to the
"mutation" in the people's consciousness. First, with its multilingual broadcasts it undermined the bifurcated colonial language
structure and thus the "tribalized" reality of colonial Algeria.
Second, it created a forum for the subaltern to speak and assisted
their desire to be involved in a dialogue. Third, it was the "useless"
static, not the radio's functionality, which helped create an institutional form, uncovering subjugated knowledges that challenged the
nationalist elite's claims to a monopoly on the truth. What becomes
important is not the radio's news report but the interpretation of
the static by the people. It was this floating signification, the space
between the reality of the event itself, the fragments and static heard
on the radio, and the manner of constructing an interpretation (as
a struggle and dialogue between the listeners and the party militant) that was a challenge to both colonial and prefigurative postcolonial rule. This process of agreeing on an interpretation, giving
voice to a concrete event, integrates it into an ideational framework.
Because we are dealing with the creative task of filling a void
created by static, and not simply a narrative of events, it becomes
clear that the process of construction apparently out of nothing (that
is, static) reflects Fanon's idea of radical mutation found in "Algeria
Unveiled." It intimates the idea of humanism that he once, quoting
Aimé Césaire, called "inventing souls," opening minds and giving
birth to a new intelligence. Radical mutation can thus be prefaced
by his concern in *The Wretched* that the people realize that the construction of reality depends on them and not any demiurge (*WE*,
197). Thus the battle of the airwaves helped liberate the people from
the old viewpoints resonating beyond the program of the FLN,
providing a much richer organizational context in which a new
democratic society was prefigured.

Finally, what becomes important is not the radio itself but the
ways in which it aids the liberation of the people. One could take
this further along a postmodern route, attaching all meaning to the
static. But this loses the social context and in fact is close to Fanon's
conception of the "hysteric" who acts on hearing voices, blows up

the local police station and declares victory (*DC*, 79).[29] In contrast the people who claim that they have heard The Voice represent a revolutionary Reason. This conscious action is not reducible to statutory rule being erected by the dominant faction in the FLN but represents something different, a process of rule established by common consent from below. The problem remained, how to institutionalize these changes.

7

Crossing the Dividing Line: Spontaneity and Organization

Because Fanon grounds the social vision in the movement's experience of radical change a vanguard party is not needed to develop the image of the future society. Instead the Fanonian organization should enlighten social experiences by bringing out their implicit meaning in a dialogue. The vision of the future society is constructed in the social relationship between the militant intellectual and the mass movement and is crucial to Fanon's conception of "radical mutation", representing for him a history in the making (*WE*, 147).

Nevertheless, the relationship between the militant and the people is a contradictory and continuing process. The dialectic of liberation is not forged in one fell swoop and the militant is posited as "an element of the contradiction," continually raising contradiction to knowledge and action.[1] It turns out, however, that the nationalist intellectual often remains far removed from the "real" struggles of the people and is still mired in the Manichean objectification of colonialism (indeed, the intellectual is very much a colonial product).

The Subject/Object Dialectic

It is rigorously false to pretend and to believe that this decolonization is the fruit of an *objective dialectic* which more or less rapidly assumed the appearance of an absolutely inevitable mechanism. (Fanon, "Unity and Effective Solidarity are Conditions for African Liberation," in *AR*)

Decolonization is a historical *process*, not a historical inevitability. Out of the timeless spatial vortex of colonial Manicheanism, with its lines of force keeping everything in place, "the thing becomes man during the same process by which it frees itself" (*WE*, 36–7); far from a simple substitution of one species for another, the very *process* of substitution indicates the transition from Manichean to dialectical logic. Such a process includes a purposeful direction toward a fully realized liberation.

Just as it is a historical process, the movement from colonial to postcolonial society is also a move away from the dominance of the spatial. Whereas Fanon's survey of colonial spacing in "Concerning Violence" powerfully portrayed the confining and repressive character of the native's quarters, Fanon's originality also lies in plotting a society liberated from colonialism where time becomes the space for human development. Embedded in Fanon's examination of colonial compartmentalization is the dialectical reordering marking out a new society:

> If we examine closely this system of compartments, we will at least be able to reveal the lines of force it implies. This approach to the colonial world, its ordering and its geographical layout, will allow us to mark out the lines on which a decolonized society will be reorganized. (*WE*, 38)

Decolonization involves more than eradicating the lines of force – the police station, barracks, and border checkpoints – that keep the zones apart. Rather there needs to be a constant reevaluation of the geographical layout, including the urban/rural divide, and a continuously unfolding dialectic and, as Marx put it, constant criticism to "transform the national revolution into a social revolution" (*DC* 169). Fanon's reference to the revolution's "form and content" and his insistence that the creation of new subjectivities are not the result of "supernatural powers" but born in the revolutionary process are reminiscent of Marx's *Eighteenth Brumaire* quoted in *Black Skin*: The revolution, Marx wrote, "cannot begin with itself before it has stripped itself of all superstitions concerning the past"; it must find its "own content" rather than "drug [itself] against [its] own content." It was the content "exceeding the form," as Marx put it, that Fanon rediscovered in radical mutations engendered by the Algerian revolution.

To find an appropriate content to transcend the colonial vortex requires emphasizing "a subjective attitude in *organized* contradiction with reality." Such a dialectic appears in Fanon's profound re-telling of the *lived experience* of anticolonial political activity. Under the pressure of his analysis, the activities described disclose an experience that "explodes the old colonial truths and reveals un-expected facets which bring out new meanings and pinpoints the contradictions camouflaged by these facts" (*WE*, 147). Spontane-ous activity, he maintains, reaches for a self-understanding not restricted by Manicheanism. In its unfolding as a self-referential absolute and in the construction of new selves without precedent, "the rebellion gives proof of its rational basis" (*WE*, 146).

Fanon's invocation "to change the world" is more than a rhetor-ical fillip to conclude his analysis of the racial Manicheanism of the colonial condition. It is often lamented that his claims about "The Revolution" creating the "new person" are naive, and even a dan-gerously utopian addendum to his explication of colonial relations. These caveats, however, betray a banal understanding. Fanon's painstaking working out of the revolution conceives the "new person," not as a miraculous creation immediately begot by violent activity, but as a product of a constant action and principled criti-cism. Such criticism is not a priori. Neither are objectives simple reflections of spontaneous activity nor pre-existing aims. Neither content with praising its strengths nor criticizing its weaknesses, this prefiguration is a fruit of the hard labor of tarrying with the problematic of violence and spontaneity in an anticolonial frame. Given the dismal, frequently horrific, consequences of revolution seen in the twentieth century, such claims for the redemptive power of revolution to transform life for the better may seem little more than dreams of another era. Nevertheless, to misrepresent Fanon as a cultural conservative upholding tradition – the common conclu-sion when Fanon is viewed as an advocate of Manicheanism – is a willful distortion since Fanon sees culture intimately connected to relations of power. "The Revolution" challenges the material/ideo-logical basis of traditional culture. Just as he proclaims in *L'An V* that the Algerian revolution has proved the truth of "the thesis that men change at the same time that they change the world" (*DC*, 30), he insists in *The Wretched* that national liberation will create radical changes in culture. What Fanon calls the radical mutations, that result in and from the process of revolution, occur, as we saw earlier, at the intersection of spontaneity and organization: organization understood both as the framework and epistemic structures of intellectual communication and exchange, as well as the resources people draw on as they reflect on their revolutionary experiences.

In other words, organization includes the organization of thought – its rational basis. The "strength of spontaneity" not only refers to mass activity, but also the meaning brought by the committed intellectual, namely Fanon, who helps those in rebellion reach beyond themselves to the type of self-understanding he describes in *The Wretched*: it is "the *essence* of the fight which explodes old colonial truths and reveals unexpected facets, which bring about new meanings" (*WE*, 147).

Some political implications of this dialectic of knowledge, action, organization and experience emerge when Fanon, neither an advocate of the introduction of modern techniques nor a traditionalist, gives us another view of "the essence of the fight" and the production of "new meanings." We saw this in the changing attitude to medicine and the radio. During the struggle these techniques are "taken over" and used in a totally different way, being stripped of their old meaning. Implicit is what he calls the "totalizing" work of "revolutionary theory" (*WE*, 304), which becomes more crucial as decolonization in Africa faces new internal contradictions and turning points. This becomes the project of *The Wretched*. Freedom *is* possible, if not inevitable. It is in fact very difficult to achieve, and the new African nation is in short "fragile and in permanent danger" (*WE*, 247).

Nodal Points

> The force of intellect increases and becomes more elaborate as the struggle goes on. (Fanon, *The Wretched of the Earth*)

The year 1960 represented a turning point for postcolonial Africa and in Fanon's thinking. It was the year 16 states became independent. But the duality of such a moment was plain when, backed by the West, the Katanga province broke away from the Congo just three days after the Congo gained its "independence" from Belgium. The Congo's Premier, Lumumba, who attempted to build a national movement across ethnic lines, was soon liquidated; and with that the second landing beach of revolutionary ideas was compromised.[2] The face of Africa's "future heaven" was already scarred. Confronted by the counterrevolution in the Congo, the assassination of Lumumba and the suppression of the Lumumbaists, Fanon deepened his conception of revolution and humanism. *The Wretched* was the product. *The Wretched* is a very different book than *L'An V*, though hardly any time separated their writing. In *L'An V* Fanon declares that France is incapable – militarily, humanly, economically and politically – of winning the war (*AR*, 130–1). He predicts an inevitable victory and encourages other African people to strike for independence. The success of the revolution seems virtually assured and the destruction of colonialism and the success of a new Algeria are proposed as a continuous movement: "colonialism has definitely lost out in Algeria, while the Algerians, come what may, have definitely won" (*DC*, 31). The new society has arrived. The difference between *L'An V*'s celebration of the festival of the oppressed and *The Wretched*'s solemnity in the face of counterrevolution is found in the muting of the claims about the instantaneous transformation of consciousness. Fanon introduces a conceptual mediation. Because the concern of *The Wretched* is with the limitations of spontaneity, we get none of the rich descriptions of change that Fanon recorded in *L'An V*. This is not because he has changed his mind. Both the focus and the problematic have changed. Compared with the central chapter of *The Wretched*, "The Pitfalls [Mésaventures] of National Consciousness," which was first presented as a seminar at a major ALN military base the same year he finished *L'An V*, *L'An V* is a lot more uncritical of nationalist movements and about the automatic establishment of the new society. There are enemies of the revolution, but these are external to the revolution rather than internal to it. The new Algeria is unproblematically apparent, already embedded in the mass movement, whose very motion has created radically different human beings. It is this that gives *L'An V* its distinctiveness, trumpeting a new Algerian nation, a new Algerian human being and a new existence (*DC*, 30). There is nevertheless an implicit critique in *L'An V*. Though Soummam's radical program had been abandoned as policy by the FLN by 1959, Fanon still clung to its vision and referred to its psychological importance (*DC*, 91). By also referring to the Soummam platform in "Algeria's European Minority" he positions himself with a minority faction of the FLN. Certainly Fanon's political ideas about minorities reflect his own position in Algeria, but what was also at stake in the minorities question was Algeria's future.

Both *L'An V* and *The Wretched* reproduce the radical agenda of the Soummam platform. Yet *The Wretched* is a lot more measured; it does not undermine the thesis of radical mutation but approaches it more critically, highlighting inherent contradictions. The new subjectivities engendered by the revolution are but bare beginnings already under threat. The new society may take a lot more time, patience, and labor of the negative for the leap ahead to be realized (*WE*, 198). *The Wretched* is an analysis of the crisis already befalling this "new reality of the nation," as a result of the conflict embedded in the epistemological and ontological problematic of the revolution's own organization.

It was in the context of the Algerian national liberation struggle, on one hand, and the Congolese counterrevolution and the murder of Lumumba, on the other, that he saw the rise of ethnic politics, expressing power in a raw form. The failure of national consciousness to deepen into humanism, to transcend the urban/rural and class divides and release the creative potentials of the rural masses violently held back by colonial despotism, would result, he predicted, in its degeneration, causing the recasting of regional, racial, and ethnic politics (*WE*, 156, 204). Faced with the ugliness of the counterrevolution, Fanon did not retreat into a bifurcated world like that of Hegel's "Beautiful Soul."[3] His Algerian experiences pushed his concept of lived experience to a more concrete expression of dialectical negativity, namely toward a critique of the revolution he himself had embraced, and tried to understand.

The Beginning of the End of Manicheanism and the Limits of Spontaneity

> Not every Negro or Moslem is issued automatically a hallmark of genuineness; and the gun or knife is not inevitably reached for when a settler makes his appearance. (Fanon, *The Wretched of the Earth*)

In "Concerning Violence," Fanon spoke of Engels's "childish position" that the success of violence was determined by its technology, contrasting it to the guerrilla warfare of the Americans against the British and the Spanish against Napoleon (*WE*, 64). In the 1850s the French, fighting their first guerrilla war in Africa in Kabylia, were forced to rethink their tactics in the face of the Kabyle strategy of war of movement. In the mountain terrain, the "unpredictable" Kabyles preferred individual rather than group action, attacking the flanks rather than head on. Patricia Lorcin points out:

> The French were struck by the involvement of the Kabyle women
> ... [T]he bloodcurdling shrieks of the Kabyle men and the ululating
> of their women, who urged them on in the midst of the mêlée, made

the obligatory hand-to-hand combat a searing experience for the French soldier.[4]

This memory is rekindled during the war of liberation, and in the djemma, the militant intellectual discovers, Fanon claims, "the substance of village assemblies, the cohesion of people's committees, and the extraordinary fruitfulness of local meetings." Each village, Fanon writes, "finds that it is itself both an absolute agent of revolution and also a link in the chain of action" (*WE*, 133).

The limit to this movement is precisely its strength, a one-sided reliance on individual action and the belief that everything can be solved by more activity. It is a "utopian atmosphere," Fanon writes, where "spontaneous impetuosity . . . is determined to settle the fate of the colonial system immediately" (*WE*, 134). Fanon's criticism of an immediacy that posits freedom without boundaries recalls Hegel's argument in the *Phenomenology* that what emerges from the previously submerged consciousness is the demand for "absolute Freedom" from all previous restrictions and cultural restraints. But freedom without a context becomes "freedom in the void." Fanon compares this to a self-determination which can set its own limits, and by setting limits comes to express the real possibility and reality of freedom. During the early period of peasant uprisings, "spontaneity is king." It rules everything. The end of colonialism seems in sight and the "art of politics is transformed into the art of war":

> On every hill a government in miniature is formed and takes over power. . . . Each man or woman brings the nation to life by his or her action, and is pledged to ensure its triumph in their locality. We are dealing with a strategy of immediacy which is both radical and totalitarian. (*WE*, 132)

At first, the leaders of the uprising are bewildered by this new experience. The defeats and setbacks are the hard facts that necessitate not only a rethinking but also a reconsideration of the people's revolutionary consciousness. The inversion of colonial Manicheanism has led to amazing results. It has brought the revolution into existence. But now the movement is suffering setbacks and its unity is crumbling; it has to understand that liberation will not be immediate.

The immediateness that characterizes both the movement's certainty and idealism constitutes its defect. Whereas Fanon had previously presented the native as one who could pass from being a colonized "thing" to being a self-determining subject "without transition" (*WE*, 35), he now argues that "the struggle for national liberation does not consist in spanning the gap in one stride." Rather the process of liberation is not simply the release of pent-up anger, or what he calls the "mirage of his muscles' own immediacy." Self-knowledge becomes critical in the development of consciousness. Resentment, hatred, and desire for revenge, which create the initial willingness to join the fight for freedom, are not enough to "sustain a war of liberation" (*WE*, 139). In fact, a war sustained on that basis inevitably leads to another form of exploitation "wearing a Black face": "The militant who faces the colonialist with the bare minimum of arms realizes that while he is breaking down colonial oppression he is building up automatically yet another system of exploitation" (*WE*, 145). This insight is absolutely critical to Fanon's critique of Manicheanism. The inversion of colonial Manicheanism which had seemed so easy leads to confusion and ruin. Because the Manichean analysis is overdetermined by the Other, it depends on the brutality of the enemy. A change in the enemy's tactics necessitates a reevaluation, and one in fact long overdue.

Fanon's awakening to the vital role of "political education" brings about a fundamental shift in his thought. Political education at first means explaining the long-term objectives of the fight. It is not merely a question of strategy. The "enlightening of consciousness" is not imposed from the outside but comes into being as a new relationship between the intellectuals and the people: "All this taking stock of the situation, this enlightening of consciousness, and this advance in the knowledge of the histories of societies are only possible within the framework of an organization and inside the structure of the people" (*WE*, 143). This enlightenment, "inside the structure of the people," faces the consequences of "primitive manicheism." For one thing, the "truth" that the native inherently and intuitively expresses has a limit, not the least because perceptions have for so long been influenced and conditioned by the Manichean structure; one cannot appeal to absolutes of truth and falsehood that a straightforward inversion of racial Manicheanism would correct. This taking stock means showing the people the limitations of the "primitive manicheism." This is not to suggest that the native is simply mired in "false consciousness" and need only turn to the organization for enlightenment. Rather than "true" or "false," Fanon focuses on the development of consciousness in relation to current exigencies that exploitation can wear a Black face and, conversely, certain Whites are prepared to fight for the people's self-determination. "In their weary road toward rational knowledge," Fanon declares, "the people must also give up their too-simple conception of their overlord" (*WE*, 145). What is required is a new, more nuanced attitude to the settler, who, in a complete turn-around from the previous confrontation, "is not simply the man who must be killed" (*WE*, 146). Immediate uncontrolled violence, which had brought things to a head, must now be controlled:

> There exists a brutality of thought and a mistrust of subtlety which are typical of revolutions; but there exists another kind of brutality which is astonishingly like the first and which is typically anti-revolutionary, hazardous and anarchist. This unmixed and total brutality, if not immediately combatted, invariably leads to defeat of the movement. (*WE*, 147)

Violence on its own can lead to defeat because the greatest barrier to the development of revolutionary consciousness is the *quid pro quo* of simply answering colonial brutality with anticolonial brutality. The negation of this negation is expressed by articulating the "positive" of anticolonial violence. The "political educator," Fanon argues, introduces "shades of meaning" and in doing so battles the organization's tendency to underestimate the peasant's reasoning capabilities and to argue that such nuances will sow confusion among the people. The political educator must understand that the people's rudimentary consciousness does not mean that they are unable to think for themselves and that the situation cannot be explained to them. On the contrary, for Fanon political education means precisely encouraging the people to think for themselves.

Of central importance, even as Fanon introduces the need for organization, is building up the self-confidence of the masses. There is "absolutely no strategically privileged position" (*WE*, 135), he argues, except the need to convince the people that everything depends on them. There is no decisive battle. The meeting of two great armies, therefore, does not take place on the field but in the mind. This "enlightenment" takes on a dialectical significance vis-à-vis the struggle. It marks a fundamental change in consciousness and represents a new type of politics which expresses the positive in the negative and prefigures the structure of the new society that is being fought for: "Political activity . . . in no way resembles the old. These politics are the politics of leaders and organizers *living inside of history* who take the lead with their brains and their muscles in the fight for freedom. These politics are national, revolutionary and social" (*WE*, 147, emphasis added).

The Making of a Radical Intellectual

Whereas "Concerning Violence" is limited by the analysis of colonial society as bipartite, inhabited by "two species" – the colonized and the colonizer – in chapter 2 of *The Wretched*, "Spontaneity: Its Strengths and Weaknesses," it is the bipartite urban/rural division which becomes a central preoccupation, influencing his idea of what constitutes revolutionary agency. It is this urban/rural dichotomy, and how it can be overcome, that Fanon alludes to when he says that "the geographical layout will allow us to mark out the lines on which a decolonized society will be reorganized" (*WE*, 38).

The urban/rural division is first presented in organizational terms as "the frequent existence of a time lag or a difference of rhythm between the leaders of a nationalist party and the people" (*WE*, 107). This difference takes on yet another dimension in the colonies, where the nationalist political organization is copied from the "mother country" and seeks its constituents in the urban areas. Often making a fetish of the methods and the form of Western political parties, these parties mimic the colonial attitude which dismisses rural society as "bogged down in fruitless inertia" (*WE*, 109).

With the development of a new relationship between urban militants and the rural masses, as well as the development of a new type of revolutionary organization, Fanon's concept of the "time lag" finds a new expression. The immediacy of mass spontaneous action against colonialism opens up a whole range of possibilities and also requires the formation of a group of militant intellectuals who are able to productively criticize the local and immediate character of the struggle and help formulate a national strategy. With a history of very little contact between the urban nationalists and the rural masses, the eventual encounter between the militant from the town and the peasant revolutionary marks an important and electric moment charged with uncertainty and potentiality. To understand the politics of the urban/rural division, Fanon reviews the relation of nationalist organizations to rural life.

During the period of late colonial rule, the country people remain suspicious of the townspeople who dress and act like the Europeans. This attitude is only reinforced when young nationalist politicos are "parachuted in" to the rural areas, expecting to be instantly embraced as leaders. Rather than carefully building up relations, they too tend to view "traditional" ways of life as inimical and so they try to act as the new modernizers.

Nationalists, even those on the left, continue to define the rural masses in colonial terms. This is an unfortunate reflex because, Fanon argues, a "reasoned analysis" would have shown the nationalist intellectual what is progressive and what is reactionary in the rural areas. A critical approach entails a double analysis, considering the effects of the colonial divide-and-rule policies, the use of "customary rule" and the structures of collaboration, as well as indicating how the peasant's will to hang onto "tradition" actually represents a source of intransigence against colonialism. However, in the first phase of nationalist activity the organization remains urban and the division between the rural population and urban nationalist organization is virtually complete.

Because colonialism has only achieved a "pseudo-petrification" of traditions, the peasantry is not a *tabula rasa* but rather an archive, one moreover that has preserved a way of life that is in many ways anticolonial (*WE*, 138).[5] When the new urban anticolonial action filters into the countryside, it finds an "echo in the heart of the peasantry." The years immediately before World War Two saw more contact between urban and rural areas because of the ability to move around the country and the growing proletarianization of the peasantry. During the period of direct action, the tradition of resistance "springs to life" and there follows a valorization of the history of resistance which is the "proof" that the "static period begun by colonization" is over and the period of "making history" – of the native "embody[ing] history" – has begun. (*WE*, 69) The notion of beginning history is important here. Fanon is arguing that the idea of liberation is not brought to the countryside from the town, but it is embedded in how rural areas cross colonial boundaries, whether intranational or international, and is intuitive among the rural masses. In the early period of revolt it is the peasants who now "substitute" themselves for the urban nationalist party and their revolt gives an elemental expression to the idea of a nationalism. This atmosphere engenders a critique within the reformist nationalist party, arising from two sources: the radical intellectuals and the rank-and-file militants. The development of the radical intellectuals also has two, though not necessarily distinct, sources. First the intellectuals, who begin to question "their party's lack of ideology and poverty of tactics and strategy," are marginalized and labelled anarchists by the party. Second, radicals among the nationalist leadership find that their time in prison helps clarify ideas.

Fanon's schema[6] is marked by the following events. A rupture occurs between the legal and illegal tendencies in the party. Those inclined toward the latter are forced underground, make contact with the radical intellectuals, and begin to form a new underground organization. The underground organization, hounded by the police and constantly on the move, is forced out of the urban areas into the countryside. Unlike the first confrontations between the urban nationalists and rural people, this new encounter upsets the peasant's preconceived ideas. News from the city also filters into the countryside; as the peasants become more informed, they now welcome revolutionaries on the run and hide them from the police. The militants, who have nowhere else to turn, re-evaluate their earlier attitude toward the country people. While they formerly dismissed them as unchanging and under the complete control of static traditions," they now "discover that the mass of the country people have never ceased to think of the problem of their liberation" (*WE*, 127). This realization marks a fundamental turning point in the dialectic of liberation. The leadership of the struggle has passed to the peasantry, who represent a more universal concept of the "nation."

Nevertheless, this new universal (which includes a new relationship between the urban revolutionaries and the rural people) has not transcended the urban/rural dichotomy. The politicos know that at some time the uprising must include the urban areas, though the militant's overtures to his former friends on the left prove fruitless. Interestingly, Fanon considers that the lumpenproletariat, the most problematic class (or non-class) in the Marxian schema, is a key to mediation between town and country.[7]

Though Fanon appears confident of the lumpenproletariat's role, one can sense an unease; and Fanon, following Marx, does acknowledge that their radicalism can be used in counterrevolutionary ways. The lumpenproletariat is always prepared for battle but "obeys its own logic" (*WE*, 130) and sometimes ends up on the wrong side.[8] Maneuvered and encouraged by colonialism, determined by its immediate situation, it can become the fodder for the counter-demonstrations and mass movements stirred up by the imperial powers to disrupt national cohesion. Fanon is aware of how the lumpenproletariat had become part of the crisis, anarchy, and disorder that the West had encouraged against Patrice Lumumba and he tied it to the ideological weakness of the movement.

Accordingly, he argued that "any movement for freedom ought to give its fullest attention to this lumpenproletariat" (*WE*, 136). With the lumpenproletariat, therefore, we reach an extreme expression of the limit of spontaneity and the problematic of organization and ideology. On the other side of the equation is the intellectual. Just as with the urban/rural problematic, Fanon schematically maps the development of the native intellectual in three stages. The intellectual is the crucial ingredient for the success of decolonization to get beyond a Manichean mind set, yet they too are mired in it.

At the heart of Fanon's idea of a fighting culture is a critique of the politics of resentment that has sustained the native during the long night of colonial rule. In Fanon's analysis the native intellectual plays both a critical and a problematic role in the movement. The intellectual, unlike the peasant, has actually embraced the civilizing mission of colonialism and has been long estranged from "traditional" life. The intellectual's "return" to roots – "going native" – is first expressed as a reaction to the colonizer in the most bald Manichean and nativist terms. However, the harsh language and styles are not simply racial, but express a "hand to hand struggle" that "must substitute itself for concepts" (*WE*, 220), as well as the exceptional sensibility resulting from the inferiority complex. Just like the native, the intellectual's pent-up anger is canalized and released through a violent style. And just as with reactive action, the intellectual often walks up a blind alley (*WE*, 220).

In the context of Africa's decolonization Fanon schematically maps out the intellectual's development by considering three phases of transformation. The first is an "unqualified assimilation" and identification with colonialism, when they throw themselves greedily upon Western culture "like adopted children" (*WE*, 218). The next two phases express reactions to, or negations of, the first phase. In the first negation, which is a reaction to assimilation, the native intellectual preoccupation with rediscovering a past is expressed in mythical terms. In the second negation, or positive stage, the intellectual seeks to join the people in developing a new culture within the context of the revolutionary movement. This is what Fanon calls a "fighting phase." It is a stage where intellectuals, instead of merely losing themselves in an abstraction of the people, act as catalysts in the people's "awakening."

The first phase, which represents the period of colonial domination, is experienced quite differently by the intellectual and the masses. While the mass of the people maintain some traditions, the intellectual is thrown into a frenzied acquisition of the culture of the occupying power. A product of assimilation, the intellectual also reflects the Manichean world: whereas the masses experience the brute force of colonialism and cultural emaciation, the intellectuals experience the cultural violence of its "civilizing mission." The intellectuals, those potential Black skins in White masks, who are products of the colonial system, have become proper little Europeans, in Fanon's view, as they imbibe Western culture. Schooled by colonialism, intellectuals are even more than its product, they are colonialism's protégés (*WE*, 46).

The intellectual's separation from the imperial country and its culture leads not only to a rejection of the settler's civilizing mission, but also to a rediscovery and even reinvention of the past. This second phase is akin to negritude.

If the intellectual wants to commit to joining the people's movement, there needs to be a painful self-analysis, and a willingness to strip naked and study the history of their body (*WE*, 211). To do so, the intellectual has to successfully break from colonialism's hold: without this the internalization of colonial ideology could have fatal psychological consequences. Colonialism tries to prevent its offspring from leaving. Claiming to protect the colonized intellectuals from themselves – their egos, their physiology, their biology, their own unhappiness, their own essence and their inferiority complexes – colonialism, like a patronizing parent, restrains its offspring from their unconscious wish to commit suicide and their self-destructive wish to join "the rebels."

In the Manichean world of colonialism, the intellectual would be rendered schizoid by the attempt to avoid this problem by becoming both Algerian and French, or both Ghanaian and English. This unwillingness to make a choice, to renounce either determining identification, opting for what they think is a "universal standpoint," is in reality a characteristically Western posture. If there is not a complete rupture with colonial thinking, the intellectual becomes rootless:

> This tearing away, painful and difficult though it may be, is however necessary. If it is not accomplished there will be serious psycho-affective injuries and the result will be individuals without an anchor, without a horizon, colorless, stateless, rootless – a race of angels. (*WE*, 218)

The claims of the "past" not only rehabilitate the nation but also its culture. The value of the past is restored, indeed even overvalued at the expense of the present. Artistic creations support this valorization. The psychological urgency of the native's intellectual and unconscious wishes are expressed in a harsh aesthetic style; art makes frequent statements of race. This style is necessary for the intellectual's development because it leads to a contact with the people even if it turns out to be a superficial advocacy expressed in the denunciatory style that still takes colonialism as its point of reference (*WE*, 239). Negritude, the "African personality," or authenticity, is a "historical necessity" but it "will tend to lead up a blind alley" if it does not evolve into a specific national and fighting culture:

> The culture that the intellectual leans towards is often no more than a *stock of particularisms*. He wishes to attach himself to the people; but instead he only catches hold of their outer garments. And these outer garments are merely the reflection of a *hidden life*, teeming and perpetually in motion. (*WE*, 223–4, emphasis added)

Fanon is criticizing the intellectual's reliance on identity, which fails to mine the deep subjugated anticolonial core of the people's culture and only scratches the surface, turning up examples and comparisons but not what is immanent in them. The intellectual's methods are hardly dialectical. This inability to get beyond the simple negation of the colonial standpoint results in several problems. The intellectual is preoccupied with a past and with traditions which, according to Fanon, are "shot through with centrifugal tendencies." Despite their anticolonial character, these traditions are in fact in flux. Making a fixed particular of them leads right back to the colonial paradigm which reified them. It is precisely this expression of the past that is praised by the colonial "expert" and patronized by anthropologists. Furthermore, a simple identification with the masses leads the intellectual toward becoming an "uncritical mouthpiece," (*WE*, 49) manifesting what Fanon calls "opportunism." The intellectual is mouthing a Manichean ideology just as the people are beginning to move on from this (op)position.

Vertiginous Intellectuals

> It is not only necessary to fight for the liberty of your people. You must also teach the people once again, and first learn once again yourself, what is the full stature of a man; and this you must do for as long as the fight lasts. (Fanon, *The Wretched of the Earth*)

Fanon's conception of a small handful of honest and radical intellectuals occupies a central but problematical place in his dialectic of organization. In the embryonic organization forged between the urban militant and the rural masses, the intellectual plays an important role in exploding the old colonial truths and bringing out new meanings inherent in the radical mutations experienced in the anticolonial movement (WE, 147). But their scripts are not readymade.

Far from a simple identity with the people, Fanon argues that it is only by realizing "the extent of the intellectual's estrangement from them" (WE, 226), that intellectuals can posit themselves as an element of the dialectic. In the colonial set-up the process of estrangement has added complications. Made intellectual by the colonial system, they have to eschew their elitism while not renouncing their education in a search for some lost authenticity. Instead, intellectuals have to put those skills "in the hands of the people" as they dive into subjugated history to bring about a cultural intersubjectivity (WE, 293). In other words, rejecting their education and "going native" would in the end reflect colonial Manicheanism. Fanon's appeals to intellectuals to recognize their "duty" to the "national cause" – though he knows full well how few are willing to relinquish their class privilege, commit class suicide, as Amilcar Cabral put it – might appear naive, yet it does have a materiality. The tension here is centered on the reliance on a group of intellectuals who have to "repudiate [their] own nature insofar as it is bourgeois" (WE, 150), as a moral ought, based on an appeal to their honesty, duty, and virtue and the "reality" of their class position. Whereas the militants expelled by the nationalist organization largely hail from the socioeconomic fringes of urban colonial society (they "are often unskilled workers, seasonal laborers" (WE, 125)), the "honest" intellectuals, like Fanon, are not necessarily the products of the native elite but children of the middle class.[9] This group's disdain for the emerging wheeling-and-dealing hucksters is often a product of moral upbringing: "The personal situation of these men (breadwinners of large families) or their background (hard struggles and a strictly moral upbringing) explains their manifest contempt for profiteers and schemers" (WE, 177).

Fanon tells us no more about the context of this moral, almost ascetic upbringing, but his description of the nationalist bourgeoisie's own nature goes further in explaining a material basis for the honest intellectual's manifest contempt, claiming that "under the colonial system, a middle class which accumulates capital is an impossible phenomenon" (*WE*, 150). In other words, the intellectual is split by competing ideologies. Colonialism prevents the bourgeoisie from truly becoming bourgeois, and thus it is somewhat in their own material interest to join the people; but ideologically the bourgeoisie is mired in inferiority complexes and mirrors the colonial elitism toward the natives. This "bourgeoisie" is therefore relatively free to discover where its "real" interests lie. In other words, in the appeal to "the national cause" the battle of ideas has a material grounding and is a material force. More precisely it the bourgeoisie's *lack* of productivity that provides the basis on which it is able to give up its nature as a huckstering class. But psychologically this lack is the problem. As a huckstering class it is willing to give up the nation for a few gleaming trinkets.

What is the intellectual's real nature? In "Colonial War and Mental Disorders" (*WE*, 249–310), Fanon analyses the native intellectual's rootlessness and alienation as an effect of colonial rule, which in extreme cases is experienced as "vertigo." Such a feeling of rootlessness was one effect of torture. If they were released from prison they are burdened by the thought that they have "spilled the beans" (*WE*, 288). Unlike the non-intellectual,[10] the arrested intellectual is asked to collaborate with army intelligence in a reasoned dialogue. It is a dialogue that presupposes an estrangement between the native intellectual and the non-intellectual, based on a condescending attitude toward the "poor mistaken" fellahs (*WE*, 287). Unlike the peasant, who knows that every relationship between colonizer and colonized is one of falsity and violence, the intellectual is less certain. The intellectual experiences interrogation as an "inability to distinguish between true and false" (*WE*, 285); a melting of all that once seemed solid.

Fanon's critical (self-)interest in this group of "honest" intellectuals was first articulated in *Black Skin*, where he spoke of the small number of intellectuals who could fully explore the negativity of Césaire's negritude. In revolutionary Algeria, this "race of angels," as Fanon describes them in *The Wretched*, comes to occupy a "zone of occult instability." Though this could be said to be a typical characteristic of the postcolonial intellectual, the proper context of the quotation reveals that Fanon is addressing the radical mutation intellectuals undergo when they enter the liberating zone of the revolution. Unlike the Manichean colonial zoning, this revolutionary zone doesn't merely transgress but breaks up old boundaries of thinking. The absolute identification with the people, Fanon maintains, calls everything into question.

The magic of this zone is simply the intellectual's discovery of the creativity of the mass movement. By entering this unstable zone and reconnecting with the people in a non-elitist way, the intellectual becomes committed and can play a mediating role in the development of a fighting culture. But by describing this zone as unstable, Fanon reminds us of the deep problematic of the intellectual. Without the organizational space where the intellectual and the people can meet on a new equal footing, the intellectual *is* decentered, rootless, unsure of what is true and false. Simply identifying with the people's culture, without a concern for political developments, can easily become opportunist or, worse, retrograde. Put another way, the vertiginous intellectual mirrors the opposition between modernity and tradition propagated by the modernization school. In a Manichean rather than dialectical fashion, the intellectual moves from embracing metropolitan "modernity" to mouthing a nativism:

> These people forget that the forms of thought and what it feeds on, together with modern techniques of information, language, and dress, have dialectically reorganized the people's intelligences and that the constant principles which acted as safeguards during the colonial period are now undergoing extremely radical changes. (*WE*, 225)

As we saw with Fanon's emblematization of the radio, these modern techniques which had hitherto been rejected by the masses are embraced during the liberation struggle. The intellectual's role as critic is to help the people move toward self-understanding. To do so does not mean telling the people what they should think but, on the contrary, helping to clarify what they already know.

First, however, the intellectual must subject habits of thought to a thoroughgoing critique by recognizing that the reactions to and against colonialism were initially cast in elitist terms. Though purporting to reflect, and reflect upon the life of the masses, the intellectual has remained quite separate from them, conceiving work in the same bourgeois "individualist" way as during the quest for assimilation. To be of any use to themselves and others, it is necessary, Fanon insists, for intellectuals to break with the bourgeois assumptions about themselves. They must reject the "dead words of European values and discover the language" and ethics "outlawed by the colonialist bourgeoisie, 'Brother, sister, friend'" (*WE*, 47). The identification with the people should not become an attempt to dredge up a purely African past and return to an invented tradition; rather, it should induce both a denial of the supremacy of the dominant power and a discovery of strength and self-definition in the actuality of the struggle: "[it] is a cultural and political recovery of the suppressed *historic possibilities* in the existence of the colonized"[11] and an overcoming of the negative inheritance that pervades the present. In other words, the intellectual's identification with the masses is part of the movement itself, without which it fails to be objective because it is only through the struggle that the people are able to become historical agents, that is, living their own, not colonialism's, history.

Contrary to the nationalist organization's elitism, the new organizational consciousness that Fanon heralds, is a product of the *experience* of those in the small illegal party as they make contact and develop a working relationship with the rural masses. It is this party that those few "honest intellectuals" join; it is this party that serves as the form in which a truly revolutionary ideology can develop. In this new situation, the whole question of audience changes. The native intellectual, instead of addressing the oppressor, now speaks directly to the people. This "literature of combat" represents the "reasoned irrevocable taking up of arms on the people's side," Fanon concludes (*WE*, 232).

Though Fanon never directly defines political ideology, for him it is clearly analogous to a vision of the future and a promotion of the people's self-reliance and creative potential. In the conclusion to *The Wretched*, it is articulated as a "new humanism" whose pedigree includes a radical critique of the liberal humanist tradition. Fanon's humanism in *The Wretched* is much sharper than *Black Skin*'s more ethical standpoint. In *The Wretched*, the need to have "an idea of man and of the future society" is quickly connected to the need to decentralize political organization "in the extreme," thus bringing full circle the dialectic of spontaneity and organization. The "dialectical leap" (*WE*, 198) is based on decision-making in democratic form and conceptualized within the Fanonian organization. Far from constituting an a priori universal, the dialectic of individual and national self-determination is not a remote prospect but a constantly developing process, figured in immediate social relations and given meaning in the organizational interrelationship between the intellectual and the mass movement. Sense and meaning are made of experience in the organization, in the "zone" where the three elements – the masses, the militants, and the intellectuals – meet and where Fanon's philosophy of liberation is made real.

Appendix: Fanon's periodization of the intellectual's relation with rural society

Historical period (approximations)	Intellectuals	Native society
Colonial domination	Some tribal chiefs as well as feudal hierarchies are co-opted	Culture becomes a stock of habits. Myths and memory take the place of real struggle as resistance is driven underground
Assimilation	Formation of colonial schools and the civilizing mission	Continued destruction of native's culture and economy. Memory and oral traditions play an important role in clandestine resistance
Initial period of nationalist activity	Imbued with notion of civilizing mission there are attempts by the newly educated middle class to achieve equality within colonialism	
Interwar years	Reaction against colonialism. Negritude and return to "roots"; valorization of the past. More militant stance by nationalist parties but still a period of near total separation from rural society which appears "inert" and backward	Stirrings in the countryside which have been continuous during the late colonial period of land seizures, forced labor and taxation. "Pacification" and development of customary rule in the rural areas
War and post–World War Two period of independence	Negritude and rejection of abstractions of negritude. Genuine (though still unstable) relationship with the masses. Creation of mass-based organizations, new national and "fighting cultures"	Open revolt. New contact between town and country and radical mutation of people's culture

8

Nationalism and a New Humanism

We must not voodoo the people.

Fanon, *The Wretched of the Earth*

An important part of my project has been to examine Fanon's cultural politics in a historical context. In my foregoing remarks on the veil and the radio, I emphasized the larger sociopolitical contexts and dynamics of Fanon's conception of national consciousness and nation-building. Here, still within the context of national consciousness, I argue that Fanon's cultural politics can lead to an understanding of his humanism. Further, if his humanism is predicated on anticolonial action, why then should it take a national form? We shall have to first discuss Fanon's conception of national liberation.

The Question of Nationalism

Fanon eschews an abstract populism which too narrowly stakes its claims in a racial reaction to White rule while too broadly taking the whole continent of Africa as its field of reference. Instead, he argues that a national culture, born in the anticolonial struggle, can provide a basis for success and lay the groundwork for a vibrant political society. It is also from this national basis that a genuine Pan-Africanism can develop. Colonialism created the national boundary, yet, Fanon maintains – though he resists an uncritical embrace of categories derived from colonialism – national liberation is the form that anticolonial struggles must take. Indeed, if the social struggle does not become a national endeavor it will inevitably degenerate along the retrograde, geographic, ethnic, and racial lines refashioned or simply created under colonial rule. He alludes to the threat of degeneration when he speculates on the likely consequences should the initial period of spontaneity not develop and the struggle remain within an elemental and local social consciousness where one group is unified in opposition to another group under the watchful eye of colonialism. If these struggles reach what Fanon calls "the stage of social consciousness before the stage of nationalism," fierce demands for social justice will be paradoxically allied with "tribalism" (*WE*, 204). Racial feeling, or a desire for revenge, might be good and cohesive enough reasons to join the struggle against colonialism, but the social consciousness it produces is rudimentary, local, and finally retrogressive.

During the Algerian war, the "nation" was, in practice, brought to life in the locality: the government is set up on the hillsides of Kabylia, for example, meting out justice in an immediate and authoritarian way, and the group is frequently held together by a "mystical body of belief" deriving in part from traditions of resistance as well as from democratic forms of local rule. This kind of local rule, which is inherently contradictory and fiercely independent, must develop into a richer and more inclusive concept of the nation. But here is where problems begin because other forces and other claims are involved in the nationalist project. With his critical insight Fanon foresaw the great potential for failure in the national movements, indicating that the test of a successful decolonization lay in the degree of human self-determination. By not making the national program explicit, by not deepening it "by a rapid transformation into a consciousness of social and political needs, in other words into humanism," he charged, it leads up a blind alley (*WE*, 204).

Some postcolonial critics claim that nationalism is alien to Africa, that it is a European idea that was adopted by anticolonial leaders to assert freedom from European domination. Certainly the nation-state in its geographical articulation was a European invention; but by the 1950s nationalism had much to do with the immediate promise that the chains of foreign rule would be shattered. Additionally, the sway of European intellectual authority continued virtually unchallenged partly because the critique of its authority lay within the Manichean thought that characterized European rule in Africa. To present an authentic African political form as *the* answer was a reaction to Manichean thinking but remained within its intellectual contours. Instead, there was a myriad of polities, some democratic and some not, and some more compromised with colonialism than others. It was necessary to see how variegated indigenous democratic forms provided a basis – while not being sufficient on their own – for nationalism to be successful. In short, Fanon's dialectic of anticolonialism is grounded in the local, but in order to defeat colonialism it moves of necessity to a centrally planned movement. This is where many nationalist movements stop. For Fanon this centralizing movement is further challenged by a return to the source, toward local decentralization enriched by the foregoing movement. Let us consider this move in more detail.

Fanon's Theory of Nationalism: Two Types of Nationalism or Three?

Let us waste no time in sterile litanies and nauseating mimicry. (Fanon, *The Wretched of the Earth*)

It has often been argued that Fanon draws a distinction between two kinds of nationalist ideology in the context of anticolonialism. There was, on the one hand, a nationalism that wanted to take power but remain virtually subordinate to external powers; and, on the other, a nationalism that wanted a genuine independence represented by such groups as the FLN. I contend that Fanon adds a third, unique conception of nationalism, which is implicitly critical of the FLN and other national liberation organizations, and is grounded in what he calls a new humanism and an internationalism.

In many cases, the development of national consciousness on the African continent depended on the reaction of the colonialists, thus in part proving Fanon's point that the degree of resistance to decolonization determines the shape and depth of the nationalist movement. In some cases, the colonialists embraced the nationalist elite and negotiated withdrawal; in others, the colonialists' refusal to recognize the nationalist elite forced it into more radical politics. These positions can be summarily contrasted as a moderate and conformist nationalism (nationalism$_1$) as opposed to a militant nationalism (nationalism$_2$). The fundamental difference between these two forms of nationalism and a third which is Fanon's (nationalism$_3$) lies not only in their reaction to colonialism but in the people's perception and consciousness of nationalism. The more the victory over colonialism is seen as the work of the people, not some elite, the more it can become decentralized in the postcolonial period and thus be identified as nationalism₃. In Gramsci's pithy hypothesis, nationalism₃ can be thought of as optimism of the will and pessimism of the intellect, a celebration of human action and a critical attention to hazards of national consciousness. This antimony can only be solved in practice, a practice which includes the work of intellectuals. But it is easy for action to be subverted and for the human will, so delicate after the colonial experience, to be crushed. Because the postcolonial situation is problematic, Fanon argues that "there must be no waiting until the nation has produced new men; there must be no waiting until men are imperceptibly transformed by revolutionary processes in perpetual renewal. It is quite true that these two processes are essential, but consciousness must be helped" (*WE*, 304). Aided by constant criticism, "revolutionary theory, if it is to be completely liberating," has to painstakingly draw conclusions; for it is revolutionary theory that can help settle problems and signals "consciousness to take another step" (*WE*, 304–5).

In the following, Fanon's conception of nationalism is further addressed in terms of self-consciousness and how this relates to his revolutionary theory, and to his plea, at the close of *The Wretched*, to work out new concepts emerging from the African struggles. "To turn over a new leaf" suggests what the anticolonial struggle seeks to produce from itself without precedent. Because the disappearance of colonialism means both the disappearance of the colonizer and the colonized, it has to include a radical reordering of the social structure to forestall a neocolonial situation. It is the complex transformation of the colonized, not the simple departure of the colonizers, that will produce the new humanity. In short, to venture beyond Manicheanism is to transform the native into an active thinking historical subject: "to rise above this absurd drama that others have staged around me . . . to reach out to the universal" of reciprocal recognition (*BS*, 197). This is in part what Fanon means by a new humanism.

We should keep in mind that Fanon's concern to establish a radically democratic polity is posed as a problematic. For example, when he raises the issue of decentralization of the party into rural areas and the village councils as a model of decision making, these councils too have to undergo a radical mutation. Fanon asks some perennial questions and suggests ways to approach them.

To go beyond Manicheanism means to end the world of colonialism and racism and to inaugurate a new human reciprocity. The proposition is tautological. Authentic termination of the colonial condition requires a new humanism and a new humanism requires total decolonization. Fanon turns away from liberal European humanism, which he considers hypocritical, but seriously attempts to create a more human and fundamentally different future from the dehumanized and violent experience of colonial rule. In part, Fanon's is a practical or ethical humanism, because it is, after all, an issue of life. Previously we saw how the prefiguring of a new humanism is expressed culturally, in the radical mutation of consciousness taking place during the revolution. The fighting culture is thus one expression of the new humanism, though in *The Wretched* it is far from complete and does not exhaust Fanon's full intended meaning. To comprehend Fanon's intention we must rigorously trace how Fanon's cultural politics leads to, and is part of, a new humanism.

Revolutionary theory requires a "total" approach and Fanon announced the theoretical frame for his cultural politics in a speech before the First Conference of Black Writers. Given soon after his self-avowed participation in the Algerian revolution, this speech champions the struggle against all forms of alienation: "The logical end to this *will to struggle* is the total liberation of the national territory. In order to achieve this liberation, the inferiorized man brings all his resources into play, all his acquisitions, the old and the new, his own and those of the occupant" (*AR*, 43). Fanon construes the struggle as part of the process by which the native becomes a *social individual*, one who has "decided, 'with full knowledge of what is involved,' to fight all forms of exploitation and of alienation of man." The goal of this plunge into struggle is "total liberation." The new humanism is "prefigured in the struggle" (*WE*, 246). For the struggle of the oppressed to become "at once total, absolute," the "practical content" – which brings all the resources of the oppressed and of the colonizer into play – must be superseded or, in other words, undergo a radical mutation. Through this dialectical supersession, we encounter the free will in a new social order, a free will that realizes (and is conscious of) its own freedom of will. The *structure and rhythm of the people*, their radical mutation, provide the structure of the new society, already in evidence in the process of "total liberation."

It was one thing to propose such a framework for the "illogical maintenance of a subjective attitude in organized contradiction with reality" (*AR*, 53) in the dark days of the Battle of Algiers, and quite another to realize it. It is the gap between Fanon's theorization of absolute liberty and the "reality" of postcolonial Algeria that is a sticking point for many critics. How could the increasingly conscious and united masses, so forcefully projected by Fanon, so quickly dissipate in the years after independence? To further plumb this question and the content of Fanon's concept of national liberation and humanism, let us first turn back to his critique of nationalism$_1$.

For the colonialist, Fanon argues that the colonial idea of humanity is realized through its civilizing mission, with its "proclamation of an essential equality between men." Appearing logical to itself, colonialism invites a handful of the native elite "to become human and take as their prototype Western humanity as incarnated in the Western bourgeoisie" (*WE*, 163). This elite adopts Western tastes, while the rest of the colonial "subhumanity" are mired in poverty. In nationalism$_1$ it is this "caste," essentially an unproductive caricature of the Western bourgeoisie, that then assumes national leadership. In this scenario, independence does not lead to decolonization but to a curious self-recolonization where a native leadership simply mimics the privileges and postures of the Europeans and follows it on the path toward "decadence" – a jet-setting, Mercedes-driving, Martini-drinking elite – while the masses sink deeper into poverty. Fanon vociferates that if one's dream is to turn Africa into Europe, then it would be better to leave Africa under the control of the Europeans. Wearing the "mask of neocolonialism," the nation is not put on a new footing but stagnates. The ruling class flocks to the capital, the urban areas, and the regions marked out for privilege under colonialism, while the "rest of the colony [would] follow its path of underdevelopment and poverty" (*WE*, 159). Under the nationalist leadership the retrogression is on all fronts: economic, social, and political. Nationalism$_1$ reflects Europe's "balkanization" of Africa, with the elite of each "country" demanding its own privileges, its own civil service, and enormous government salaries, while resisting African unity. Fanon calls this type of nationalism "anti-national":

> The nationalist bourgeoisie with practically no economic power . . . not engaged in production, invention, construction or labor . . . enters, soul in peace, on the terrible anti-national path of a bourgeoisie, flatly, stupidly, cynically bourgeois. For them nationalization does not mean governing the state with regard to new social

relations ... [but] quite simply the transfer into native hands of those unfair advantages which are legacies of the colonial period ... Enormous sums are spent on displays of ostentation, cars, houses ... They will prove themselves incapable of triumphantly putting into practice a program with even a minimum humanist content, in spite of fine-sounding declarations ... that come straight out of European treatises on moral and political philosophy. (*WE*, 149–63)[1]

This prescient analysis sums up the subsequent and saddening experience of a host of countries, including ones that had started along the track of a more militant nationalism.[2]

Even worse, not only have the nationalist leaders become Westernized in superficial though insidious ways, but they also accept European racial philosophy "in its most corrupt form." The rhetoric of bourgeois humanism is easily turned into a rhetoric of African uniqueness, and the "Africanization of the ruling class" heralds the culmination of a racist policy whose whole philosophy is really no more than the slogan "replace the foreigner."

The emptiness and danger of such nationalism is exposed as interracial and interethnic rivalries appear, created and recreated by colonial rule and classifications, and "African unity takes off its hollow mask"; soon, nationalist sentiment degenerates into racism. The rationalism that the masses had attained by confronting colonialism now dissipates, fierce old enmities are encouraged, and in place of a national consciousness religious identity and spiritual cults "show a new vitality." In short, the policies of nationalism$_1$ lead to stagnation, regression, fragmentation, and starvation. Sadly such xenophobia as the basis for politics has not diminished. Citizenship in many postcolonial African countries has become reduced to colonial classifications. Such politics, and the legacies of colonial rule, were found in the most extreme and tragic form in Rwanda, where "replace the foreigner" was used as a justification for genocide.

Nationalism$_2$: The Overworked Peasant and the Lazy Intellectual

The unpreparedness of the educated classes, the lack of practical links between them and the mass of people, their laziness, and, let it be said, their cowardice at the decisive moment of the struggle will give rise to tragic mishaps. (Fanon, *The Wretched of the Earth*)

Let us suppose that we would have produced as human beings . . .
In the individual expression of my own life I would have brought
about the immediate expression of your life, and so in my individual activity I would have directly *confirmed* and *realized* my authentic nature, my *human, communal* nature. Our productions would be
as many mirrors from which our natures would shine forth. (Marx,
"Excerpts from James Mill's *Elements of Political Economy*")

Fanon's singular critique of the more militant nationalism$_2$ gives
us an insight into the dialectical character of his concept. Unlike
nationalism$_1$, which is led by a kleptocratic, self-interested elite,
nationalism$_2$ articulates a genuine desire to modernize and develop
the nation. However, rather than developing new relations with
the peasants and workers and genuinely involving them in the
decision-making process, nationalism$_2$ regards them merely as the
means to accumulate the capital needed for "modernization."

The colonial master's familiar complaint that the native is slow
and lazy is repeated by the nationalist leaders with a new ideological twist: now they should sacrifice for the nation. "Development"
by any means becomes the new fetish, which, with the lack of technology to increase surplus value, can only be accomplished by labor
which is in plentiful supply.[3] This call by the nationalist$_2$ leaders to
make "colossal efforts" for the nation accommodates various and
often conflicting ideological determinations – negritude, African
personality, or pan-Arabism, as well as various forms of "socialism," and "modernization." But among the variables, there is one
constant: pressure on the peasantry to sacrifice *even more* than they
did in the colonial period: "The exploitation of agricultural workers
will be intensified and made legitimate. Using two or three slogans,
these new colonists will demand an enormous amount of work
from the agricultural laborers, in the name of the national effort of
course" (*WE*, 154–5). The leader, in whose person the populace
found a representative of national unity against colonial domination, inevitably becomes a new source of domination, overseeing
the accumulation of capital. The term "leader" refers to a driver of
animals, but Fanon reminds us, "the people are no longer a herd
[and] do not need to be driven" (*WE*, 184).

Fanon's critique of nationalist bourgeoisie (as huckstering,
greedy, and useless) is often associated with the underdevelopment
school which sees colonialism as the expropriation and *underdevelopment* of Africa by the West, with the unequal exchange
in global capitalism determining and even undermining class rela-

tions. Yet unlike the dependency theorists' preoccupation with external relations, Fanon's dialectic enabled him to discern internal social conflicts. Choices can be made even in the vortex of the world market. This is a crucial consideration. The situation is far from perfect but for Fanon it is, in part, how and under what conditions people work that becomes a measure of independence and an important element in his critique of nationalism$_2$. Fanon compares the simple adoption of the productivist model and the colossal efforts demanded of the masses with his call for a new paradigm (*WE*, 100). Rather than a "developed" country, he argued, such exploitation created a devolved human being, a being turned animal because he or she is treated as such. Rather than worry about the withdrawal of capital, or primitive accumulation, Fanon voices concern in *The Wretched* about the withdrawal of the human being, the "very concrete question of not dragging [people] towards mutilation, of not imposing upon the brain rhythms which very quickly obliterate and wreck it" (*WE*, 187). Condemning forced labor in the name of the nation, he insists on the laborer's self-determination as an important step toward actualization. There are no stages of liberation, whereby the nation develops its economic basis first and then liberates the people second. Body is given to national consciousness only when "men and women are included on a vast scale in enlightened and fruitful work" (*WE*, 204). Other projects are fruitless.

Fanon's attention to the conditions of labor is reminiscent of Marx's contention that the realm of freedom is based on the transformation of alienated labor into a form of self-realization. "If conditions of work are not modified," Fanon warns, "centuries will be needed to humanize this world which has been forced down to animal level" (*WE*, 100). The necessary modifications can only be effected through people making decisions, experimenting at a local level, learning by mistakes and "starting a new history" (*WE*, 99, 188–9). Such a goal resides not in some utopian distance but in immediate development; thus he speaks of the Algerian experience as a "new beginning." Moreover, Fanon views work not as external compulsion but as an expression and act of creation of the social individual. From a psychological point of view, non-alienating labor is essential to the individual sense of self. The new social relations of work engender at the same time the reproduction of a newly created self who understands that "slavery is opposed to work, and that work presupposes liberty, responsibility, and consciousness." He claims that "in those districts where we have been able to carry out successfully these interesting experiments, we have watched man being created by revolutionary beginnings" (*WE*, 192). This is quite a different discourse of nationalist politics. In Fanon's mind national production actually rises rather than declines if the people take control. With the focus on the whole human being, not simply the immediate functioning of muscles, with meetings between producers and consumers during the Algerian war of liberation, the caloric intake in the liberated areas reached unheard of levels: "The fact is that the time taken up by explaining, the time 'lost' in treating the worker as a human being, will be caught up" (*WE*, 192). The problem remained, however, how to take this idealism of the war of liberation into the postindependence period.

Fanon can be considered a Marxist humanist in the sense that he is not championing a static notion of human nature, but a notion of human potential "created by revolutionary beginnings."[4] Rather than viewing Fanon's Marxism simply in terms of stretching class categories in the colonial context, what is especially provocative is the expression of the creativity of ideological intervention as a political act. In *The Wretched* he calls this intervention "political education," which he defines as opening the people's minds, "awakening them, and allowing the birth of their intelligence" (*WE*, 197). This birth is central to Fanon's conception of a national culture and is made possible by the transformation of consciousness catalyzed by the revolutionary struggle; and here that consciousness is created in a flash of common sense so straightforward that it seems extraordinary: "the peasants have very clearly caught hold of the idea that the more intelligence you bring to your work, the more pleasure you will have in it" (*WE*, 192).

In contrast, the nationalist$_2$ organization has an administrative attitude toward labor. They might eschew "technicians and planners coming from big Western universities" (*WE*, 192), but they have the same attitude to "human resources." What makes this so pernicious, in Fanon's mind, is the separation it introduces between organization and the revolutionary principles, and between organization and masses.

The division between the nationalist leaders and the masses, following so soon after independence and appearing so evident in retrospect, was neither automatic nor passive; it was the result of an intense class struggle where workers' organizations were banned and oppositions destroyed. It represents something of a counterrevolution. Stanching the free flow of ideas that had given impetus to the independence process, the party disintegrates into a "trade union of individual interests" and an "empty shell," used by the nationalist leadership to form a "screen" between it and the masses. Unwilling to expand democracy, the party becomes authoritarian and systematically eliminates all opposition: "The embryo opposition parties are liquidated by beatings and stonings. The opposition candidates see their houses set on fire. . . . All the opposition parties . . . have been, by dint of baton charges and prisons, condemned first to silence and then to clandestine existence" (*WE*, 182). Fanon's prediction would soon be seen in Algeria, where political dissidents were silenced, radicals purged, and strikes were termed labor "indiscipline" and declared not to be in the national interest.[5]

The question of organization provides a powerful lens for focusing the degeneration of nationalism$_2$. Again Fanon presciently describes the postcolonial African situation. Though helping to fulfill the "historical mission" of ridding the nation of the colonialists, the organization all too frequently metamorphoses into a bureaucratic dictatorship. Invariably centered in the urban areas, where it becomes increasingly corrupt, it degenerates into a dictatorship of party officials. Embracing a military model, it frequently acts like a "common sergeant-major," ruling from the top. It demands of the people "silence in the ranks," predicts Fanon: increasingly separated from all decision-making, the masses are sent back, intellectually and physically, "to the caves."

Fanon's project of deepening the anticolonial revolution into humanism is reminiscent of Marx's point in the *Eighteenth Brumaire* that proletarian revolutions move forward through a process of constant criticism. For national consciousness to be "deepened" into a humanism, there needs to be a different conception of time and development. It is no use importing capitalist notions; rather production needs to be considered in terms of human development. People must understand that a new social agenda will follow a novel timetable, often improvised, tempered by patience and fortitude, especially since "the spirit of discouragement, which has been rooted in people's minds by colonial domination, is still very near the surface" (*WE*, 194). Such discouragement can, and Fanon fears will, lead to an all-too-quick retrogression.

The profundity of Fanon's critique of the separation between leaders and ranks, and the lack of practical connections between them, has been borne out by the early years of African independence. Genuine commitments to agricultural cooperatives have failed. Often targeted from the urban center, the peasantry has been permitted no voice, no representation, being placed at the receiving end of "collectivization." The emphasis on cash crops rather than food crops has often led to food shortages and increased dependence on imported foods, and has been tacitly determined by a characterization of the peasants not as valuable in themselves but as mere producers of value. The authoritarian character of the implementation of the plan led "to the triumph of a dictatorship of civil servants" (*WE*, 180). Even attempts to reduce the growing government bureaucracy through decentralization, as in Nyerere's Tanzania, did not halt "the process of its own contradictions" (*WE*, 165) but only increased the regional bureaucracy. Politics were directed at the symptoms rather than the underlying causes. Part of the problem resulted from the assertion that the capitalist, or the landed exploiter, was unknown to traditional African society.[6] This perspective led to a rather naive and uncritical attitude toward incipient class divisions emerging most profoundly in the organization. In many cases, harking back to "traditions" became part of an ideology used to mask new divisions between leaders and masses, and put an end to dialogue, discussion, and the "free exchange of ideas" (*WE*, 170). While nationalization transferred to the elite the unfair advantages which are legacies of the colonial period, privatization has not challenged this legacy but only helped produce more inequality and poverty. Projects of "African socialism" were genuine if bureaucratic; neo-liberal capitalistic "structural adjustment," on the other hand, is nothing but systematic exploitation.

Humanism and Ideology

> [The] clarity of ideas must be profoundly dialectical. The awakening of the whole people will not come about all at once; the people's work in the building of the nation will not immediately take on its full dimensions. (Fanon, *The Wretched of the Earth*)

Reluctant to produce an abstract "treatise on the universal," Fanon's attention to the centrality of labor in the independence context attempts to create meaning for lived experience and gain insight into African processes of national reconfiguration. Fanon's dialectic can perhaps be approached by remembering his engagement with Hegel. Axel Honneth argues that *The Wretched* "is an anticolonialist manifesto that attempted to explicate the experience of the oppressed Black Africa by drawing directly on Hegel's doctrine of recognition."[7] Honneth grasps a truth, but in almost too simple a fashion, ellipsing Fanon's sharp critique of Hegel and thereby reducing Fanon's innovative recreation of the Hegelian dialectic of recognition to the experience of oppression. For Fanon the paradigmatic development of reciprocity that Hegel develops has to be remapped in the colonies. When the slave is also colonized the development of recognition through labor is blocked off. Fanon offers another route through the development of national consciousness. In other words, rather than equate reciprocity with identity which inevitably annulled the Other, Fanon grounded mutual recognition in the moment of alterity, and called for recognition from the Other while demanding it not be reduced to the same. This dialectic of reciprocity, made concrete in terms of a national liberation movement against colonialism, is not reducible to the dialectic of labor. Fanon is not simply replacing one dialectic (the anticolonial) for another (the class struggle) but, through a system of interpenetration, deepening each. The result is, as we saw in his critique of Sartre, a much more open-ended or, as Fanon would put it, "untidy" dialectic, which can be best understood in the social context. At least that is where Fanon saw the possibility of freedom. For such a possibility is never automatically realized; indeed, "philosophical thought teaches us," Fanon observed in *The Wretched*, that "the consciousness of the self is not the closing of the door to communication, but guarantees it" (*WE*, 247). This "self" which does not close the door to communication develops by undergoing mediation (and therefore self-negation) and only then embraces the other in mutual recognition.

The movement of the dialectic in *The Wretched* is first expressed by Fanon's profound retelling of the *experience* of anticolonial political activity. It is an experience that destroys old colonial truths and a hermeneutic that reveals contradictions that have been hidden by colonialism. Spontaneous activity, as we saw earlier, reaches for a self-understanding based on action not hemmed in by Manicheanism. In fact, Fanon argues that it is "the rebellion" itself that "gives proof of its rational basis" (*WE*, 146). The power of this drive to self-understanding is, however, impeded by the "laziness" of the intellectuals, who continue to insist on a Manichean analysis when "shades of meaning" are needed. Optimism in the possibility of African freedom is a result of revolutionary action based on a vital transformation in the character of subjectivity. But, and here he marks a new theoretical warning, "colonialism and its derivatives do not, as a matter of fact, constitute the present enemies of

Africa . . . [T]he deeper I enter into the culture and political circles the surer I am that the great danger that threatens Africa is the absence of ideology" (*AR*, 186).[8] What is of overriding importance to Fanon's conception of ideology was its relation to revolution. That was exactly why the young Fanon criticized Bantu Philosophy as a closed epistemology which placed disproportionate value on the externals of culture (*WE*, 234); summing up the dialectic of culture and liberation in *The Wretched*, he noted, "The struggle for freedom does not give back to the national culture its former values and shapes."

One important turning point of *The Wretched* is when he charts the challenge to theory, schematically mapping the development of a small group of revolutionary intellectuals who help the development of "new meanings" inherent in the spontaneous activity. Hounded by the authorities in the town and isolated in the nationalist party, this group of what we have called "honest intellectuals" (who have begun to learn a new ethics in prison), are forced underground. Their estrangement and distrust of the mainstream nationalist party drives them to the countryside. Whereas earlier contacts between the urban militant and the peasantry had resulted in mutual distrust, this second meeting results in a "radical mutation." The intellectual, who had previously seen the peasant as backward, sees them as spontaneously anticolonialist. The peasant, on the other hand, who hates the colonial police machine, welcomes with open arms these militants on the run. Fanon looks for a solution to this pressing problem of the relationship between urban and rural and mental and manual labor, to express the Marxian problematic, by considering the *experience* that the handful of intellectuals have in the small illegal party as it makes contact and develops a working relationship with the rural masses. It is these relationships that he thinks can be pressed by demanding a process of organizational decentralization, and that can create the atmosphere for developing the revolutionary ideology that has been so sorely absent. The intellectual's "instinctive distrust of the race for positions" (*WE*, 177) provides the basis for a new type of organization and is key to the postcolonial situation.

Nevertheless there still remains the question: what is the place of the intellectual in the discovery of what constitutes the national? It is a question that returns to the problematic of the absence of ideology. For Fanon, ideology is the development of a new humanism built around and promoting the people's self-reliance and creative potential. An important indicator of this relationship, nevertheless, is the language of politics. His concern for a common language turns on the way in which the politicos speak to the masses, and the type of language they use, which is quite different from the liberal discourse of "individual rights" spoken by the nationalist elite. Fanon is mapping out new terrain in which the narrative of the honest intellectual's development is seen in the very method of *The Wretched*. Honesty produces commitment but it does not, of itself, produce the exploration of social relationships, and the practical-critical activity that Fanon is asking for.

It needs to be stressed that Fanon's concern that the intellectual be aware of *what happens after* decolonization leads him to criticize the very Manicheanism that had first motivated the mass movement. Thus Fanon does not support any and every peasant–intellectual interaction. First, he is critical of the intellectual's elitism toward the masses (inculcated by Western culture), and thus the intellectual's first rule should be to emphasize that the whole political project is based on the masses coming to realize that the future of the nation depends on themselves. Second, he is critical of the intellectual's rejection of their Western experiences, which leads them to make sacred, almost uncritically, any manifestation of native culture, which has been seriously compromised during the period of colonialism. Such a valorization can lead to reactionary consequences. Fanon's claim that *The Wretched* is directed to his African comrades, not to the West, should be taken seriously. Certainly "The Pitfalls of National Consciousness" and "On National Culture" are pointedly addressed to that small group of committed intellectuals; they are also critiques of a Manichean "Africanist" bootstrap ideology which says no to foreign influences but hounds the peasantry to work harder, to make "colossal efforts" for the nation (*WE*, 154–5). The "optimism of the will and pessimism of the intellect" of this small band of revolutionaries is not equivalent to Che Guevara's focoism, or to Plato's "philosopher Kings,"[9] but rather they are a group willing to tip the scales of destiny through painstaking work. A philosophy born of struggle also means that philosophy has a role to play in the struggle.

For Fanon the appellation *nation* was not a strategic move to intervene in metropolitan debates. The importance of the rural in Fanon's conception of national consciousness problematizes such intellectual discourse. Indeed, for Fanon national consciousness was a unifier, it crossed urban and rural and tribal and ethnic barriers and racial and religious categories, either invented or reinforced by colonialism, and it was the only possible political form that could successfully challenge colonialism. He attacked those leftists who thought that the stage of national liberation could be bypassed in the colonies,[10] as though it was a "phase that humanity has left behind." National liberation met a need of people long denied such recognition, and without it, social and political demands would tend toward racism. This is no better seen than by the passion with which the native intellectual defends the existence of a national culture in the face of being "swamped" by "Western culture." This reaction, which is a response to the colonialist theory of precolonial barbarism, represents a psychological need. Fanon maintained that national liberation, which was not nationalism, was more than a necessary moment, but he was also perceptively aware of the problematic. While he was ready to concede on the factual plane that the glories of past African civilizations do not help the starving peasant today, he regarded their existence in other times as both rehabilitating and a justification for the future. This work of discovery is of "dialectical significance," opening up space for a new national culture to be reconstituted through new connections between cultural historians and the new cultural voices emerging in the liberation struggle. These new relations are essential to Fanon's project and, inverting the familiar complaint about the laziness of the peasant, Fanon placed blame for the "tragic mishaps" of the liberation struggle on the laziness of the nationalist intellectual.

Political Education: How National Consciousness can Deepen into a Humanism

> Now, political education means . . . to teach the masses that everything depends on them; that if we stagnate it is their responsibility, and if we go forward it is due to them too, that there is no such thing as a demiurge, that there is no famous man who will take responsibility for everything, but that the demiurge is the people themselves. (Fanon, *The Wretched of the Earth*)

Looking at Europe, its styles and techniques, Fanon argues that he sees only "a succession of negations of man, and an avalanche of murders," and a bourgeoisie which proclaims the "essential equality between men" (*WE*, 163) while murdering everywhere (*WE*, 311). However, even though its Enlightenment claims to universalism specifically excluded Africa, Fanon does not reject the positive project of human equality:

All the elements of a solution to the great problems of humanity have, at different times, existed in European thought. But the action of European men has not carried out the mission which fell to them . . . [i.e.] bringing the problem of mankind to an infinitely higher plane. (*WE*, 314)

Europe must be rejected not because it speaks of humanism, and not only because it speaks hypocritically, but because its promise, its intellectuals and its workers, on whose shoulders the task has rested of breaking with its narcissism and its imperialist spirit, have also failed. Europe must be forsworn because there the dialectic of liberation has become "the logic of equilibrium." The dialectic, which never belonged exclusively to the Europeans anyway, has to be delinked from a Europe which has become antidialectical.[11] The European is no longer the site for ideas of liberation. Hitler's concentration camps gave notice that the idea of Europe as the site for the human project had come to an end, but the anticolonial movements had uncovered the real source of its barbarity. Fanon's conceptual new leaf, his new humanism, is intimately connected to conscious action and critical of any action that "does not serve to reconstruct the consciousness of the individual."[12] This is the challenge to Africa and to Africana philosophy.

When Fanon writes that his philosophy is "an untidy affirmation of an original idea propounded as an absolute" (*WE*, 41), he is not making claims about universal human development. He is insisting that it is only through conscious, reflective activity that the "question of mankind," and indeed the "rehumanization" of humanity, can be discussed (*WE*, 314). He does believe that it is the human's essence to be free, but his idea of humanism is not based on uncovering an essentialist idea of the human being. The *creation* of the liberated human being must be fabricated by conscious work.

While Fanon argued that not experiencing a nationalist period represented a serious deprivation, an unwise shortcut, with perhaps dire consequences, he clearly differentiated between a narrow, racially defined nationalism and a national (antiracist) consciousness that wanted to "open out" to the "truth of the world." It claims "universality" only because he locates it in a "decision to recognize and accept the reciprocal relativism of different cultures, *once* the colonial status is irreversibly excluded" (*DC*, 44). The road to this universality is through national consciousness. The irreversible exclusion of colonial ideology, including any movement toward establishing a neocolonial social structure, means for Fanon that the ultimate goal cannot reside in taking over existing institutions with their exploitative practices (*WE*, 144–5). Fanon's new humanism develops during the struggle for freedom, beginning as a reaction to the Manichean status quo, with the native "vomiting up" the Western values force-fed by the colonialists. This development results not from the cognitive persuasiveness of some humanist treatise; rather, it is compelled by a visceral reaction to colonialism's actual dehumanization. If not exhausted by Manichean agitation, the native's energies can lead to the reconstruction of the consciousness of self. Independence and reciprocity are the necessary conditions for freedom. It is only when the native gets beyond Manichean action, an action determined by the Other, that he or she can truly be considered self-acting.

When Fanon argues that "national consciousness, which is not nationalism, is the only way to give us an international dimension" (*WE*, 247), he is not merely communicating the need for national recognition on the international stage. He is also declaring that the native's struggle for freedom could start a new world history. Though this new history might find some use for Europe's "prodigious theses," Fanon's proclaimed intention to enlighten the world and create a basis for a new human reciprocity represents a new beginning. At the same time, his internationalism is revolutionary, for his idea of national liberation was explicitly continental: he wanted to "carry Algeria to the four corners of Africa," assembling revolutionary Africa across the desert and thereby creating a continent (*AR*, 180).

While the concept of radical mutation is bound up with the development of indigenous intellect, the philosophic basis, on which the intellectual makes a "reasoned analysis" and aids the indigenous intellect, needs to be further explored. The principal aim of a national culture is to encourage and assist self-understanding, which cannot come all at once. Because self-understanding is a "profoundly dialectical" process, Fanon stresses its development through facing contradictions. Still, some notion of where one is going – what sort of society one is trying to create – has to be spelled out in some conceptual form. This is what Fanon means when he says, "we must work out new concepts, and try to set afoot a new man" (*WE*, 316).

Taken out of context, Fanon's assertion that "Africa will not be freed through the mechanical development of material forces," and his concentration on a mental and cultural revolution, seem to wash out a concern about material conditions. Profoundly concerned with life, he is not antidevelopment. Instead of addressing change as a machine, he insists on the human aspect and in a Marxian way stresses the ideal unity of mental and manual labor: "It is the hand of the African and his brain that will set into motion and implement the dialectics of liberation of the continent" (*AR*, 173). The "practice of action" affects the mind and also is a product of the mind. The radical mutation in consciousness which is a result of the revolutionary struggle is not only an act directed at the externality of objective conditions, but it also supplies the impetus for the revolutionary subject to seek self-development.

Implicit in Fanon's conception of national culture is its organization, especially in the sense of creating "practical links" between intellectuals and the masses. The masses seek self-clarification and understanding of the workings of the objective world. They seek this self-clarification from an organization that can analyze the contradictions in the revolution from *within* the revolution. In Fanon's mind, this working relationship between the intellectuals and the masses is crucial to the survival, self-determination, and development of a truly independent society.[13] The extent to which the masses continue to play a central role in the postcolonial society determines the success of – indeed defines – Fanon's new humanism. And the part played by revolutionary intellectuals, insofar as it bolsters and sustains the masses' efforts, performs a crucial function.

The process whereby colonized people come to understand that "everything depends on them" involves a degree of spontaneity and a process of enlightenment. As we have already seen, to transcend the limitations of Manicheanism created by colonialism depends on what Fanon calls political education. Yet understanding is still grounded in action. What is required, Fanon suggests, is a real working relationship between the dissident intellectuals who bring their "knowledge of the practice of action" and the masses who have decided to "embody history." This does not necessarily mean that intellectuals do the thinking. Fanon challenges both the colonial idea that the masses have no thoughts of their own, and the intellectual's uncritical celebration of any subjugated idea.

Intellectuals must undergo a profound sense of alienation from themselves as products of the colonial civilizing mission. Without this experience, the intellectual, in one way or another, will tend to be set apart and antagonistic to the people's aspirations. This process is not a straightforward one. Most obviously, the eyes of the first type of nationalist intellectual (nationalist$_1$) are focused more on the "mother country" than on their own people. They are the enfranchised slaves of *Black Skin* who never fought for their freedom and remain indebted to their colonial masters. This type of nationalism is merely the empty sentiment of flag waving. More interesting is the plight of the nationalist$_2$ who, while hoping to make the nation matter on the world stage of nations, wants more than juridical recognition. Here the organization plays a centralizing role, bringing together all the fragmented and diverse anticolonial struggles. Under the banner of liberation, this centralizing role is a "natural" one for the nationalist$_2$ intellectual, who is wont to speak *for* the masses and to suppress differences for the sake of unity. Disagreements are submerged to buoy up the national cause. Both the vanguard party and nationalism are homogenizing forms. While this strategy is an important one for the success of the anticolonial struggle, it creates a "sclerosis" (*DC*, 66). It can lead to the rights of different groups being trampled on and an exaggerated importance being placed on the ethnicity of the leaders. In the name of the "nation," one ethnic or religious group can come to dominate.

The tricky problem is to judge the differences and how to allow them expression. When Fanon speaks of deepening national consciousness into a new humanism, it is precisely this problem he is addressing, because he wants the most democratic and pluralistic culture – where "minorities" and genuine differences are allowed full expression – to emerge. This problem is not worked out, but he claims that individual liberation does not automatically follow as a consequence of national liberation; rather, individual liberation emerges as part of a process: "The liberation of the individual does not follow national liberation. An authentic national liberation exists only to the precise degree to which the individual has irreversibly begun his own liberation" (*AR*, 103).

National culture takes as its point of departure the "fighting culture" developed during the anticolonial period and thus Fanon does not pretend that a national culture is innocent of suppressing those differences that hinder the development of the national cause. Nor does he look uncritically at the indigenous culture that had survived under colonialism. Tribal, racial, and ethnic identifications, often encouraged or even fabricated by colonialism, pose barriers to national and individual self-determination. Instead of uncritically embracing either traditions or modernity as external unifiers, Fanon turns to the revolutionary movement as the source for creating an entirely new context. If national struggle makes possible the development of a social consciousness, then culture is simply "a whole body of efforts made by a people in the sphere of thought to describe, justify, and praise *the action which the people has created itself*," because it "takes its place at the very heart of the struggle for freedom" (*WE*, 233). Dehumanized by colonialism, the native is newly individualized, Fanon argues, by the experience of being part of the struggle for freedom. It is through the activity of self-creation that the social individual comes into being:

> Individual experience, because it is national and because it is a link in the chain of national existence, ceases to be individual, limited, and shrunken . . . during the period of national construction each citizen ought to continue in his real, everyday activity to associate himself with the whole of the nation, to incarnate the continuous dialectical truth of the nation and to will the triumph of man in his completeness here and now. (*WE*, 200)

Far from reflecting an a priori, the dialectic of self-determination of the individual and self-determination of the nation is, in Fanon's view, not something put off for the future but is a constantly developing process. This process is expressed through the individual's experience in building up the nation. Fanon uses the example of building a bridge. He says that if it does not enrich the awareness of those who work on it, then it ought not to be built (*WE*, 200-1). Successfully carrying out a program is by no means the proof of the program's worth or merit. In Fanon's ethos, financial or utilitarian standards of value count for little: human activity must first and foremost enrich human awareness. Fanon's liberatory ideology is a practical matter, it fulfills the task of criticizing other ideologies (colonial and nationalist) and gives meaning to events. This latter process does not come from the intellectual's head but from a back and forth between people and militants in a working group. Liberatory ideology seeks to uncover the mystifications that block the people's self-activity. Fanon's example of the building of a bridge is also a metaphor for the practical matter, of the building of bridges between the organization and the people.

Liberation is an ongoing project. No plan, no leaders, no temporary strategic necessity can take its place: "If we stagnate it is [the people's] responsibility, and if we go forward it is due to them too." The individual's self-understanding becomes inseparable from their quest for liberation. There is also, for Fanon, an important concomitant process between the activity of individual liberation and the release of a people's inherent intelligence which needs further clarification.

If the emphasis on the people's self-creation leaves room for individual self-determination, there still remains the question: what is the place of the intellectual in the discovery of what constitutes the national? In fact, the intellectual's interpretation of the "national" can lead to confusion and obfuscation if it does not take into account a "conception . . . of the future of humanity" (*WE*, 234–5).

It seems at first glance that Fanon assumes as given, or at least as unproblematic, the value of the expertise or knowledge that the intellectual has "snatched" from the West. Nevertheless, we have seen that Fanon does not intend intellectuals to educate in the same fashion as they have been educated; the educator becomes newly educated by challenging preconceived ideas about the backwardness of the masses. It is only in this context that a mutual education can take place.

Fanon introduces the question of political education to criticize how the nationalization of the economy benefited an oligarchical government of privileges. Instead "public business should be the business of the public," carried out on a "democratic basis," with the mass of people taking part in its running. The greatest challenge to Fanon's fundamental humanist belief that "everything can be explained to the people, on the single condition that you really want them to understand" (*WE*, 189) is to ensure that the lines of communication are open, and that new ears are found to listen to the so recently voiceless and dehumanized. The task of political education is not the practical administration of things but enlightenment. It involves a fundamental questioning and rethinking of every aspect of life, beginning "everything all over again" (*WE*, 100). Far from proposing a return to an idyllic past, Fanon is speaking of a thorough reexamination of production and human relations, questioning the environment which has been detrimentally used by the "economic channels created by colonialism." Because its central credo is the self-activity and self-determination of the masses, "political education" must be profoundly democratic, encouraging meetings and discussion where the people are "able to speak, to express themselves, and to put forward new ideas" (*WE*, 195). It requires a new patience on the part of the intellectual, whose "return to the source" is also a turn to an oral culture and history not judged as the past but in the making.

The move toward an engaged intellectual is seen from the shift from the abstractions of the "poet's Africa" to the concrete of revolutionary Africa. Fanon's change in attitude can be seen in the different approaches taken in *Black Skin* and in his Mali notebooks ("This Africa to Come," in *AR*, 177–90). In *Black Skin* he writes that "The discovery of the existence of a Black civilization in the fifteenth century confers no patent of humanity on me. Like it or not, the past can in no way guide me in the present moment" (*BS*, 225). In the midst of his revolutionary reconnoitre of the Southern Front Fanon changes his focus. The issue now is not the meaning of African civilizations for Fanon's own sense of self, but the need to know the histories of the peoples of Africa to work out postcolonial problems: "In Kidal I plunge into some books on the history of the Sudan. I relive, with the intensity that circumstances and the place confer upon them, the old empires of Ghana, of Mali, and Gao, and the impressive Odyssey of the Moroccan troops with the famous Djouder. *Things are not simple*" (*AR*, 185).

Because things are not simple, Fanon does not operate under romantic illusions that there will be an immediate understanding of the most complicated problems. This is why he emphasizes a dialectical process, a deepening spiral rather than a straight line, a working through contradictions rather than a static subject/object identity. Because self-consciousness does not come about all at once, the intellectual's role is to destroy the ideology that characterizes the masses as backward and incapable of governing themselves. Fanon's faith in the ability of the masses to understand everything does not imply a withdrawal of the intellectual and the advocacy of the type of autarkic economy where specialist knowledge and technology is shunned and the regime is based on "miserable resources" (*WE*, 103). Fanon is neither a voluntarist[14] nor an anti-intellectual. Nor is he suggesting that the division between the intellectuals and the masses is bridged by the intellectual performing manual labor. The point is not that the masses' thoughts are more relevant than those of the intellectual, but because of the masses' lack of esteem for their own ideas, the intellectual is crucial in eliciting and explaining their subjugated knowledge. This is what Fanon means when he says that the intellectuals should put themselves "to school with the people."

The intellectual's job is to make the *social* individual's own self-understanding the basis for understanding the world: "Political education is the . . . birth of their intelligence" (*WE*, 197); it is not about applying knowledge, but helps the immanent development of the indigenous reason. In other words, it helps the reason that is born in the decolonization struggle to test itself out, raise itself to truth, and set about learning about the world and acquiring genuine content. By helping reason reflect on its (Manichean) certainty, political education helps develop the truth of the anticolonial struggle. This is the intellectual's main role. "The nation does not exist in a program which has been worked out by revolutionary leaders"; it is created by "the muscles and brains of the citizens" (*WE*, 203, 201). Implicit here is that the intellectual's theoretical work will foster national liberation.

What Type of Organization for the Postcolonial Future?

> For the people, the party is not an authority but an organism through which they as the people exercise the authority and express their will. (Fanon, *The Wretched of the Earth*)

In contradistinction to the formal questions of organization, Fanon was concerned with its nature and the relations of power that it expresses. For Fanon the political organization is a "living party," an *organism* that encourages an exchange of ideas elaborated by the needs of the people. This new type of organization is quite different from the imported Western model. Fanon criticizes the nationalist elite's "fetish of organization" that often takes precedence over "a reasoned study of colonial society" (*WE*, 108), which is of much greater consequence than the existence of a formal organization. The problem, then, is how to give an organizational form to a "reasoned study." Such a study should not be confined to a strategic interpretation of alienated conditions of the moment; it should seek to understand and explain the epoch of decolonization. Where Fanon had previously postulated a "time lag" between the rural masses and the urban nationalists, he now speaks of a different register of time needed to make a reasoned analysis – to take stock and think critically of the situation.

Despite the centrality of the intellectual, Fanon's dialectic of organization does not grant a privileged site to ideas *per se*. In fact, Fanon implies that the intellectual is not necessarily the bearer of the intellect since the *practice of action* itself is the source of a new way of knowing. It is through reflection on such action that unexpected details and new meanings are discovered, and it is through this self-reflected knowledge that the colonized come to be freed from the colonial condition and conditioning. Although the activity of the revolutionary intellectuals makes it possible for the masses to "understand social truths," the development of the indigenous intellect requires constant dialogue.

Fanon presents a number of practical ways for the form of organization to foster indigenous intellect and stymie intellectual elitism. His conception of organization is highly democratic and encourages the free exchange of ideas. In its first appearance during the early stages of revolt, the organization necessarily assumes a centralizing character in order to unify the colonized to counter the tactics of the colonialists, but in the postcolonial period it is desirable for the organization to be "decentralized in the extreme." It is from below "that forces mount up which supply the summit with its dynamic, and make it possible dialectically for it to leap ahead" (*WE*, 198). Whereas the town-based nationalist parties had "show[n] a deep distrust towards the people of the rural areas" (*WE*, 109), the Fanonian organization bends the stick the other way as it avoids the capital "like the plague" and is headquartered, or decentralized into the countryside. Regionalism and tribalism need to be confronted, but Fanon does not believe that they can be tackled from above by a centralized and an urbanized organization which would tend to disregard the real concerns of the people. It is at the local level that the new society is created and the "decentralized despotism"[15] of the colonial legacy confronted.

The problem is that, like colonial forms of governance, old ideas and cultures – along age and gender lines – have been challenged but not completely uprooted. It is a ticklish problem because in many cases these forms have been a bulwark against colonialism during the early period of resistance. In the most practical sense the Manicheanism that exists after liberation can only be addressed with great patience. In part this is often one of the legacies of "late colonial rule" where urban civil society is deracialized but where "despotic" customary rule is kept in place in rural areas. By considering the peasant as the central protagonist of national liberation, Fanon has in part approached the problematic of postcolonial Africa, making land and labor central to the rights of the nation's citizens. It is in the rural areas that the success of national liberation can really be judged by the challenge to "customary rule."

Fanon's call for a breaking down of the distinction between town and country, and for the extreme decentralization of the organization, echoes his belief (albeit undeveloped) that the degenerating communal form might be reinvigorated during the independence struggle and become an element on which a future decentralized state and nation might be based. Fanon understands that, though there is no going back, the democratic polities that existed in many African societies should be regenerated. However, Fanon's fundamental point is to identify the "enlightened action" of the people with the "nation":

> The flag and the palace where the government sits cease to be the symbols of the nation. The nation deserts these brightly-lit, empty shells and takes shelter in the country, where it is given life and dynamic power. The living expression of the nation is the moving consciousness of the whole of the people; it is the coherent, enlightened action of men and women. (*WE*, 204)

On an individual level, Fanon deplores madness as a loss of liberty; on the social level, colonialism has created a form of madness and enforced a loss of liberty. The conclusions to *Black Skin* and *The Wretched* are remarkably similar. The question of human reciprocity that dominates *Black Skin* is approached in *The Wretched* from the perspective of a historicized consciousness, which becomes responsible for its own action. Throughout, Fanon remained committed "to educate man to be actional, preserving in all his relations his respect for the basic values that constitute the human world" (*WE*, 200). Thus the organization must not block this historical and social self-consciousness. The organization, he says, should "not [be] an authority but an organism through which . . . a people exercise their authority and express their will" (*WE*, 185). Fanon argues for a separation of organization and administrative body. The party leaders should not have any administrative powers: "The party should be a direct expression of the masses. The party is not an administration responsible for transmitting government orders . . . we must rid ourselves of the very Western, very bourgeois and therefore contemptuous attitude that the masses are incapable of governing themselves" (*WE*, 187–8).

Once again we return to the proposition that the people can and should govern themselves. This principle battles the "spirit of discouragement" drummed into the colonized during the period of colonialism. It is on this basis that the organization can remain an "incorruptible defender of the masses." The reasoned analysis and rethinking of social conditions and political exigencies must be worked out through a dialogue, and at the same time this working out of what to do immediately and practically must be informed by "an idea of man and the future of humanity" (*WE*, 203). It is the activity from below that makes possible the "dialectical leap," but it depends on a free flow of ideas between the rank and file and the leadership. Each side, on its own "would split apart in incoherence and anarchy."

Fanon's approach to nationalism is dialectical. Nationalism is both an imported European idea and a product of opposition to the colonial regime. As such, it can undergo a dialectical development and be taken over and used against the colonialists. Moreover, for Fanon, a national consciousness, which he argues is not nationalism, signifies the form, not the goal, of postcolonial society. The struggle for independence looks forward but also backward, and part of its goal is to invent a history and a tradition. Fanon's concept of national liberation is an attempt to transcend this Manichean problematic where the backward-looking tendency of nationalism can easily degenerate into racism. It is not possible to return to a precolonial standpoint (often promoted to a separatist and authoritarian nationalism that looks to the past and seeks cultural regeneration),[16] and nor is it desirable to approach the future in mimicry of the West (nationalism$_1$ often unites both these tendencies, with the mimicry of the colonialist administration often also echoing attitudes to the "customary"). The decolonized society has to find its own way. Such self-consciousness provides a form which can open out to other cultures and becomes continental. Fanon is perhaps a perceptive critic of the rhetoric of the "essential African" that cloaks its racist paradigms, and its politics of ethnic cleansing, behind a mask. There is nothing essentially progressive, therefore, about African essentialism.[17] The point was not only to uncover a neocolonialist conspiracy behind the "African" mask, but to highlight the internal problematic of African decolonization.

In Place of a Conclusion

Part of Fanon's dilemma is a result of the important role he reserves for the intellectual, who is potentially the most unstable element in the Fanonian scheme. Yet in helping create a national consciousness through a new cultural politics and in encouraging the masses' self-certainty, intellectuals contribute greatly to stability. They play a central role in either the development or the failure of a new humanism. If a new humanism is to develop and succeed, then the intellectuals themselves must also develop, discarding the universals inculcated through colonial training; their development is both a practical rather than theoretical matter, a physical and a cerebral experience. In the new movement, the liberated voice of the radical intellectual "gives rise to a new rhythm of life and to forgotten muscular tensions, and develops the imagination" (*WE*, 177).

The African movements for freedom opened up a new dialectic and page in history. Today, Fanon's ideas might seem overly idealist, but he was, in fact, a consummate realist. Sadly his predictions about postcolonial Africa have often proved correct: Africa is worse off than it was over 40 years ago. On the other hand, the revolutionary pressures in Africa have not ceased. It is the unfinished nature of decolonization that continues to haunt Africa in this present moment of decomposition. Fanon's conceptualization of development, with its focus on labor (more often female in contemporary Africa), is no more "idealist" than it was 40 years ago. The hard facts of twenty-first century Africa tell a different story. The last 25 years have seen life expectancy fall, the health care and education systems in crisis and food production decline. There is a growing gap between rich and poor. There has been hardly a positive from structural adjustment. Who but the ideologues believe that Africa can now "develop" along capitalist lines? Fanon's prognosis, however incomplete, remains eerily concrete. His point was not merely to foretell the crisis in Africa and the degeneration of the independence movements, but to intervene and affect the process. To tap into the vast reservoir of popular resistance and to try and "put Africa in motion . . . behind revolutionary principles" – that was his self-assignment.

Yet perhaps Fanon's most enduring legacy today is to have formulated a series of problematics rather than answers. Thus when Fanon asks in the middle of *The Wretched*, "Do I exist?" "In reality, who am I?" (*WE*, 250), the question touches both ontological and epistemological issues; the fragmentation of identity as well as the uncertainty of binary concepts that are to be employed to understand the postcolonial social situation. Rather than celebrate their certainty or ambiguity, or back away to a "neutral" standpoint, Fanon engages these categories, understanding that they are products of power. Human freedom remained central to Fanon's dialectic. Humanity is also yes-saying, he says in *Black Skin*, and thus he rejected the idea that the individual is powerless to change reality or to construct a self. But it is never enough to dismiss a way of thought without engaging the social condition that produces it. Fanon's postcolonial imagination is a challenge; an insistence that one confronts the here and now. Rather than a technological solution, his idea of the future Africa rested on the hand and brain of the African. Imagination may seem a sorry answer to the powerful forces of neoliberal globalization that attempt to discipline Africa today, yet Fanon's insistence on bringing "invention into existence" and to imagine a future is in fact a concrete response to the threadbare technical economic authoritarianism of structural adjustment, the grim reaper which continues to haunt the continent.

Notes

See also p. xii for the abbreviations for Fanon's works.

Introduction

1 Homi Bhabha's preface is reprinted in Nigel C. Gibson (ed.), *Rethinking Fanon: The Continuing Legacy* (Amherst: Humanity Books, 1999). Edward W. Said's *Culture and Imperialism* (New York: Knopf, 1993) should be noted here as an important and much more politically engaged reading of Fanon to which I am indebted.

2 See Lewis R. Gordon, *Fanon and the Crisis of European Man* (New York: Routledge, 1995); Ato Sekyi-Otu, *Fanon's Dialectic of Experience* (Cambridge: Harvard University Press, 1996).

3 The title of the US edition of 1965, *Studies in a Dying Culture*, is a little misleading. The book is a study not so much of a dying colonial culture, or *Studies in a Dying Colonialism*, its current title, as a study of the coming alive of a new national Algerian culture, and could be named "Studies in a Fighting Culture." It was originally published in France, *L'An V de la révolution algérienne* – Year 5 of the Algerian revolution – referring to the revolutionary calendar, with the start of the revolution as Year 1. Apart from specific citations from the translation, abbreviated as *DC*, I shall often use the more appropriate title, *L'An V*.

4 Fanon's experience in the Free French army was also metaphysical. He wrote to his parents in April 1945 that he had been wrong to leave Fort-de-France to defend the "obsolete ideal" of French civilization. For the fight against fascism for liberty and equality did not include Blacks.

5 Banania refers to a breakfast drink made from banana flour, cocoa and sugar. The Banania tin carries a picture of a smiling African with the caption "Y'a bon" (an interpretation of the native's slang for "C'est

bon"). Launched in 1917 with a Senegalese soldier spooning Banania into his mouth, the frightening "savage" soldier became a sympathetic figure during the war. Over the years the smiling full figure of a Senegalese militia man sitting on a box had lost his legs and arms, and by 1980 he had become a caricature with his head transformed into the B of Banania. See Jan Nederveen Pieterse, *White on Black: Images of Africa and Blacks in Western Popular Culture* (New Haven: Yale University Press, 1992), pp. 162–3, and www.ucad.fr/pubgb/virt/mp/banania for an assortment of Banania tins.

6   Mustafah Dhada, *Warriors at Work: How Guinea was Really Set Free* (Niwot, Colo.: University Press of Colorado, 1993), p. xii.

7   He was correcting the proofs on his deathbed. For further biographical information, consult David Macey, *Frantz Fanon: A Life* (London: Granta Books, 2000). For a more politically engaged short biography, see Emmanuel Hansen, "Frantz Fanon: Portrait of a Revolutionary," reprinted in Gibson, *Rethinking Fanon*, pp. 49–82.

8   The first use of the term Manichean was connected to Fanon's discussion of Mayotte Capécia in *Black Skin*. He later references "manicheism delirium" in the 1922 work of Maurice Dide and Paul Guiraud, *Psychiatrie du médecin praticien* (*BS*, 183). Whether or not *The Second Sex* (1949) had any influence on Fanon, Simone de Beauvoir had used the term to describe women's position (see *The Second Sex* (New York: Vintage, 1989), p. 451).

9   For example, the character Martin in Voltaire's *Candide*. Martin's cynicism is refreshing after Pangloss's optimism, but it remains as depressingly negative and one-dimensional whatever the situation.

10 Fanon does not dismiss the "Enlightenment" *in toto*, and he uses the term enlightenment in *The Wretched* in the popular sense of educating and shedding light. To speak of "Black enlightenment" is a paradox. Fanon realized this in *Black Skin*; indeed part of that project was to criticize a certain kind of Black enlightening, that is a physical and psychological Whitening.

11 See Achille Mbembe, *On the Postcolony* (Berkeley: University of California Press, 2000). Hegel says that "the Negro is an example of animal man in all his savagery and lawlessness, and if we wish to understand him we must put aside all our European attitudes . . . All that is foreign in man in his immediate existence, and nothing consonant with humanity is to be found in his character" (*Lectures on the Philosophy of World History* (Cambridge: Cambridge University Press, 1975), p. 177).

12 Hegel recognized in the *Encyclopedia of the Philosophical Sciences* that "they" – "the Negroes" – "cannot be denied a capacity for education" and have even formed a state in Haiti on Christian principles (para. 393). It should not be forgotten that Hegel's "master/slave dialectic" was written under the impact of the European enslavement of Africans, the slaves' revolt in Haiti, as well as the French revolution.

13　Such as Algeria, Kenya, and South Africa. Violence remains near the surface in many postcolonial regimes.

14　Freud offers a very different account of object relations than Hegel's concept of reciprocity, though love plays an important role in both (the early "theological" writings of Hegel had also emphasized "love" as the key element of genuine reciprocity). If Fanon's critique of Hegel is that the master/slave dialectic doesn't apply when race is added, then love relations between Whites and Blacks are similarly compromised.

15　"Islam," "North Africa," and "violence." This elective affinity formed the bedrock of colonial theory about Algeria and the "Algerian personality" and still remains powerful today. The categories are far from neutral; they are constructed and contested and have a violent history. Their meaning is not explicit and the categories themselves are often intellectually constraining. The division of Africa by the Sahara often obscures rather than clarifies the historical and social processes and the complex linkages within and between regions.

16　Pierre Bourdieu's critique is reported in James D. Le Sueur, *Uncivil War: Intellectuals and Identity Politics during the Decolonization of Algeria* (Philadelphia: University of Pennsylvania Press, 2001). It is interesting to note that in the medieval period it was the presumed identification of the Black African with the Muslim which fashioned the European image of Black Africans as the impersonation of sin, evil, and inferiority (see I. Hrbek, "Africa in the Context of World History," in E. Elfasi (ed.), *The General History of Africa: Africa from the Seventh to the Eleventh Century* (London: Heinemann, 1988). Only later was a distinction made between the "white moor" and the "blackamoor."

17　See John Ruedy, *Modern Algeria: The Origins and Development of a Nation* (Bloomington: Indiana University Press, 1992), p. 136. In chapter 5, I discuss the different tendencies in the Algerian nationalist movement from 1919 to 1954. Ferhat Abbas represented the assimilationist Fédération des Élus Indigènes.

18　The Islamic Reform Movement under Ben Badis was the first to say that Algerians were a distinct nation.

19　The most radical and nationalist of the Algerian opposition was the Étoile Nord-Africaine, founded in France with Communist Party support in 1926, with Messali Hadj as General Secretary.

20　I am using inverted commas around the term to indicate my awareness of its problematical character. Scholars have become critical of the term, stressing both its invented character and the ways in which tradition, rather than being static, changes. Nevertheless, such processes depend on autonomy. In the context of the extreme violence of colonial Algeria, one of Fanon's points is that the native's indigenous culture has been broken, becoming rigid and inert (to use Fanon's language). "[T]raditions need autonomy," writes Jan Vansina. "The peoples who carry them must have the power of self-determination. A tradition is maimed when autonomy is lost. Given its capacity to accept, reject, or modify innovation, a tradition will not be over-whelmed by another major tradition as long as its carriers still retain enough liberty of choice" (*Paths in the Rainforests: Toward a History of Political Tradition in Equatorial Africa* (Madison: University of Wisconsin Press, 1990), p. 259). Thus, when considering "tradition" in Fanon's writing we must bear in mind that it is the destruction of "liberty of choice" that grounds his analysis.

21 Jack Woodis, *Four Revolutionary Theories* (New York: International Press, 1974).

22 Christopher Miller, "Ethnicity and Ethics," *South Atlantic Quarterly*, 87, no. 1 (1989).

23 Marie-Aimée Helie-Lucas, "Women, Nationalism and Religion in the Algerian Liberation Struggle," in Gibson, *Rethinking Fanon*.

24 For example, Mervat Hatem, "Toward the Development of Post-Islamic and Post-Nationalist Feminist Discourses in the Middle East," in Judith E. Tucker (ed.), *Arab Women: Old Boundaries, New Frontiers* (Bloomington: Indiana University Press, 1993).

25 See the discussion in Irene Gendzier, *Frantz Fanon: A Critical Study* (New York: Grove Press, 1973), pp. 231–60.

26 Both these positions are referenced by Le Sueur who makes the accu-sation that "Fanon was without question one of the intellectuals who helped ensure the perpetuation of violence in the postcolonial era" (*Uncivil War*, p. 293).

27 For example, Mohammed Harbi, an activist in and archivist of the Algerian revolution, should not be considered a neutral source. Yet he is very often cited uncritically and used against Fanon as if the understanding of events by participants were not also contested and political.

28 Skinner's essay "Meaning and Understanding in the History of Ideas" is reprinted in James Tully (ed.), *Meaning and Context: Quentin Skinner and his Critics* (Cambridge: Polity, 1988); see also Skinner's introduc-tion to Skinner (ed.), *The Return of Grand Theory in the Human Sciences* (Cambridge: Cambridge University Press, 1985).

29 John Keane, "More Theses on the Philosophy of History," in Tully, *Meaning and Context*, p. 204.

30 This can be seen in a discussion on Fanon and Islamic fundamental-ism which has been especially important over the past 20 years and represents, in some part, the historic failure of the nationalist project in the postcolonial period. It is a failure that is both ideological and practical, which returns us to the period of decolonization and to Fanon's contributions.

Fanon said little directly about Islam, but he understood the retro-grade features of any fundamentalism as a part of what he called the "lack" of a liberatory ideology in Africa's decolonization movements. The cultural reformation of Islam was taking place in the cities that had always been its centers. And though Fanon repeated the FLN's criticism of the collaboration of the rural Sufi brotherhoods with the colonial regime, and went as far as to dismiss traditional practice, it did not mean he supported claims to orthodoxy. Fanon's critique was quite different. Those claiming Islamic orthodoxy viewed the fiercely independent rural areas, where Islam coexisted with local beliefs and practices which included women working on the land without being veiled, as heretical. Fanon was critical of the collaboration of the local marabouts with colonialism, but whereas the Koran had little positive to say about the peasantry, he proclaimed it revolutionary because it had resisted colonial intrusion. The problem was how to organize this spontaneously anticolonial and independent people into a social and national movement.

31 It was international in a very narrow sense, following the old colonial routes to the Western metropoles. Fanon argues that this bourgeois "cosmopolitan mold" of the national middle class is a result of the easiness of getting rich by becoming a "comprador" caste.

32 See Nigel Gibson, "Ideology, Political Education and South Africa's Transition from Apartheid," in Stephen N. Ndegwa (ed.), *A Decade of Democracy in Africa* (Leiden: Brill, 2001).

33 One recurring criticism is Fanon's apparent praise of violence as psychologically liberating. Fanon's opening chapter of *The Wretched*, "Concerning Violence," has been controversial ever since its publication and continues to be a preoccupation today. For example, see "The Doctor Prescribed Violence," Adam Shatz's review in *New York Times* book review section, Sept. 2, 2001.

Chapter 1   The Racial Gaze: Black Slave, White Master

1 Thinking was dividing into two irreconcilable camps, "Everything was classified in Manichean terms," opines the historian Tony Judt. "Communists/capitalists, Soviet Union/United States, right/wrong, good/evil, them/us . . . It was once again Sartre who gave this idea its most rarified expression. Hell being other people" (Judt, *Past Imperfect: French Intellectuals, 1944–1956* (Berkeley: University of California Press, 1992), p. 54).

2 The first few issues contained articles by Jean-Paul Sartre, Simone de Beauvoir, Richard Wright, Raymond Aron, Maurice Merleau-Ponty, Claude Lefort and Jean Genet. Hyppolite's translation of Hegel's *Phenomenology of Spirit* appeared soon after the war, and Heidegger's critique of Sartrean existentialism in his "Letter on Humanism" in 1948.

3 Edited by Alioune Diop and with writings by Gwendolyn Brooks, Albert Camus, David Diop, Michel Leiris, Jacques Rabémananjara, Jacques Roumain, Abdoulaye Sadji, Jean-Paul Sartre, Leopold

Senghor, and Richard Wright in the first two issues. "Thanks to Alioune Diop's magazine," writes Fanon, "I have been able to coordinate the psychological motivations that govern men of color" (*BS*, 53).

4 The first issue emphasized this presence in the titles of articles, "Présence noire" by Sartre and "Présence africaine" by Pierre Naville.

5 Bernard Mouralis, "Présence Africaine: Geography of an Ideology," in V. Y. Mudimbe (ed.), *The Surreptitious Speech: Présence Africaine and the Politics of Otherness* (Chicago: University of Chicago Press, 1992), p. 4.

6 His use of the authorial "I" should be considered akin to that employed by Sartre in *Being and Nothingness* (1943; New York: Washington Square Books, 1966) or Merleau-Ponty's *Phenomenology of Perception* (1945; London: Routledge, 1962).

7 Fanon had left Martinique for Paris in 1947, but had quickly quit the capital for Lyon. He had first enrolled in dentistry school in Paris, thinking it would provide a solid professional career, but after three weeks of introductory courses he left abruptly, complaining there were too many "niggers" in Paris (that is Blacks with "white masks – Martinican évolués who spoke only French and believed they were proportionately Whiter and more civilized the more fluent their French). Lyon, without a psychoanalytic institute, was a very different kind of place than Paris. His arrival in Lyon coincided with a series of militant strikes as well as celebrations of the hundredth anniversary of the *Communist Manifesto*. According to Peter Geismar, Fanon attended worker and Trotskyist meetings (Geismar, *Frantz Fanon* (New York: Grove Press, 1969)).

8 An interesting tension is evident in the dialectic of *Black Skin* between the decultured but "civilized" Martinican and the uncivilized but cultured Arab, Senegalese, or Malagasy in the sense that they have a written culture, poetry and an art that can be *translated* into French.

9 Jean-Paul Sartre, *The Anti-Semite and the Jew*, trans. G. Becker (New York: Schocken Books, 1976), p. 108.

10 Ibid., p. 79.

11 Ibid., p. 135.

12 Steve Biko spoke in similar terms in *I Write What I Like* (London: Heinemann, 1978): "Does this mean I am against integration? If by integration you understand a breakthrough into White society by Blacks, an assimilation and acceptance of Blacks into an already established set of norms and code of behavior set up by and maintained by Whites, then YES I am against it" (pp. 38–9).

13 Ibid., p. 35.

14 A typical expression is that "they" should assimilate and stop behaving like Jews.

15 Sartre, *The Anti-Semite and the Jew*, p. 135.

16 Ibid., pp. 137, 134.

17 Ibid., p. 137.

18 The Antilles becomes paradigmatic of Europe's colonies and a certain type of postcolonial situation. In a repressive settler society, like Algeria, he finds how this aggression is directed back onto the community.

19 Sartre writes, "Recall the portrait of the philosopher that Plato sketches in the Phaedro: how the awakening to reason is for him the death of the body . . . this is the sort of disincarnation that certain Jews seek. The best way to feel oneself no longer a Jew is to reason" (Sartre, *The Anti-Semite and the Jew*, p. 111).

20 Sander Gilman, "Black Bodies, White Bodies: Toward an Iconography of Female Sexuality in Late Nineteenth-Century Art, Medicine and Literature," in Henry L. Gates Jr (ed.), *"Race," Writing and Difference* (Chicago: University of Chicago Press, 1986).

21 Ibid., p. 167.

22 The relationship with the Jew is caricatured in some nineteenth-century illustrations as taking on Black African characteristics. This is to say nothing about the possibility of African Jews, see "DNA Backs Tribe's Tradition of Early Descent from the Jews," *New York Times*, May 9, 1999.

23 G. W. F. Hegel, *Lectures on the Philosophy of World History* (Cambridge: Cambridge University Press, 1975), p. 177.

24 Achille Mbembe, *On the Postcolony* (Berkeley: University of California Press, 2000), p. 184.

25 As Karen Blixen puts it: "What I have learned from the game of the country is as useful to me in my dealings with the native people" (Isak Dinesen, *Out of Africa* (New York: Random House, 1972), p. 23).

26 See Gilman, "Black Bodies, White Bodies."

27 Whereas the retranslation of "L'expérience vécue du Noir" emphasizes the existential lived experience, Charles Lam Markmann's translation, "The Fact of Blackness," caught the facticity of Blackness both as a social and historical construction and as a constructed fact that emphasizes not "the Black" *qua* being but Blackness *qua* existence, as a lived fact. What Markmann's translation signals (which could be lost in a mere accounting of lived experiences) is Fanon's concern to create a new fact and a new way of life. Such a conceptualization is attained by thinking of lived experience not only as a social construct reflecting reality, but also dialectically (a subject/object in Merleau-Ponty's terms, of the body in the world, of touching and being touched, of seeing and doing (*Phenomenology of Perception*, pp. 94–5)) embodying tensions and contradictions that necessitate struggles to shape new realities.

28 Merleau-Ponty, *Phenomenology of Perception*, pp. 99–100.

29 Ibid., p. 143. Merleau-Ponty argues that sensory organs can have the same ontological status as instruments, so that the prosthetic becomes an extension of the body. My four year old insisted that he could see through his prosthetic "painted eye." With reality, the social world, the perception is adjusted toward what we would include as "normal."

30 Ibid., p. 101.

31 Ibid.

32 Namely an awareness of the other's awareness of my self, the third term that mediates and makes concrete "in-itself" and "for itself."

33 Merleau-Ponty, *Phenomenology of Perception*, p. 122.

34 Sartre, *Being and Nothingness*, p. 555.

35 See Lewis R. Gordon, *Bad Faith and Anti-Black Racism* (Atlantic Highlands: Humanities Press, 1995).

36 Fanon (following Kojève) uses "master/slave" rather than the more correct "Lord and Servant" (for a discussion of the terms see Michael Hoffheimer, "Translating *Knechtschaft*," *Owl of Minerva*, 32, no. 2 (Spring 2001)). However, when Fanon speaks of the Black slave he is not primarily thinking of the plantation slave but the mental condition of the Black in post-emancipation Martinique.

37 Hegel had written in the section of the *Phenomenology*, "Absolute Freedom and Terror," that "when in revolt it [self-consciousness] adopts a language of its own" (G. W. F. Hegel, *Phenomenology of Spirit*, trans. A. V. Miller (Oxford: Oxford University Press, 1971), para. 520). In *The Wretched* this idea of "a language of its own" is seen in the form of the struggle itself which suggests new social relations (*WE*, 47).

38 Edward W. Said has pointed to the importance of reciprocity in Fanon's "rescription" of Hegel's dialectic, arguing that in *The Wretched* Fanon attempts to create "a non-adversarial community of awareness and anti-imperialism" binding together "the European as well as the native" (*Culture and Imperialism* (New York: Knopf, 1993)), pp. 210, 274; also see Said, "Traveling Theory Reconsidered," in Nigel C. Gibson (ed.), *Rethinking Fanon* (Amherst: Humanity Books, 1999).

39 H. S. Harris notes of Hegel that "there is nothing in his logical theory to warrant the belief that the motion of consciousness must always be progressive" (*Hegel: Phenomenology and System* (Indianapolis: Hackett, 1996), p. 107). Sartre formulated the "progressive-regressive method" as a fundamental heuristic in *Search for a Method* (1958; trans. Hazel Barnes (New York: Vintage, 1968)). In contrast to Hegel and Sartre, however, Fanon is arguing that the regressive method is the only way out of the impasse in the dialectic. That is, the only move is backward.

40 Jürgen Habermas, *The Philosophical Discourses of Modernity* (Cambridge, Mass.: MIT Press, 1987), p. 7.

41 See Lou Turner, "On the Difference of the Hegelian and Fanonian Dialectic of Lordship and Bondage," in Lewis R. Gordon, T. Denean Sharpley-Whiting, and Renée White (eds), *Fanon: A Critical Reader* (Oxford: Blackwell, 1996).

42 Cf. Sartre, *Being and Nothingness*, pp. 252–302.

43 G. W. F. Hegel, *Philosophy of Mind* (Oxford: Oxford University Press, 1971), p. 177.

44 "The Kojève/Strauss Correspondence," in Leo Strauss, *On Tyranny* (New York: Free Press, 1991), pp. 142–3.

45 Alexandre Kojève, *Introduction to the Reading of Hegel*, ed. Allan Bloom (New York: Basic Books, 1969), pp. 46–7.

46 J. M. Bernstein, "From Self Consciousness to Community," in Z. A. Pelczynski (ed.), *The State and Civil Society: Studies in Hegel's Political Philosophy* (Cambridge: Cambridge University Press, 1984), p. 20.

47 The phrase comes from G. A. Kelly's discussion of Raya Dunayevskaya's *Philosophy and Revolution* in *Hegel's Retreat from Eleusis* (Princeton: Princeton University Press, 1978), p. 239.

48 G. A. Kelly, "Notes on Hegel's 'Lordship and Bondage,'" in Alasdair MacIntyre (ed.), *Hegel: A Collection of Critical Essays* (Garden City: Anchor Press, 1972), p. 213.

49 Hegel, *Phenomenology of Spirit*, para. 196.

50 Specifically, Fanon speaks of the "French" Black. He argues that the "American Black is cast in a different play. In the United States, the Black battles and is battled" (*BS*, 221).

51 Hegel, *Phenomenology of Spirit*, para. 187.

52 Ibid., para. 196. This attitude might be applicable to the Black who has not experienced the "anguish of liberty" but has instead donned a White mask; but it has little in common with the attitude to freedom found in "freedom and self-consciousness," which is more akin to negritude.

53 Kojève, *Introduction to the Reading of Hegel*, p. 55.

54 Hegel, *Phenomenology of Spirit*, paras 197, 193.

55 Ibid., para. 231.

56 Ibid., para. 192.

Chapter 2   Psychoanalysis and the Black's Inferiority Complex

1 Paulette Nardal, "The Awakening of Race Consciousness," translation of "Éveil de la conscience de race," *La Revue du Monde Noir*, no. 6 (1932), in Robert Bernasconi (ed.), *Race* (Oxford: Blackwell, 2001), p. 108. For a diagnosis of the time, see Diedrich Westermann, *The African Today* (London: Oxford University Press, 1934).

2 The exaggerated importance of Lacan in Fanon's work has resulted in the project of fitting Fanon into a Lacanian frame. Ironically, Fanon is supposed to be employing Lacanian concepts that were only fully worked out *after* he had written *Black Skin*. Lacan's influence on *Black Skin* is restricted to before Lacan's 1953 "return to Freud."

Fanon's only citation is to Lacan's 1938 article "La Famille. Le complèxe, facteur concret de la psychologie familiale" (The family: the complex, a concrete factor in familial psychology) in *Encyclopédie française*, vol. 8, sec. 40 (La vie mentale) ed. A. de Mounzie (Paris: Société de gestion de l'Encyclopédie française). Fanon does not cite the "mirror stage." It should be noted that Lacan refers to the mirror stage in "La Famille" but that his 1936 paper on the mirror stage was indexed (as the Looking-Glass Phase) but was not published in the

International Journal of Psychoanalysis. The more widely known and revised version of the paper was delivered in Zurich in 1949 and is published in *Écrits: A Selection* (New York: Norton, 1977).

   Lacan brings us back to a discussion of Hegel. The "mirror stage" is influenced by Lacan's involvement in Kojève's lectures on Hegel. In 1936 Kojève and Lacan had decided to collaborate on a project entitled "Hegel and Freud: Attempt at a Comparative Interpretation." The project, however, did not get off the ground. David Macey notes that to reread Kojève after reading Lacan is "to experience the shock of recognition, a truly uncanny sensation of déjà vu" (*Lacan in Context* (London: Verso, 1988)). The Kojèvean–Hegel reference is a "central element" in Lacan's article "La Famille" where Lacan attributes to Hegel the notion that "the individual who does not struggle for recognition will never become a personality before he dies." The idea is central to Fanon's engagement with Hegel in *Black Skin* where the individual who has not staked his life, quoting Hegel, "has not attained the truth of recognition as an independent self-consciousness" (*BS*, 219). While Fanon finds in reworking Hegel's dialectic of reciprocity the possibility of "the open door of every consciousness," Lacan, on the other hand, credits Hegel with providing an "iron law for our time": "the ultimate theory of the proper function of aggressivity." ("Aggressivity in Psychoanalysis" (1948), in *Écrits*, p. 26). Following Kojève he adds, "From the conflict of Master and Slave he deduced *the entire* subjective and objective process of our history." While Fanon might agree that true freedom stemmed from a consciousness of the lack of freedom, he was unhappy to leave it as such. *Black Skin* is a mirror, Fanon claims, not a mirror stage; the apparent fragmentary commentary has a "progressive infrastructure" under the imprimatur of the need for social change.

3 Hussein A. Bulhan, *Frantz Fanon and the Psychology of Oppression* (New York: Plenum Press, 1985), p. 73.

4 Alfred Adler's "Feeling of Inferiority and the Striving for Recognition" seems to have had a particularly important impact (in Adler, *Understanding Human Nature* (New York: Fawcett, 1956)).

5 On watching a documentary film on Africa in the Antilles the Martinican laughs, but watching the film in France the Martinican is petrified: "There he had no more hope of flight: He is at once Martinican, Bushman, and Zulu" (see *BS*, 152 n15). The Antillean in France experiences a profound psychological shock. The inner structure of "his world" – formed by the internalization of Europe's collective unconscious – is uncoupled and then turns into a void.

6 Freud's theory of human civilization is based on a notion of development from primitive society. The development of the race is recapitulated in the development of the individual. The subtitle of *Totem and Taboo* "Some Points of Agreement between the Mental Lives of Savages and Neurotics" not only prefigures colonial psychology of the

interwar years, but also expresses the idea of sexual perversity among "savages," the loss of which is the cost of civilization.

7   The book won the Grand Prize for Antillean Literature in 1948 (the jury was made up of 13 French men!). See T. Denean Sharpley-Whiting, *Frantz Fanon: Conflicts and Feminisms* (Lanham: Rowman and Littlefield, 1998), ch. 2.

8   This formulation is repeated in *The Wretched*, stretching the Marxian idea of base and superstructure: "You are rich because you are white, you are white because you are rich" (*WE*, 40).

9   Saint-Louis, an island in the Senegal river, boasted a large population of Europeans in the eighteenth century. During this period Wolof and Lebou women had considerable autonomy as traders with European men, which resulted in cohabitation and "mulatto" offspring.

10 This "reactional phenomenon" is not unique to Blacks. Fanon quotes Sartre's argument from *The Anti-Semite and the Jew* (*BS*, 182) that in order to react against anti-Semitism, the Jew becomes an anti-Semite.

11 Octave Mannoni, *Prospero and Caliban: The Psychology of Colonization*, trans. from *Psychologie de la colonisation* by Pamela Powesland (Ann Arbor: University of Michigan Press, 1999).

12 See Elisabeth Roudinesco, *Jacques Lacan and Company: A History of Psychoanalysis in France 1925–1985* (Chicago: University of Chicago Press, 1990), p. 234.

13 Mannoni, *Prospero and Caliban*, pp. 5, 34.

14 Ibid., p. 6.

15 Mannoni wasn't the only one for whom African colonial experiences were therapeutic. In Lord Lugard's case it was a failed love affair that put his African colonial adventure into motion. He dropped out of the army (the best place for people like him, he had thought) and tried to snuff out his burning desire by becoming a fireman. Seeing Zanzibar on a map he decided instead on that direction. Though denied a chance to join the Italian campaign to invade Ethiopia, he was lucky enough to come across Rider Haggard's *The Witch's Head*. The hero who, "crossed in love," seeks adventure in central Africa spoke directly to Lugard. Reading the book on the boat to Zanzibar while he felt he was going mad, Lugard gave up religion and "struggled with self-destruction," writes his biographer Margery Perham: "still in a pathological mental state Lugard reached the scene of his first African adventure" (Perham, *Lugard* (London: Collins, 1960), p. 105). From Mannoni's point of view, Lugard would be a marvelous example of a type of inferiority complex.

16 Mannoni, *Prospero and Caliban*, pp. 86, 85.

17 Ibid., pp. 22, 34.

18 See ibid., p. 111 n1.

19 Ibid., p. 122.

20 Maurice Bloch, Introduction to ibid., p. vii.

21 Mannoni, *Prospero and Caliban*, p. 135.

22 Bloch insists that Mannoni's belief that the revolt followed a liberal-ization of French policy is "at best a gross oversimplification and, at worst, a self-serving dissimulation of the situation, one much encour-aged by the French at the time" (Introduction to ibid.).

23 Mannoni, *Prospero and Caliban*, p. 136.

24 In order for the colonialists to regain their feeling of superiority, 100,000 Malagasies were slaughtered. In the penultimate chapter of his book, titled, "What Is To Be Done," Mannoni suggests the solution to the problem lies in the proper education of the colonial administra-tion. Mannoni proposed the development of a new enlightened colonial administrator, which depended on the inclusion of modern, perhaps Mannonian, psychology in their education.

25 Mannoni, *Prospero and Caliban*, pp. 87–8.

26 Ibid., p. 204.

27 Ibid., p. 32.

28 See ibid., p. 100, and *BS*, 107.

29 The nationalist leadership said that they had tried to prevent the upris-ing, though the French hardly believed them. Rabémananjara received an amnesty in 1960 and became a minister in the Madagascan gov-ernment. Despite his early radical politics, he became a conservative politician always willing to accommodate France, and he served as an architect for a dialogue with apartheid South Africa. This accommo-dation with France over Algeria was noted by Fanon in *The Wretched* when Rabémananjara was still perceived as a radical (see *WE*, 235).

30 Mannoni, "Epilogue to Part I: Dreams," in *Prospero and Caliban*, pp. 89–93.

31 Ibid., p. 89.

32 Mannoni, *Prospero and Caliban*, p. 70.

Chapter 3   Negritude and the Descent into a "Real Hell"

1 Quoted by Lilyan Kesteloot, *Black Writers in French: A Literary History of Negritude* (Philadelphia: Temple University Press, 1974), p. 53.

2 The term was invented by Césaire in 1935. Earlier, the Nardal sisters had spoken of a "Negro humanism" and had been part of the short-lived, radical *Review of the Black World* (1931–2). Césaire first uses the term "negritude" in *Cahier d'un retour au pays natal* (*Notebook of a Return to the Native Land*) when he speaks of Haiti standing up and believing in its humanity. The term is based on the derogatory "nègre"; a modern-day equivalent might be "niggas with attitude."

3 Césaire, Senghor and Damas were born within six years of each other (between 1906 and 1913) and in three different French colonies (Martinique, Senegal, and French Guinea). Each became a political actor, and after World War Two all three were elected to the National

Constituent Assembly as deputies, from Martinique, Senegal, and French Guinea respectively.

4 Damas, brought up to think of himself as a white Frenchman, published his first book of poems, *Pigments*, in 1937.

5 The commonality could be questioned: color was common only in as far as it was considered "non-White," the colonial background only in as far as it was French. Yet it was precisely from this negative commonality that negritude derived its power and its limitations.

6 Quoted in Janet G. Vaillant, *Black, French, and African: A Life of Leopold Sedar Senghor* (Cambridge: Harvard University Press, 1990), p. 97.

7 "Interview with René Depestre" (1967), in Aimé Césaire, *Discourse on Colonialism* (New York: Monthly Review Press, 1972), p. 67.

8 Kesteloot argues that "for the creators of [the wartime Martinican magazine] *Tropiques*, the word surrealism was synonymous with revolution; if they preferred the former, it was not only because of political censorship, but because they wanted to show that it referred not merely to social reform but to a more radical change aimed at the very depths of individual awareness" (*Black Writers*, p. 263).

9 Quoted in ibid., p. 257.

10 Fanon notes that under Vichy, racist French sailors were stationed in Martinique, see *Toward the African Revolution: Political Writings* (*AR*, 23).

11 René Ménil, "L'Action foudroyante," quoted in Kesteloot, *Black Writers*, p. 259.

12 Quoted in Kesteloot, *Black Writers*, p. 261.

13 Peter Geismar argues that rum was the opiate of the masses, who were "continually appeased by the liberal distribution of the territory's one important manufactured product" (*Frantz Fanon* (New York: Grove Press, 1969), p. 20).

14 The metaphors of islandness, which operates as a continuing theme at different levels throughout the poem, and of the diaspora (the transplanted slaves from Africa) are also elements which figure with different emphases in Césaire's negritude. Negritude itself is, to employ Hegel, "an island of safety for the spirit."

15 Aimé Césaire, *Return to my Native Land*, bilingual edn, trans. Émile Snyder (Paris: Présence Africaine, 1971), p. 64. A more recent bilingual edition is Aimé Césaire, *Notebook of a Return to my Native Land*, trans. Mireille Rosello with Anne Pritchard (Newcastle upon Tyne: Bloodaxe Books, 1995). Beneath Martinique lurks the illusory, never to be retrieved, Mother Africa. Césaire's notion of the "future" is not, in fact, rooted in Africa but in a "new humanism" – at the "rendezvous of victory." Despite *Return*'s rhetoric of solidarity with Africa, Césaire remains cocooned in his Islandness.

16 Ibid., p. 66.

17 "Interview with René Depestre," p. 74.

18 Césaire, *Return to my Native Land*, p. 33.

19 Ibid., p. 103.

20 Ibid., p. 73. "Que l'arbre tire les marrons du feu" can be translated as "plucking the chestnuts from the fire." However, "marron" can also mean a fugitive Black slave, a maroon. Césaire coined the neologism "marronner" as a command to the slave to escape. See A. James Arnold, *Modernism and Negritude* (Cambridge: Harvard University Press, 1981), pp. 148–9.

21 Fanon imitates this "supposed irrationality" in *Black Skin*: "since no agreement was possible on the level of reason, I threw myself back toward unreason."

22 Césaire, *Return to my Native Land*, p. 74.

23 Ibid., p. 70.

24 Clayton Eshleman and Annette Smith, Introduction to *Aimé Césaire: The Collected Poetry* (Berkeley: University of California Press, 1985), p. 13.

25 Arnold, *Modernism and Negritude*, p. 151. Fanon is critical of Césaire's "African period" in his 1955 essay "West Indians and Africans": "the West Indian, after the great white error, is now living in the great Black mirage" (*AR*, 27).

26 "No, we've never been amazons of the King of Dahomey, nor Princes of Ghana with eight hundred camels," writes Césaire, directing us instead to the contemporary working-class Black reality: "I may as well confess that we were at all times pretty mediocre dishwashers, shoeblacks without ambition, at best conscientious sorcerers and the only unquestionable record that we broke was that of endurance under the cat-o-nine-tails" (Césaire, *Return to my Native Land*, p. 97).

27 Arnold, *Modernism and Negritude*, p. 158.

28 Mazisi Kunene, Introduction to Césaire, *Return to my Native Land* (London: Penguin, 1969), p. 22.

29 Césaire, *Return to my Native Land*, bilingual edn, pp. 147–8.

30 Ibid., p. 166.

31 Arnold, *Modernism and Negritude*, p. 168.

32 Césaire, *Return to my Native Land*, p. 85.

33 See S. Okechukwu Mezu, *The Poetry of Léopold Senghor* (Rutherford, N.J.: Fairleigh Dickinson University Press, 1973), p. 87.

34 See Vaillant, *Black, French, and African*, p. 263. Senghor attended Catholic elementary school and wanted to become a priest. He entered a seminary in Dakar but was told he had no vocation. Later he became President of a predominantly Muslim country, Senegal.

35 Vaillant, *Black, French, and African*, p. 244.

36 Senghor, "Planification and Moral Tension," quoted in Irving Markovitz, *L. S. Senghor* (New York: Atheneum, 1969), p. 71.

37 Paulin Hountondji, *African Philosophy* (London: Hutchinson, 1983), pp. 159–60.

38 David Caute, *Frantz Fanon* (New York: Viking, 1970), p. 62; *DC*, 139.

39 Leopold Senghor, "Problematics of Negritude," quoted in Margaret Melady, *Leopold Sedar Senghor: Rhythm and Reconciliation* (South Orange: Seton Hall University Press, 1971), p. 27.

40 Jean-Paul Sartre, *Black Orpheus*, trans. S. W. Allen (Paris: Présence Africaine, 1965). (An alternative translation of the essay appears in R. Bernasconi (ed.), *Race* (Oxford: Blackwell, 2001).)

41 L. S. Senghor, *Anthologie de la nouvelle poésie nègre et malagache de langue française* (Paris: Presses Universitaires de France, 1948); Sartre, *Black Orpheus*, pp. 30–1.

42 *Black Orpheus*, pp. 42–3.

43 Ibid., p. 39.

44 Ibid., p. 41.

45 Sartre comments in an aside about the contempt the White worker has for the Black. But this insight is not developed (cf. ibid., p.16), and neither is a moment when Sartre wonders what will happen to Black consciousness, but quickly adds, "it does not matter" (ibid., pp. 64–5). It doesn't matter because race is deemed particular and subjective whereas class is objective and universal. As Clayton Eshleman and Annette Smith put it, the Black is to enact a "sacrificial ritual." Black destiny is to suffer for the world and for the "sins of the white race" (Eshleman and Smith, Introduction to *Aimé Césaire*, p. 7).

46 Sartre, *Black Orpheus*, pp. 44–5.

47 Ibid., p. 45.

48 Ibid., pp. 16–17.

49 Ibid., pp. 56–7.

50 Ibid., pp. 59–60.

51 Ibid., pp. 60, 62.

52 Jean-Paul Sartre, *Being and Nothingness* (1943; New York: Washington Square Books, 1966), p. 243.

53 Ibid.

54 On the relationship of negritude and modernity see Arnold, *Modernism and Negritude*.

55 See G. W. F. Hegel, *Phenomenology of Spirit*, trans. A. V. Miller (Oxford: Oxford University Press, 1971), para. 173.

56 Ibid., para. 193.

57 Ibid., para. 232.

58 Jean Hyppolite, *Genesis and Structure of Hegel's Phenomenology of Spirit* (Evanston: Northwestern University Press, 1974), p. 229.

59 Focusing for the moment on the *attitude* to freedom, Fanon draws implicit parallels between Black consciousness and what Hegel calls the Skeptical consciousness which follows the dialectic of Lordship and Bondage. The problem with this attitude to freedom is that the slave finds a sort of freedom "within the sphere of bondage," and though the slave appears to rise above both Lordship and Bondage, the social conditions remain just as they were. It is skeptical about everything except itself. The pitfall of this introverted type of consciousness, however, is that it fails to recognize how consciousness itself is also determined by those external fluctuating realities. Such

self-centeredness can lead to complacency, to the "isle of repose," as in Hegel's "Beautiful Soul."

60 "Even the tom-toms will have learned the language of the Internationale / For we have chosen our day / The day of the dirty niggers / Of the dirty Indians / Of the dirty Malays / Of the dirty Jews / Of the dirty Proletarians / And we rise up / All the wretched of the earth" (Jacques Roumain, "Sales Nègres," quoted by David Macey, *Frantz Fanon: A Life* (London: Granta Books, 2000), p. 178.

61 Jock McCulloch, *Black Soul, White Artifact* (Cambridge: Cambridge University Press, 1983), p. 53.

62 One way of expressing the different aspects of negativity in *Black Skin* and in *The Wretched* is to consider Fanon's "reading" of Césaire's *Les Armes miraculeuses*. In *The Wretched* Fanon interprets the passage literally as an example of the enlightening potential of violence to which Césaire gives "prophetic significance" (*WE*, 86). In *Black Skin*, Fanon views violence metaphorically as part of the development of Black consciousness. The self-discovery and development of the sense of one's own identity necessitated laying bare and killing the white man *within*. It is, using Césaire's words, an "internal revolution" that creates the "leap" in self-consciousness so that one emerges from the "black hole" to shake the pillars of the world (*BS*, 198–9). In *The Wretched* it is an "external" revolution.

63 Suzanne Césaire, "1943: le surréalisme et nous," *Tropiques II* (Paris: Éditions Jean Michel Place, 1978).

64 Even if the colonial administrator differentiates the degree of civilization of the Arab and the Kabyle in Algeria, or the Sudanese, the Masai and the Kikuyu in Kenya, all are in need of White governance.

65 Hegel, *Phenomenology of Spirit*, paras. 195–6.

Chapter 4 Becoming Algerian

1 John Ruedy, *Modern Algeria: The Origins and Development of a Nation* (Bloomington: Indiana University Press, 1992), p. 79.

2 Passed as a temporary security measure in the 1870s, the Code de l'Indigénat made illegal such offenses as speaking disrespectfully to or about a French official, defaming the Republic, and travelling without a permit. In practice the Algerian courts were presided over by Europeans and in the countryside by local caïds appointed by the administration.

3 See Dr Eugène Boudichon, *Considérations sur l'Algérie* (Paris: Comptoir Central de la Librairie, 1845). Boudichon suggested that "noncivilizable Arabs" be eliminated.

4 Lévy-Bruhl's generalizations had a powerful influence on intellectuals in the interwar period, including psychologists, and theorists of "Bantu philosophy" and negritude, as well as the Algiers school.

5   A. Porot, "Notes de psychiatrie Musulmane," *Annales Médico-Psychologiques*, 1 (1918), pp. 377–84.
6   J. C. Carothers, "Frontal Lobe Function and the African," *Journal of Mental Science*, 97 (1951), pp. 12–47. See *The African Mind in Health and Disease: A Study in Ethnopsychiatry*, sponsored by the World Health Organization (1953). For a discussion of Carothers see Jock McCulloch, *Colonial Psychiatry and the African Mind* (Cambridge: Cambridge University Press, 1995).
    At the first Congress of Black Writers and Artists in Paris in 1956 (*AR*, 31–44), Fanon mentioned how Carothers's " 'scientific argument' in support of a physiological lobotomy of the Black African", is not simply a relapse to an early vulgar racism but is analogous to the new culturalist stage of racism. In the context of the objective "destructuration" of the colonized, there is an appeal to a "less crude, more subtle, more 'cultivated' direction" that appeals to "democratic and humane" values. In other words, the very success of the civilizing mission was the cultivation of an urban colonized elite who are the object of inferiority complexes but who also only come into being with the destruction of the indigenous economy.
7   Porot first put forward his idea of an "Algerian personality" in his 1918 article "Notes de psychiatrie Musulmane" (Notes on Muslim psychiatry) and continued publishing into the 1960s. Porot drew on "older" theories of climate and psychosocial development which positioned Arabs in the "hot" zone, creating a quick, hot-tempered, violent, criminal, and homicidal type, on the one hand, and an inactive, lazy type that shuns labor, on the other. Viewed not as one of the major revealed religions, but as a paralyzing agent that induced fatalism, Islam reinforced this thesis.
    Porot's contribution to the theory of the Arab personality was to underline the excitability and fanaticism of the Arab, who, he argued, was a congenital thief, pillager, and murderer. For Porot: "The suggestibility of the indigenous people indicates a similarity to the classic medieval hysterias in that it is frequently collect with easy generalization through contact" (ibid.). The Arab is subject to violent mood swings. The Arab is passive and childlike, governed by a "fatalistic metaphysics" but also prone to rage, violence, fanaticism, and criminality.
    Porot continued to embellish his thesis, suggesting a causality for the Algerian's murderous nature and impulse in the nondevelopment of cortical functions. The native's life is primarily vegetative and instinctual, he argued, dominated by the diencephalon. Porot's descriptions are reproduced in the opening pages of *The Wretched* as "zoological": the settler speaks of "the reptilian motions . . . of breeding swarms, of foulness, of spawn, of gesticulation . . . that laziness stretched out in the sun, that vegetative rhythm of life" (*WE*, 42).
8   The school remained commanding and unyielding for 40 years and its influence was significant up until the 1970s. Porot's in-depth "scien-

tific" studies of the Algerian revealed that, unlike the European, the North African did not have a cerebral cortex. However absurd these theories seem today, we must remember that they were not marginal but the mainstream and dominant ideas held by leaders in the field of Anglo and Francophone "scientific" studies of "the African mind." Fanon, on the other hand, published in less mainstream and more peripheral journals.

9   In the concluding pages of "Colonial Wars and Mental Disorders" in *The Wretched of the Earth* Fanon quotes an article that Porot co-authored with his student Sutter in 1939, which recapitulated Lévy-Bruhl's idea of the primitive mentality, with the psychobiological addition that North Africans are deprived of certain critical activities of the cortex. Fanon responds that on the biological level the native's laziness is in reality a "remarkable system of auto-protection" and on the conscious level a "sabotage of the colonial regime." Responding also to Carothers, Fanon argues that the native who is a good worker is a pathological case (*WE*, 294). It is in fact quite normal that under the colonial regime "what is true for the Arab and for the Black is that they should not lift their little fingers nor in the slightest degree help the oppressor" (*WE*, 294). What Carothers saw as cultural rigidity, Fanon saw as a form of sabotage. For Fanon, cause and effect had changed places: it was the colonial destruction of indigenous cultures and the internalization of the colonial ways of seeing them that led to schizophrenia. Resistance was manifested in frustrating ways for the investigator of native ways of life, and it was logically adopted. As Fanon put it, "the colonized does not let on, does not confess himself in the presence of the colonizer" (*DC*, 127 n2).

10 A. Porot and D. C. Arrii, "L'Impulsivité criminelle chez l'indigène algérien," *Annales Médico-Psychologiques*, 90 (1932), pp. 588–611.

11 C. L. Razanajao, J. Postel, and D. F. Allen, "The Life and Psychiatric Work of Frantz Fanon," *History of Psychiatry*, 7 (1996), p. 522.

12 F. Fanon and J. Azoulay, "La Sociothérapie dans un service d'hommes musulmans," *L'Information Psychiatrique*, 30, no. 9 (1954), pp. 349–61; repr. in vol. 51, no. 10 (Dec. 1975).

13 Ibid., p. 355.

14 Ibid., pp. 355–6.

15 Ibid.

16 In the article Fanon returns to Merleau-Ponty's maxim that "to speak a language is to support the foundations of a culture" (ibid., p. 359).

17 Ibid., p. 358.

18 Albert Memmi's accusation that Fanon's "refusal" to learn the language of the patients he was treating constituted a "psychiatric scandal" (Memmi, "Frozen by Death in the Image of Third World Prophet," *New York Times Book Review*, March 14, 1971), p. 5) is unfair. Fanon did try to learn Arabic, but moreover was clearly aware of the problem in a wider sense.

19 See Frantz Fanon and Charles Geronimi, "Le TAT chez femme musul-mane. Sociologie de la perception et de l'imagination," for Congrès des Médecins Aliénistes et Neurologues de France et des Pays de Langue Française, 54th session, Bordeaux, Aug. 30–Sept. 4, 1956.

20 C. Razanajao and J. Postel, "La Vie et l'oeuvre psychiatrique de Frantz Fanon," *L'Information Psychiatrique*, 51, no. 10 (1975), p. 508.

21 F. Fanon and F. Sanchez, "Attitude du Musulman maghrébin devant la folie," *Revue Pratique de Psychologie de la Vie Sociale et d'Hygiène Mentale*, 1 (1956).

22 Fanon's study of a Sufi mystic, "Le Marabout de Si Slimina," does not survive. In an unpublished paper, Fanon, Sanchez and Azoulay wrote about the cultural context of the spiritual world and sexual dysfunc-tion and impotence. Rather than an organic problem and a visit to the doctor, especially a European one, North African men saw the issue in terms of an "evil eye" and preferred to consult a local wise man or Marabout. ("Introduction aux troubles de la sexualité chez Nord-Africain," MS, see David Macey, *Frantz Fanon: A Life* (London: Granta Books), 2000), p. 236).

23 F. Fanon and R. Lacaton, "Conduites d'aveu en Afrique du Nord," for Congrès des Médecins Aliénistes et Neurologues de France et des Pays de Langue Française, 53rd session, Nice, Sept. 5–11, 1955, repr. in *L'Information Psychiatrique*, 51, no. 10 (1975).

24 F. Fanon and S. Asselah, "Le Phénomène de l'agitation en milieu psy-chiatrique," *Maroc Médical*, 36, no. 380 (1957), p. 22.

25 F. Fanon and C. Geronimi, "L'Hospitalisation de jour en psychiatrie. Valeur et limites," *Tunisie Médicale*, 38, no. 10 (1959), pp. 689–732. This two-part article is divided between an empirical section and a theo-retical section. Bulhan points out that the seriousness with which Fanon treats the empirical section debunks the opinion that Fanon was not interested in facts (Hussein A. Bulhan, *Frantz Fanon and the Psychology of Oppression* (New York: Plenum Press, 1985), p.167).

26 Fanon and Geronimi, "L'Hospitalisation de jour en psychiatrie," p. 732.

27 Ibid., p. 690.

28 Ibid., p. 717.

29 Bulhan notes that his approach to psychotherapy would be considered eclectic today, but that he "adopted Sandor Ferenczi's psychoanalyti-cal techniques in which the therapist takes an *active* and *involved* role in therapy" (*Frantz Fanon*, p. 245). This active role includes issues of transference and countertransference.

30 Fanon and Geronimi, "L'Hospitalisation de jour en psychiatrie," p. 721.

31 Ibid., p. 719.

32 Ibid., p. 721.

33 General Bugeaud, *L'Algérie. Des moyens de conserver et d'utiliser cette conquête* (Paris: Dantu, 1842), p. 67.

34 Ibid., p. 40.

35 Quoted in G. A. Kelly, *Lost Soldiers: The French Army and the Empire in Crisis, 1947–1962* (Cambridge, Mass.: MIT Press, 1965), p. 143.
36 Quoted in Rita Maran, *Torture: The Role of Ideology in the French–Algerian War* (New York: Praeger, 1989), p. 52.
37 Ibid., p. 48.
38 Quoted in ibid., p. 47. The French denied torture throughout the war and only in October 1999 did the French National Assembly decide to officially permit the term "Algerian War." In November 1999 *Le Monde* reported that Jacques Massu, who in 1957 was in charge of the notorious "Paras" (10th Parachute Division), and his deputy, Paul Aussaresses, then director of the French secret service in Algiers, admitted that over 3,000 prisoners considered to have "disappeared" at that time had in reality been executed. Aussaresses explained that in 1957 torture and murder were an integral part of France's war policy. He boasted that methods were employed that were not covered by the conventions of war, that he had given his subordinates orders to kill and had personally liquidated 24 FLN members. His memoir (Paul Aussaresses, *Services spéciaux. Algérie 1955–1957* (Paris: Perrin, 2001)) sheds some light on the deaths of the Battle of Algiers leader, Larbi Ben M'Hidi, who was, in fact, strangled to death at Aussaresses' command.
39 See Maran, *Torture*, pp. 11–23.
40 Macey notes a meeting with FLN representatives at Fanon's home in February 1955 and adds that "Fanon did apparently contemplate taking up a gun and going into the mountains as early as January/February 1955." As Fanon was a decorated World War Two veteran, the claim was not an empty one (see Macey, *Frantz Fanon*, p. 265).
41 Generally considered the "mastermind" of the Soummam and the instigator of the "Battle of Algiers," Abane is identified as advocating indiscriminate urban terrorism. Quandt argues that "according to many who knew him, [Abane] was decisive without being authoritarian and was able to command the respect of those around him. Although a Kabyle, Abane is held in high regard by Arabs as well as Kabyles, and several elite members claim that he might have been the one Algerian who could have held the elite together after independence" (W. B. Quandt, *Revolution and Political Leadership: Algeria, 1954–1968* (Cambridge, Mass.: MIT Press, 1969), p. 100). The latter statement is perhaps all the more problematic since it was the elite who conspired to remove him in the first place.
    A serious critique is still to be written in English of Abane, the figure Lacoste, the "liberal" French governor-general of Algeria, called the movement's "best brain."
42 Lou Turner, "Fanon and the FLN," in Nigel C. Gibson (ed.), *Rethinking Fanon: The Continuing Legacy* (Amherst: Humanity Books, 1999).
43 Ben Khedda and Abane Ramdane were the ideological heirs of the radical intellectuals in the Central Committee of the Messalist MTLD (Movement for the Triumph of Democratic Liberties), formed in 1946 by Hadj Ben Ahmed Messali, considered the founder of Algerian

nationalism, and a figure who was active in the Communist Party of France in the mid 1920s. In 1927 Messali's Étoile Nord-Africaine organized a League Against Colonial Oppression. Their demands included independence, universal suffrage, freedom of the press, access to education for all, and the creation of Arabic language schools. Later, economic demands, such as the nationalization of banks, large industry and national rural projects, were added.

Hussein Ait Ahmed, one of the intellectual leaders and a founder of the FLN, argued that "the revolutionary must . . . descend from the pedestal of his theory to root himself in concrete life, in order to draw upon it and to verify there his principles of action" (Joan Gillespie, *Algeria: Rebellion and Revolution* (London: Ernest Benn, 1961), p. 80). Ait Ahmed was a mentor to Abane who, in the Kabyle tradition of the Djemma, or democratic Berber assembly, favored collective leadership, and a secular state. Although, with the Soummam declaration, the personalization of power in the hands of a single charismatic leader, like Messali, was challenged, it would remain a dogged problematic of Algerian postcolonial politics (see Turner, "Fanon and the FLN").

44 Rather than the "Kabyle myth," what was at stake were political tendencies. Often associated with "Berber separatism," some of the most left-wing and secular leaders of the FLN were from Kabylia, which also meant that as the revolution moved into a more accommodationist pose, with conservative and Islamicist nationalist elements, these leaders were threatened, as was the case with Abane Ramdane. Located as he was in Blida, it is interesting to note Fanon's close proximity to Kabylia, his interest in the Djemma as a possible local democratic form that could be reinvigorated through the revolution and the secular politics of its leaders. Just as Fanon spoke of the importance of "minorities" in the Algerian revolution – European and Jewish supporters – one cannot help but think also of the Kabyle militants as both the extreme left wing of the revolution, and the problematic at the heart of Algerian nationalism. It was not coincidental that Soummam criticized both the regionalism of some of the Wilayas and the authoritarianism of Messali.

45 Edward Behr, *The Algerian Problem* (London: Penguin, 1961), pp. 111–12, 114.

46 Quoted in Maran, *Torture*, p. 44.

47 Simone de Beauvoir, *Hard Times: Force of Circumstance, II* (New York, Paragon, 1992), p. 317.

Chapter 5   Violent Concerns

1 Fanon echoes Freud's terminology. Freud argues that the most important inhibition that "civilization employs" is the individual's internalization of aggressiveness toward his own ego (*Civilization and its*

Discontents (New York: Norton, 1989), pp. 83–4). Like the libido, violence can be considered economically. That is why the internalized violence created by the colonial regime has to be turned outward, to its "proper place," the real source of the native's oppression.

2   One problem of reading Fanon's "Concerning Violence" is Sartre's introduction, which at the time of the book's publication gained more notoriety than *The Wretched* itself. For example, Jean Daniel created the "Sartre–Fanon phenomenon," making Fanon a crude devotee of Sartre's *Critique of Dialectical Reason* (London: Verso, 1991) and finally calling him a "redemptive assassin" (Daniel, *La Blessure* (Paris: Grasset, 1992), p. 69; see also his review of *The Wretched* in *L'Express*, Nov. 30, 1961). Sartre provided some of the theoretical language and framework for thinking about the violence and fraternity (see *Critique*, p. 733), though Fanon did not need Sartre to tell him what was going on. In fact it was perhaps the other way around.

   Fanon's critique of Western morality in *The Wretched* is just as devastating as Sartre's. In contrast to the egotistical individualism of the colonialist bourgeoisie whose "brother is my purse," Fanon argues that the new morality is simply that the interests of one will be the interests of all and that "everyone will be massacred or everyone will be saved" (*WE*, 44–7). It is public rather than private, communal rather than narrowly individual, open rather than concealed, self-critical rather than self-serving. Democracy does not have to be imported from outside but is embedded – even if implicitly and problematically, especially after the decades of colonial rule – in many indigenous institutions and practices where members have the right to free opinion, and collective decisions are made after long discussion. Yet, if Sartre had provided a framework for Fanon to discuss colonial Manicheanism, by stressing the "end of the dialectic" (*WE*, 31) he had missed how Fanon attempted to go past Manicheanism while at the same time seeking to understand it.

3   See Daniel, *La Blessure.*

4   Hannah Arendt, "On Violence," in *Crisis of the Republic* (New York: Harcourt Brace Jovanovich, 1972), p. 116 n19, and p. 162.

5   Albert Memmi, "Frantz Fanon and the Notion of 'Deficiency,'" in *Dominated Man: Notes toward a Portrait* (New York: Orion, 1968), p. 88.

6   See Mahmood Mamdani, *When Victims Become Killers* (Princeton: Princeton University Press, 2001), pp. 10, 13.

7   As Abdallah Laroui has put it, "It was not enough to drive the Maghrebi once again . . . into the desert . . . it was necessary also to deprive him of his religion, language, and historic heritage, so producing a man free from culture, who could then be civilized" (*The History of the Maghrib* (Princeton: Princeton University Press, 1977), pp. 342–3). Colonialism exiled the colonized to the desert historically, psychologically, and sociologically. The process of destruction was not without terrible human cost. For example, the initial suppression of

the Algerian resistance during the years 1830 to 1852 reduced the Algerian tribes from 6 million to 2.5 million.

8 Peter Knauss argues that "French cultural imperialism in 'French Algeria' was more totalitarian in its scope and more intensely implemented than in Morocco and Tunisia" (Peter Knauss, *The Persistence of Patriarchy: Class, Gender and Ideology in Twentieth Century Algeria* (New York: Praeger, 1987), p. 22).

9 The native zone's division between the urban masses and that small elite striving to cross the border and to become European does not represent a development outside of Manicheanism.

10 Lord Lugard, *Dual Mandate in British Tropical Africa* (London: Frank Cass, 1965), p. 148.

11 Or as he ventriloquizes, " 'Let's each one of us take ten of them and bump them off and you'll see the problem solved' " (*DC*, 56).

12 Freud speaks of "free" and "bounded" energy, the former discharging in the easiest and speediest manner, the latter being controlled and checked. Bounded energy as a more advanced stage of psychical development has a resonance with Fanon's idea of re-redirecting toward the "real" source of the problem.

13 Which underlines the native's anxiety about the security and policing of the borders between his and the colonized "zones."

14 Fanon's examples, zombies, voodoo, and vampirism, are all from the Caribbean.

15 He praises "Mau-Mau," but says little about any religious practices associated with it. On the other hand he is critical of Sufi Islam (especially "Marabout confraternities") insofar as its cultural practice obscures the "real" condition. Religion is judged in terms of political action.

16 In the context of the revolutionary struggle, Fanon argues that dancing, singing, and traditional ceremonies manifest a "new vigor" and express the coming revolt (*WE*, 243).

17 The issue is a lot more complicated, as the extent of liquidation of "collaborators" included political opponents who were liquidated by the FLN. Many were Algerians working for the colonial government and members of the MTLD or later FLN opponents. During the first two and a half years of the revolution the FLN killed six Muslims to every one European.

18 While in retrospect all the signs can be read, the answer cannot be known beforehand. In the final chapter of the *Science of Logic*, Hegel argues that every beginning is made from the Absolute though it "must be inherently defective [and] must be endowed with the impulse of self-development."

19 For example, see Emmanuel Hansen, *Frantz Fanon* (Columbus: Ohio State University Press, 1977) and Marie B. Perinbam, *Holy Violence: The Revolutionary Thought of Frantz Fanon* (Washington DC: Three Continents Press, 1983).

20 Aristotle located catharsis in tragedy, clearing, or illuminating the mind. Irene Gendzier, *Frantz Fanon* (New York: Grove Press, 1973), pp. 201–2.

21 See Hussein A. Bulhan, *Frantz Fanon and the Psychology of Oppression* (New York: Plenum Press, 1985), p. 147; and case 3, Series A (*WE*, 261–4) for Fanon's discussion of the psychosis of violence.

22 The cases in Series A in "Colonial Wars and Mental Disorders," in *The Wretched*, indicate aspects of post-traumatic stress.

23 Fanon only uses the term "inferiority complex" once in *The Wretched* and then as a critique of new sociological studies produced in the colonial metropole during the struggle and embedded in the problematic of violence.

24 Some critics maintain, perhaps all too simply, that the Kojèvean emphasis on the slave's "work" as central to the process of liberation is translated by Fanon's preoccupation with the peasant's potential for violence (see Perinbam, *Holy Violence*, p. 81). Renate Zahar also maintains that Fanon's conception of violence is "unadmittedly derived from Hegel" (Zahar, *Colonialism and Alienation* (New York: Monthly Review Press, 1974), p. 78). She maintains that instead of asserting his "true self" through work, the colonial bondsman finds a psychological emancipation through violence (p. 79).

   Because of an emphasis not on "work" qua work, but on the work of consciousness that withdraws from "work," Fanon's conception is actually quite similar to that of Hegel, who writes in the *Phenomenology*: "The consciousness which withdraws from its work is in point of fact universal – because it becomes, in this opposition between work and consciousness, absolute negativity, the process of action – and stands over against its work, which is determinant and particular" (G. W. F. Hegel, *Phenomenology of Spirit*, trans. A. V. Miller (Oxford: Oxford University Press, 1971), para. 405).

   With Fanon, the opposition between work and consciousness is reproduced as a creative principle latent in the native's refusal to labor. In *Black Skin*, he argues against Hegel, that the slave has to turn away from work toward the master. There is a second shift in *The Wretched*, where Fanon argues that the withdrawal from work, misconstrued by the colonialists as the "laziness" of the worker, is in fact a form of resistance (*WE*, 294). The work Fanon sees as the agency of liberation is the work of turning *against* the master and rising up in a liberation struggle. He reasserts the notion of liberation through work which he had earlier abandoned, reinterpreting it as working for the death of the master. More importantly, he revalues the turn toward the master, not as the object, but as the source of internal anguish which must be destroyed. Fanon's analysis is consonant with Kojève's. Work now becomes the work of the revolutionary: the "absolute negation" of the master's world. Work, Kojève argues, "presupposes the 'negation,' the non-accepting of the given World *in its totality*. And the origin of this

ation can only be the absolute dread inspired by the given
re precisely, by that which, or by him who, dominates
by the master of this world" (Alexandre Kojève,
the Reading of Hegel, ed. Allan Bloom (New York: Basic
~~~, p. 29).

Certainly Fanon thinks that the "native's" liberation must be gained
through self-activity, yet *working* for freedom should not be immediately translated either into actual labor or physical violence. The
master's death is both actual and metaphorical. In "Decolonization
and Independence" (1958), for example, he leaves aside a consideration of violence and simply declares that the only work that the
oppressed have is the work of their own liberation (*AR*, 105).

25 It is communicated well in Pontecorvo's film *Battle of Algiers* when Ali
La Pointe's loyalty to the organization is tested by being told to kill a
police officer. The unloaded gun is a test of loyalty.

26 The phrase "le racisme anti-raciste" is translated by Constance
Farrington as "racial feeling, as opposed to racial prejudice" (*WE*, 139),
rather than Sartre's phrase "antiracist racism."

Chapter 6   Radical Mutations: Toward a Fighting Culture

1 An interesting analogy could be made to the controversy around
Mbeki's resistance to accepting a "scientific" answer to HIV/AIDS in
South Africa.

2 Hussein A. Bulhan, *Frantz Fanon and the Psychology of Oppression* (New
York: Plenum Press, 1985), p. 96.

3 See Lynette Jackson, "The Story of Chibheura (Open Your Legs)
Exams," in George C. Bond and Nigel C. Gibson, *Contested Terrains and
Constructed Categories: Africa in Focus* (Boulder: Westview, 2002).

4 Gayatri Chakravorty Spivak, "Can the Subaltern Speak?" in Cary
Nelson and Lawrence Grossberg (eds), *Marxism and the Interpretation
of Culture* (London: Macmillan, 1988).

5 Pierre Bourdieu, as a sociologist doing fieldwork in the late 1950s in
Kabylia, chronicled the radical changes taking place: "*No one* is
unaware of the fact that a deep gulf now separates Algerian society
from its past and that an irreversible change has taken place ...
The Revolutionary situation has upset the former social hierarchies,
now associated with the system of outmoded values, and has sub-
stituted for them new men to whom authority was granted for
reasons other than birth, wealth, or moral or religious ascendancy"
(Bourdieu, *The Algerians* (Boston: Beacon Press, 1962), p. 182).
Bourdieu also commented on the veil as a social mutation in "Guerre
et mutation sociale en Algérie," *Études Maghrébibes*, 7 (Spring 1960),
pp. 25–37.

6 Many of his articles were collected in *Toward the African Revolution* (*AR*). Two articles are omitted from the English-language edition, the statement at the Accra conference, 1958, "Accra. L'Afrique affirme son unité et definit sa stratégie" (*El Moudjahid*, 1, no. 34 (Dec. 24, 1958)) and "Culture nationale et guerre de libération" (*El Moudjahid*, 2, no. 39 (Apr. 10, 1959)).

7 *El Moudjahid*, the central organ of the FLN, was reorganized by Fanon in 1957. Edited in Algeria, it had become increasingly difficult to publish and only appeared sporadically. Toward the end of 1957 it moved to Tunis and there under Fanon's editorship it came out more or less biweekly (there were 48 issues between September 1957 and January 1960).

8 Francis Jeanson saw the poverty among the Algerians during the war and criticized the massacre at Sétif. He lived in Algeria in 1948, returning to become one of the leading critics of French Algeria. Supportive of the FLN, he and Colette Jeanson wrote *Algérie-hors-la-loi* in 1955 (Paris: Éditions du Seuil, 1965). The book reproduced FLN leaflets and an interview with an anonymous FLN spokesman, who might well have been Abane. In 1956 Jeanson began working with the FLN and created the "Jeanson Network" to support the struggle for independence. Members of the "Jeanson Network" were tried in a military court in September 1960. Jeanson, in absentia, and others in the network were found guilty of offenses against state security.

Earlier, he was an editor at Seuil, the publishing house with which Fanon published *Black Skin*. Interested in the book, Jeanson met with Fanon, but the meeting did not go well. Jeanson recounts in an afterword to the 1965 edition: "In 1952 we almost broke off our relations . . . Having found his manuscript exceptionally interesting, I committed the error of telling him so, which made him suspect me of having thought, 'for a Negro, that wasn't so bad.' As a result of which, I showed him the door and expressed my own reaction in the liveliest terms – which he had the good sense to take."

9 Fanon has been criticized for not providing a sociological dimension for the Algerian woman, and not distinguishing between the rural and the urban, or between the petty bourgeois and poor women, see Madhu Dubey, "The 'True Lie' of the Nation: Fanon and Feminism," *Differences: A Journal of Feminist Cultural Studies*, 10, no. 2 (1998), pp. 2–28. For a defense of Fanon see T. Denean Sharpley-Whiting, "Fanon's Feminist Consciousness and Algerian Women's Liberation: Colonialism, Nationalism and Fundamentalism," in Nigel C. Gibson (ed.), *Rethinking Fanon: The Continuing Legacy* (Amherst: Humanity Books, 1999), pp. 329–53, and Sharpley-Whiting, *Frantz Fanon: Conflicts and Feminisms* (Lanham: Rowman and Littlefield, 1998). The focus of "Algeria Unveiled" is the urban woman (Fanon admits, "We do not consider here rural areas where the woman is often unveiled. Nor do

we consider Kabyle woman who, except in large cities, never wears the veil" (*DC*, 36)).

10 In a note Fanon states that there is an "important piece of work to be done on the woman's role in the Revolution" and he sets out a number of chapter headings – woman in the city, in the djebel, the prostitute gathering information, the woman in prison – that would be essential for the "history of the liberation struggle" (*DC*, 60n).

11 The appendix to "Algeria Unveiled" was originally printed just after the Battle of Algiers in the Morocco-based journal *Résistance Algérienne*, May 16, 1957.

12 See Zouligha, "Challenging the Social Order: Women's Liberation in Contemporary Algeria," in Nigel C. Gibson (ed.), *Rethinking Fanon: The Continuing Legacy* (Amherst: Humanity Books, 1999), pp. 354–66.

13 See the essays collected in *Rethinking Fanon* by Marie-Aimée Helie-Lucas, Anne McClintock, Diana Fuss, and T. Denean Sharpley-Whiting, as well as Winifred Woodhull, "Unveiling Algeria," *Genders* 10 (Spring 1991), Jeffrey Louis Decker, "Terrorism Unveiled: Frantz Fanon and the Women of Algiers," *Cultural Critique*, 20 (Winter 1990), and Dubey, "The 'True Lie' of the Nation."

14 While McClintock adds that Fanon rejects the "western metaphor of the nation as a family," Diana Fuss sees in Fanon's "Algeria Unveiled" the veiled woman as a stand-in "metonymically for the nation."

15 While in hindsight nationalism might appear simply as a European creation, equated with the development of a nation-state mimicking the European, this viewpoint forgets other nationalisms in Africa (and other earlier state forms), equating the project of national liberation with the consolidation of local elites in a neocolonial frame. This type of thinking elides the ways in which subjugated notions of national identity were products of anticolonial struggles sometimes quite outside the control of the nationalist elites and the programs of nationalist organizations.

16 These measures went much further in Algeria than in Morocco and Tunisia. In Algeria an attempt was made to assimilate Algeria's economic, social, and cultural infrastructure into France.

17 Assia Djebar, "A Forbidden Glimpse, a Broken Sound," in Elizabeth Fernea (ed.), *Women and the Family in the Middle East* (Austin: University of Texas Press, 1985), p. 343.

18 Peter Knauss, *The Persistence of Patriarchy: Class, Gender and Ideology in Twentieth Century Algeria* (New York: Praeger, 1987), pp. 23–4.

19 Ibid., p. xiii. Islamic observance in Algeria at independence was fairly weak in the urban areas and far from "orthodox" in the rural areas, which were influenced by Sufism.

20 The Manichean atmosphere produced another expression of the lack of reciprocity between the (male) native and (male) colonizer, but this time with a different twist. To the colonizer, veiled women look the same, but the *refusal* of the colonized woman to be revealed frustrated

the colonizer in another way: "they can see our women, we can't see theirs." The struggle over the veil had more than mild erotic overtones for the Frenchman; it spoke directly to his virility – as Alistair Horne puts it, "the Arab had a plurality of wives, and therefore was possibly more virile . . . and with the demographic explosion spawned by his potency, he was threatening to swamp the European by sheer weight of numbers" (*A Savage War of Peace: Algeria 1954–1962* (London: Macmillan, 1977), pp. 46, 55).

21 Marnia Lazreg, "Gender and Politics in Algeria," *Signs: Journal of Women in Culture and Society*, 15, no. 4 (1990), p. 767.

22 David Caute, *Frantz Fanon* (New York: Viking, 1970), p. 52.

23 An overemphasis on the veil itself aids the erasure of a discussion of the change in subjectivity. Fanon notes that during the war of liberation, the Kabyle women's action has "likewise assumed an absolutely original aspect" (*DC*, 36).

24 Women played a leading and public role in stopping the factional fighting on the onset of independence, and women's freedom still posed a threat after independence. See Cherifa Bouatta, "Feminine Militancy: Moudjahidates during and after the Algerian War," in Valentin Moghadam (ed.), *Gender and National Identity: Women and Politics in Muslim Societies* (London: Zed Press, 1994), p. 25.

25 Ato Sekyi-Otu, *Fanon's Dialectic of Experience* (Cambridge: Harvard University Press, 1996), p. 225.

26 Knauss, *The Persistence of Patriarchy*, p. 78.

27 Ulama, a cultural organization founded in the 1920s, did not take an explicitly political position against colonialism, though it did articulate a belief in a distinct nation. Its main concern was establishing Koranic schools and fighting the marabouts and Sufism. It officially joined the FLN in 1956. FLN conservatives systematized their cultural credo with the old Ulama slogan, "Islam is our religion, Arabic our language, Algeria our fatherland." What this credo means is far from self-evident. What kind of Islam would be practiced? Would more than one school be allowed? Would secular Muslims be tolerated? What would be the relationship of Islam to politics and economics between the state formation and the rights of people? What social relations, gender, class and ethnic hierarchies would Islam justify? What groups would it seek to suppress?

On the question of language, for example, what form of Arabic would be chosen, classical or modern? Since French colonialism had destroyed Algerian literacy, what other languages would be official? What about Berber languages? What about French? What about the hybrid "Algerian"? On the question of the "fatherland," would a free Algeria be free for non-Arabs and non-Muslims, for the French and European Algerians or the Jews? Would Algeria be free for women?

It is not an accident that these questions were addressed at the Soummam conference and reworked in Fanon's *L'An V*.

28   In a note, Fanon describes that in Kabylia in "groups of scores and sometimes a hundred around a receiver, the peasants listen religiously"; though "few understand the literary Arabic" a few expressions are enough to "keep alive the faith of victory" (*DC*, 87 n6).

29   He adds that the difference between the hysteria of the dominant group and that of the colonized was that "the colonizer always translated his subjective states into acts, real and multiple murders" (*DC*, 79). He then proposes a study to "deal with these different problems, arising out of the struggle for liberation . . . directly based on psychopathology." Unfortunately, apart from the case studies in the final chapter of *The Wretched*, Fanon never wrote such a study.

Chapter 7   Crossing the Dividing Line: Spontaneity and Organization

1   See A. Gramsci, *Prison Notebooks* (London: Lawrence and Wishart, 1971), p. 405.

2   The first "landing beach" for Fanon was, of course, Algeria. For Fanon, the failure to open up a "second front" would have a profoundly detrimental effect on the first.

3   See "Teacher" in Ayi Kwei Armah's *The Beautyful Ones Are Not Yet Born* (London: Heinemann, 1981).

4   P. Lorcin, *Imperial Identities: Stereotyping, Prejudice and Race in Colonial Algeria* (London: I. B. Tauris, 1999), p. 28.

5   Rural violence against *colons* increased between 1878 and 1900, and increased again in the 1930s through the early 1950s. The governor-general of Algeria, Jacques Soustelle, commented that when he first went to the Aurès (scene of the initial revolutionary outburst in the winter of 1954–5), "No one spoke. The administration and the Army had seen information dry up [and] any native suspected of friendly relations with the authorities ran the fear of assassination or mutilation" (quoted in Edward Behr, *The Algerian Problem* (London: Penguin, 1961)). B. Marie Perinbam adds, "perhaps Fanon was right. . . . The evidence suggests that [the growing correlation between stress and violence] increased in those areas where the French presence was heavily concentrated . . . or among those tribes who had suffered heavily from land sequestration."

6   The schema loosely follows the postwar experience of Algerian nationalism but could be applied elsewhere. In Algeria three quasi-nationalist movements developed in the 1920s. The Fédération des Élus Indigènes represented a French educated elite who wanted to gain equality and representation in Parliament. Their main goal was assimilation with France. Ferhat Abbas emerged from this organization.

An urban-based cultural organization, Ulama, called for a purification of Islam, criticizing the assimilationism of the évolué. It attacked Sufism and the marabouts as heretical, and attempted to "separate the rural believers from the popular, indigenous forms of their religion" (Ruedy, *Modern Algeria*, p. 135).

Messali's Étoile Nord-Africaine was an important training ground for the FLN militants. Messali was born to a lower middle-class family and earned an elementary education at a colonial school. He served three years in the French army, and returning to France in 1923 joined the Communist Party. The Étoile was formed in 1926 and from its early days separated itself from other nationalist (including cultural) organizations by being anticapitalist and being concerned with life in the rural areas.

It was Messali's organization, the Party of the Algerian People (PPA), that called for the insurrection on May 8, 1945 that led to the Sétif massacre. Fanon's description of the intuitively nationalist peasants, who had kept their traditions of resistance intact and were only waiting for a signal, is captured by the historian John Ruedy: "Quite apart from the PPA, peasant villagers, seeing the outbreak of warfare and the startling breakdown of French authority, descended on the colonial settlements to begin wreaking vengeance on their tormentors, much in the manner of their ancestors a century earlier" (ibid., p. 150). Ruedy continues, highlighting the distance between the nationalists and the rural masses: "The events in northern Constantinois marked for the first time that the dispossessed and pauperized masses of the countryside, the principal victims of the colonial system, had linked up for meaningful action with the nationalist movement that urban Algerians had created and which had been spreading in the cities for fifteen years" (ibid.).

This was the highpoint for Messali's organization, which was reconstituted as the Mouvement pour le Triomphe des Libertés Démocratiques (MTLD) in 1946. Out of the PPA also came the Organisation Spéciale (OS), a clandestine paramilitary organization whose leaders included many of the early members of the FLN (which was first known as CRUA, Comité Révolutionnaire d'Unité et d'Action). A number of faction fights destroyed the PPA-MTLD in 1948–9, turning on issues of the inclusiveness of Algerian nationalism, including questions of the place of Islam and the use of the term "Arab" (rather than Algerian). CRUA emerged in early 1954 out of the dispute between the central committee (called centralists) and Messali, who was accused of creating a cult of personality. Structured on the same lines as OS, its members believed that the PPA-MTLD was no longer a viable organization. The MTLD remained an important force in France, and a bloody struggle ensued between it and the FLN in 1958. In Algeria after 1955, many of the members joined the FLN, which labeled the PPA-MTLD counterrevolutionary.

7 It was key to the Battle of Algiers, where about a third of the workforce was unemployed.

8 The unstable character of the lumpenproletariat, who are desperately in need of political education, is reflected in Fanon's characterization of them as "turn[ing] in circles between suicide and madness." Nevertheless, he is hopeful that they will "recover their balance . . . and march proudly in the great procession of the awakened nation." See also Fanon's concern with the African youth who are impressionable in the face of the assaults made by Western consumer culture. This moral question is a result of "the universe of the perceptions [being thrown] out of focus" by the collision of two worlds (*WE*, 195).

9 Ruedy puts the number of "upper bourgeoisie" at 5–6,000. While not all of them were French educated, French education gave the bourgeoisie its tone. In 1920 they wore the fez as a sign of class distinction and cultural inheritance; by 1954 they dressed in European style. The much larger middle class of 200,000, which included the liberal professions, middle-level civil servants, and craftsmen, were the fertile ground for nationalism (*Modern Algeria*, pp. 124–5).

10 "Subjectivity is . . . taken as the starting point for modifying the attitude" of the intellectual; for the non-intellectual "the body is dealt with" (*WE*, 288–9).

11 Tsenay Serequeberhan, *The Hermeneutics of African Philosophy* (London: Routledge, 1994), p. 105 (emphasis added).

Chapter 8   Nationalism and a New Humanism

1 Fanon's idea of premature senility of the nationalist bourgeoisie is brilliantly rescribed by Ayi Kwei Armah in *The Beautyful Ones Are Not Yet Born* (London: Heinemann, 1981) when he describes birth to death in seven years, mirroring the short time between Ghana's independence from the British and its degeneration under Nkrumah and the coup against him.

2 Ngugi wa Thiongo has quite aptly characterized the literature about postcolonial Africa as a "series of imaginative footnotes" to Fanon's "Pitfalls" chapter (see Ngugi's "The Writer in the Neo-colonial State," in *Moving the Centre* (London: Heinemann, 1993), p. 66).

3 A theory propounded by W. A. Lewis, "Economic Development with Unlimited Supplies of Labour," *The Manchester School of Economics and Social Studies*, 36, no. 1 (Jan. 1958).

4 I am using the term "potential" guardedly, but I think it gestures to a more dialectical rather than a static view of an unchanging human essence merely being uncovered by revolution. A material reordering (to use Fanon's words) releases human potential. Fanon, like Marx, called his philosophy a "new humanism." Tony Martin argues that Marx's *Eighteenth Brumaire*, especially Marx's idea that people make history but not in the circumstances of their own choosing, "had a special attraction for Fanon . . . [and] provided him with the *leitmotif*

of his philosophy" (Martin, "Rescuing Fanon from the Critics," in Nigel C. Gibson (ed.), *Rethinking Fanon: The Continuing Legacy* (Amherst: Humanity Books, 1999).

5 Likewise in Nkrumah's Ghana, the right of workers to strike against the new government was disallowed.

6 For example see Julius Nyerere, "Les Frondements du socialisme africain," reprinted in *Freedom and Unity: A Selection from Writings and Speeches, 1952–1965* (Dar es Salaam: Oxford University Press, 1966).

7 Axel Honneth, *The Struggle for Recognition: The Moral Grammar of Social Conflict* (Cambridge: MIT Press, 1996), p. 160. Of course, the experience was limited to the racial designation "Black Africa."

8 Fanon does not think that there are simply no ideologies; there are plenty of "morbid symptoms," as Gramsci put it, to choose from, but these are all retrogressive. The problem is a lack of revolutionary ideology (or perhaps more appropriately revolutionary theory) grounded in the anticolonial social movements and with a vision of the future. "Ideology" is needed to counteract the hollow rhetoric of the nationalist middle class and the romanticized, and potentially retrograde, negritude ideology, which includes appeals to "traditions," including religion.

9 See L. Adele Jinadu, *Fanon* (London: Kegan Paul International, 1983).

10 Lenin also emphasized the importance of national liberation in his conception of social revolution: "To imagine that social revolution is possible without revolts by small nations in the colonies . . . is to repudiate social revolution. So one army lines up in one place and says, 'We are for socialism,' and another, somewhere else says, 'We are for imperialism,' and that will be a social revolution! . . . Whoever expects a 'pure' social revolution will never live to see it. Such a person pays lip service to revolution without understanding what it is" (V. I. Lenin, "The Discussion of Self-Determination Summed Up," in *Collected Works*, Vol. 22 (London: Lawrence and Wishart, 1964), p. 355).

11 Cf. Jean-Paul Sartre, *Critique of Dialectical Reason* (London: Verso, 1991), pp. 726–7. Nevertheless, Fanon had not totally given up on the Europeans. If they want to be involved in "reintroducing mankind to the world . . . [they] must first wake and shake themselves" out of their stupor (*WE*, 106). Europeans might disagree though it was the anticolonial revolts in Luso-Africa that shook Portugal out of its stupor.

12 Found in Fanon's "Blida notes" (1955), quoted in Peter Geismar, *Frantz Fanon* (New York: Grove Press, 1969), p. 197.

13 Fanon defines "intellectual resources" as "engineers and technicians" (*WE*, 152) but includes poets, some of whom became political leaders.

14 Fanon perceptively notes that "men and women, young and old, undertake enthusiastically what is in fact forced labor, and proclaim themselves slaves of the nation," but he adds perceptively that "we

cannot believe that such an effort can be kept up at the same pace for very long."

15 See Mahmood Mamdani, *Citizen and Subject: Contemporary Africa and the Legacy of Late Colonialism* (Princeton: Princeton University Press, 1996).

16 Christopher Miller's view that Fanon's attitude is "massively ethnocentric," because he views precolonial society as having no history, is based on several misquotations. The idea of precolonial traditions can also be "massively ethnocentric." Rather than talked about in generalities, each "tradition" and its history needs to be discussed. Miller, who consistently wants to find some African essence, ends up privileging "ethnicity" over "nation." But he fails to understand how ethnicity is also manipulated by colonialism (Miller, "Ethnicity and Ethics," *South Atlantic Quarterly*, 87, no. 1 (1989)). In Fanon's time, it was clearly the ethnic entrepreneurs who were used to destroy Lumumba.

17 His penetrating critique of Leopold Senghor, the President of Senegal, who heralded African humanism while supporting the French in Algeria, pointed to the problematic of negritude in power.

Bibliography

Only works by Fanon or books and collections of essays on Fanon are included here. See the notes for other works cited in the text.

Works by Frantz Fanon

Books

Peau noire, masques blancs (Paris: Éditions du Seuil, 1952); trans. Charles Lam Markmann as *Black Skin, White Masks* (New York: Grove Press, 1967), also published with an introduction by Homi K. Bhabha (London: Pluto Press, 1986), introduction repr. in Nigel C. Gibson (ed.), *Rethinking Fanon* (see secondary works below).

L'An V de la révolution algérienne (Paris: Maspero, 1959); repr. as *Sociologie d'une révolution* (Paris: Maspero, 1966), trans. Haakon Chevalier as *Studies in a Dying Colonialism* (New York: Monthly Review Press, 1967; London: Earthscan, 1989), introd. A. M. Babu. Includes "Algeria Unveiled"; "This is the Voice of Algeria"; "The Algerian Family"; "Medicine and Colonialism"; "Algeria's European Minority."

Les Damnés de la terre (Paris: Maspero, 1961); trans. Constance Farrington as *The Wretched of the Earth*, including introduction by Jean-Paul Sartre (New York: Grove Press, 1968; Harmondsworth: Penguin, 1970). Includes "Concerning Violence"; "Spontaneity: Its Strength and Weakness"; "The Pitfalls of National Consciousness"; "On National Culture"; "Colonial Wars and Mental Disorders".

Pour la révolution africaine. Écrits politiques (Paris: Maspero, 1964); trans. Haakon Chevalier as *Toward the African Revolution: Political Essays* (New York: Grove Press, 1967; Harmondsworth: Penguin, 1970). Includes, as well as articles from *El Moudjahid*, "The 'North African Syndrome'" (1952);

"West Indians and Africans" (1955); "Letter to the Resident Minister" (1956); "Racism and Culture" (1955); "This Africa to Come" (1959).

Selected articles and essays not included in books

Readers should consult the special edition of *L'Information Psychiatrique*, 51, no. 10 (Dec. 1975), which collected a number of Fanon's writings to celebrate his fiftieth year.

"Le Trouble mental et le trouble neurologique," *L'Information Psychiatrique*, 51, no. 10 (1975), an extract from Fanon's 1951 thesis entitled "Altérations mentales, modifications caractérielles, troubles psychiques et déficit intellectuel dans l'hérédo-dégénération spino-cérébelleuse. Un cas de maladie de Friedrich avec délire de persécution," Faculté Mixte de Médecine et de Pharmacie, Lyon, Nov. 29, 1951.

"La Sociothérapie dans un service d'hommes musulmans," with Jacques Azoulay, *L'Information Psychiatrique*, 30, no. 9 (1954), repr. in vol. 51, no. 10 (Dec. 1975).

"Aspects actuels de l'assistance mentale en Algérie," with J. Dequeker, R. Lacaton, M. Micucci and F. Ramée, *L'Information Psychiatrique*, 31, no. 11 (1955), repr. in vol. 51, no. 10 (Dec. 1975).

"Conduites d'aveu en Afrique du Nord," with R. Lacaton, for Congrès des Médecins Aliénistes et Neurologues de France et des Pays de Langue Française, 53rd session, Nice, Sept. 5–11, 1955, reprinted in *L'Information Psychiatrique*, 51, no. 10 (1975).

"Attitude du Musulman maghrébin devant la folie," with F. Sanchez, *Revue Pratique de Psychologie de la vie Sociale et d'Hygiène Mentale*, 1 (1956).

"Le TAT chez femme musulmane. Sociologie de la perception et de l'imagination," with Charles Geronimi, for Congrès des Médecins Aliénistes et Neurologues de France et des Pays de Langue Française, 54th session, Bordeaux, Aug. 30–Sept. 4, 1956.

Le Phénomène de l'agitation en milieu psychiatrique. Considérations générales, significations psychopathologiques," with S. Asselah, *Maroc Médical*, 36, no. 380 (1957).

"A propos d'un spasme de torsion," with L. Lévy, *La Tunisie Médicale*, 36, no. 9 (1958).

"L'Hospitalisation de jour en psychiatrie. Valeur et limites," *La Tunisie Médicale*, 38, no. 10 (1959), repr. in *L'Information Psychiatrique*, 51, no. 10 (Dec. 1975).

"The Stooges of Imperialism," *Mission in Ghana, Information Service*, 1, no. 6 (Dec. 1960).

Selected Secondary Works

Alessandrini, Anthony C., *Frantz Fanon: Critical Perspectives*. London: Routledge, 1999.

Bulhan, Hussein A., *Frantz Fanon and the Psychology of Oppression*. New York: Plenum Press, 1985.

Caute, David, *Frantz Fanon*. New York: Viking, 1970.

Frantz Fanon, Panaf Great Lives. London: Panaf Books, 1975.

"Frantz Fanon; Forty Years Later." *Philosophia Africana*, 4, no. 2 (Aug. 2001); papers from symposium on A Dying Colonialism at Columbia University, Nov. 15, 1999.

Geismar, Peter, *Frantz Fanon*. New York: Grove Press, 1969.

Gendzier, Irene, *Frantz Fanon: A Critical Study*. New York: Grove Press, 1973; repr. 1985.

Gibson, Nigel C. (ed.), *Rethinking Fanon: The Continuing Legacy*. Amherst: Humanity Books, 1999.

Gordon, Lewis. R., *Fanon and the Crisis of European Man*. Routledge: New York, 1995.

Gordon, Lewis R., T. Denean Sharpley-Whiting, and Renée White, (eds), *Fanon: A Critical Reader*. Oxford: Blackwell, 1996.

Hansen, Emmanuel, *Frantz Fanon: Social and Political Thought*. Columbus: Ohio State University Press, 1977.

History of Psychiatry, 7, no. 28 (1996).

Jinadu, L. Adele, *Fanon: In Search of the African Revolution*. London: Kegan Paul International, 1986.

McCulloch, Jock, *Black Soul, White Artifact: Fanon's Clinical Psychology and Social Theory*. Cambridge: Cambridge University Press, 1983.

Macey, David, *Frantz Fanon: A Life*. London: Granta Books, 2000.

Mémorial international Frantz Fanon. Paris: Présence Africaine, 1984.

Onwuanibe, Richard, *A Critique of Revolutionary Humanism: Frantz Fanon*. St Louis: Warren H. Green, 1983.

Perinbam, B. Marie, *Holy Violence: The Revolutionary Thought of Frantz Fanon*. Washington DC: Three Continents Press, 1983.

Read, Alan (ed.), *The Fact of Blackness: Frantz Fanon and Visual Representation*. London: Institute of Contemporary Arts; Seattle: Bay Press, 1996.

Sekyi-Otu, Ato, *Fanon's Dialectic of Experience*. Cambridge: Harvard University Press, 1996.

Turner, Lou and John Alan, *Frantz Fanon, Soweto and American Black Thought*. Chicago: News and Letters, 1986; repr. in Gibson (ed.), *Rethinking Fanon*.

Zahar, Renate, *Frantz Fanon: Colonialism and Alienation*. New York: Monthly Review Press, 1974.

Zairek, Eva (ed.), "Frantz Fanon and the Impasses of Modernity," *Parallax*, no. 23 (2002).

Index

Frantz Fanon is "F" in various subentries

abandonment neurosis 51, 53, 55–6
  see also Guex, Germaine; Mannoni,
    Octave
Abane Ramdane 98, 99, 100, 102
  see also Soummam conference
absolute 74, 75–6, 153
  as new beginning 31, 40, 76, 77,
    134, 185, 194
  descent from 118–20
  relativity at the heart of 103–6
  see also dialectics; negativity
absolutism 129
abuse 7
Accra 5, 124
Adler, Alfred 43, 46, 47, 48, 51
affect 43, 81, 86, 170–3
Africa 15, 21–2, 62, 177, 178
  civilizations in 67, 71, 82, 192, 199
  decolonization 12, 137, 169
  Europe's "balkanization" of 182
  first "day hospital" 5
  postcolonial 4, 105, 201, 204
  "return" to 63, 67
  revolutionary 194, 198–9
  see also Angola; Congo; Ghana;
    Guinea; Kenya; Madagascar; Mali;
    Mozambique; Rhodesia; Senegal;
    South Africa; Tanzania
Africanism 66

Africanization, ruling class
  183
Afrikaners 135
agency 4, 7, 104, 117
aggression 14, 44, 45, 109, 110, 116
Algeria 1, 55, 56, 57, 115, 123, 134,
  161, 185
  political dissidents 187
  women 22, 138, 139–48
  see also Blida-Joinville
"Algeria Unveiled" (F) 137, 138, 139,
  140, 148, 155
"Algeria's European Minority" (F)
  134–5, 161
Algerian revolution 3, 5, 8, 11, 40, 80,
  159, 173
  criticisms directed at F's analysis of
    10–14
  social transformations engendered
    by 14, 127–56, 158
Algiers School 84–90, 91, 93, 100, 102
  see also Porot, Antoine
alienation 17, 18, 19, 31, 32, 48, 51, 62,
  65, 89
  authentic 40–1
  F's conceptualization 16
  intellectual 3, 78
  see also humanism, new
Alleg, Henri 93

ALN (Armée de la Libération Nationale) 98, 125, 127, 133, 136
alterity 39, 54, 57
  see also Other
anger 13, 14, 66, 169
Angola 121
anthropology 44, 72
Antilles/Antilleans 16, 17, 19, 44, 46, 47–8, 49, 50, 63, 65, 70
anti-Semitism 18, 20, 21
  Jewish type of 19
  see also Jews
anxiety 22
apartheid 108
AR (*Toward the African Revolution*) 63, 86, 94, 97, 100, 102, 127, 161, 181–2, 190, 194, 195, 196, 198
Arabic language 88, 153, 154, 223 n18
"Arabization" 149
Arabs 5, 10, 90, 93, 94, 97, 147
  Europeans want to kill 126
  hordes 138
  "scientific" designation of 84
  viewed as not civilizable 85
Arendt, Hannah 104
Aristotelian logic 114–15
assimilation 11, 18, 19, 64, 88, 133, 169, 170
authenticity 18, 18, 106, 172
authority 44, 151, 152
  patriarchal 147
  symbol of 17, 33
authority complex 54, 56
  see also Mannoni, Octave
Azoulay, Jacques 87, 88

Baartman, Sarjie 22
bad faith 26, 28
bad instincts 20
Banania 206–7
Bantu society 57
barbarism/barbarity 10, 14, 81, 123, 124, 135
Battle of Algiers (1956) 98, 99–102, 121, 128, 144, 182
Beauvoir, Simone de 28, 102, 134
Behr, Edward 100–1
Belgium 160
Ben Bella, Ahmed 99
Bhabha, Homi 2

Biko, Steve 18, 211 n12
bitterness 51
Black consciousness 11, 29, 31, 38–9, 63, 72, 82
  dialectics of 40, 67, 73–8, 136–7
  Jews and 18–24
  separatism 72
  see also negritude
Blackness 21, 22, 26, 51, 71, 80, 81
  European representations of 23, 42, 46, 48, 49
Blackphobia 48, 52
  see also "negrophobia"
Blacks 3, 4, 7, 8, 16, 17, 18, 24, 25, 26, 27, 46, 51, 52, 55, 57, 62, 63, 64, 72, 77, 82
Blida-Joinville 5, 85, 86–7, 89, 91, 95, 96, 100, 107, 134, 135
Bloch, Maurice 55
body image 26
Bonaparte, Marie 20
Bordeaux 65
Bourdieu, Pierre 208 n16, 230 n5
bourgeoisie 3, 12–13, 82, 94, 112, 113, 173, 174
  Algiers Muslim 101
Bresson, Yvon 135
Breton, André 63
brutishness/brutality 36, 66, 84, 94, 107, 124, 126
BS (*Black Skin, White Masks*) 1, 2–3, 4, 5, 8, 9, 10, 15–52, 54, 55, 57, 58, 59–60, 61, 73–4, 75–7, 78, 79, 80–1, 82, 83, 106, 109, 110, 112, 124, 126, 130, 132, 134, 136–7, 140, 143, 153, 158, 173, 180, 196, 202, 204
Bugeaud, Thomas-Robert 92, 102

Capécia, Mayotte 50, 113
capitalism 37, 184, 205
Carothers, J. C. 42, 85, 222 n6
castration 20, 23
catharsis 44, 118
Caute, David 70
Césaire, Aimé 4, 7, 42, 54, 58, 61, 70, 82, 108, 110, 155
  negritude 71–3, 78, 80–1, 173
Christianity 69, 93, 107
circumcision 20

citizenship   5, 15, 84 199
civilization   17, 21, 22, 83, 148, 153
  African   67, 71, 82, 192,
  colonization and   92
  European   23, 48, 49
  universal   71
  White   51
class   74, 83, 112
  African societies and   188
coition   72
Cold War   1, 15
collaborators   56, 111
collective unconscious   47, 48, 49
colonialism   2, 8, 10, 12, 13, 15, 38–9,
    42, 55, 72, 79, 81, 90, 92, 94, 107,
    109, 110, 114, 117, 119, 123, 125, 131,
    132, 135, 152, 158, 161, 163, 170
  hygiene   131, 133
  Manichean world of   27, 170
  violence and   6, 7, 92–7, 101, 102,
    103–12, 119
colonized elites   61, 62, 65, 112, 172,
    173, 174
color *see* skin color
complexes   23
  see also authority complex;
    dependency complex; inferiority
    complex; Oedipus complex
"Confession in North Africa" (F and
    Lacaton)   89–90
Congo   6, 66, 67, 160, 162
Conrad, Joseph   23, 49
consciousness   27, 28, 68, 105, 125,
    136, 143
  African   137
  alienated   32, 152
  double   22, 35
  false   164
  indigenous   33
  organizational   175
  radical mutation of   10, 14, 113, 125,
    161, 163, 165
  social   24, 155, 178
  third person   26
  "unhappy"   77
  see also Black consciousness; Hegel;
    Kojève; master/slave dialectic;
    national consciousness
cosmopolitanism   146

counterrevolution   162
counterterrorism   14, 138
counterviolence   14, 80, 103, 115, 119
  see also violence
Cournot, Michel   23
cowardice   66, 67, 81, 100
cultural creativity   147
cultural relativism   45, 88
cultural unity   81
culture(s)   5, 7–8, 9, 17, 27, 100, 109,
    169
  African   82
  Black   69, 79, 82
  European   48
  fighting   82, 127–56
  French   17
  indigenous   30, 33
  language   29
  Manichean   132
  national   13, 132, 140, 177
  phenomenological view of   45
customs   54, 71, 81, 107

Damas, Leon   62
DC (Studies in a Dying Colonialism)   4,
    82, 86, 88, 93, 94, 95, 120, 124,
    128–56, 158, 206 n3
death rate   86
decolonization   4, 12, 14, 132, 137, 158,
    169
  achieved without transition   143
  intellectuals and success of   169
  internal dialectic of   133
  native's certainty during modern
    period of   39
  unfinished nature of   138
  violence and   106, 111, 112, 113, 114,
    116, 117, 122, 126
dehumanization   6, 11, 13, 54, 57, 89,
    95, 107, 131, 134
delirium   48
delusion   60
dependency   52, 58
dependency complex   16, 42, 53, 54,
    57
depersonalization   96, 97, 140, 144
deprivation   14, 114
desire   9, 22, 23, 35, 36, 47, 59
  dreams   9, 58–60, 110, 111, 112, 116

despair 65
dialectic 3, 4, 8, 10, 25, 44, 65, 80, 135,
  140, 144
  Black consciousness 40, 67, 73–8,
    136–7
  blocked 9, 32
  liberation 168
  master/slave 27, 29–30, 31, 33–4,
    37, 75, 77
  national culture 132
  negative 30–3
  negativity 74, 162
  open-ended 133
  recognition 153
  subject/object 157–60
  subjective, existential 28
  synthesis 74, 76, 125
  unchained 37–41
  untidy 189
Dien Bien Phu 96, 98, 136
Diop, Alioune 57
disalienation 16, 63, 83
  authentic 40
  see also alienation
dissidents 187
Djebar, Assia 141
Djemma 98, 163, 180, 225 n43,
  226 n44
Djouder 198
doctors 86, 129–30, 133
  Nazi 94
domination 22, 54, 56, 106, 131, 132
  racial 46
dread 36, 51

ego 75
  collapse of 48
  weakening of 44
  withdrawal 17, 35
El Moudjahid 4, 5, 93, 102, 124, 134
emotion 19, 69, 79
empathy 69, 89
Engels, Frederick 136, 162
enlightenment 6, 21, 165, 192, 207 n10
envy 1, 13, 114
epidermalization 21, 43, 52
equality 19, 26, 46, 117, 146, 147
eroticism 22, 141
Esprit (magazine) 86

essence 5, 25, 26, 71, 72, 94
  existence precedes 26
  imposed 81
essentialism 70, 72
ethnopsychiatry 89
Étoile Nord-Africaine 225 n43, 234 n6
Eurocentrism 54
Europe 44
Europeanization 140, 144
evil 6, 20, 115
  Black symbol of 24
  Blackness as 48
  Blacks the principle of 23
  quintessence of 107
évolués 52, 62, 64, 79
existence 35
  Bantu 57
  being and 53
  corporeal 24
  outside of external appearance 20
  possibility of 37, 59
  precedes essence 26
existentialism 28, 67, 74, 75, 77
exploitation 62, 85, 188

family structure 45, 46, 49
fanaticism 85, 86, 100
Fanon, Frantz
  abbreviated biography 4–6
  works/writings *see* "Algeria
    Unveiled"; "Algeria's European
    Minority"; *AR*; *BS*; "Confession in
    North Africa"; *DC*; *L'An V*;
    "Racism and Culture";
    "Sociotherapy in a ward of
    Muslim men"; *WE*
fantasy 90
  infantile 45, 50
  sexual 22
fatalism 86, 111, 130
Fédération des Élus Indigènes 234 n6
flight 18–19
FLN (Front de la Libération Nationale)
  4, 5, 97, 98, 99, 100, 101, 120, 134,
  135, 142–3, 145–6, 151, 155, 161,
  179
  see also ALN; Soummam conference;
    nationalism
focoism 191

forced labor   15, 38, 55, 56
France   10, 48, 63, 101, 108
  assimilating Algeria into   84
  being Black in   2
  "civilizing mission"   62, 66, 92–3,
    94, 102, 112,
  incapable of winning war in Algeria
    161
  political left   4, 134, 135
  Vichy   4–5, 56, 206 n14
Frenchness   2, 19, 48
"Free French"   4, 56
freedom   1, 9, 31, 33, 34, 35, 38, 39, 40,
    76, 89, 110, 138
  absolute   27
  cycle of   80
  dialectic   31
  given by colonial master   20
  memory   67
  Merleau-Ponty's conceptualization
    27
  national   58
  psychiatric patient's   91
French army   95
Freud, Sigmund   6, 9, 23, 43, 44, 45,
    48, 51, 60, 109
frustration   32, 50

Gallieni, General   54, 55
Gao   198
Gaulle, Charles de   70, 145
gender relations   11, 138
Geronimi, Charles   91, 92, 101, 135
Ghana   4, 5, 6, 170, 198
Gilman, Sander   21
globalization   1, 13, 204–5
Gobineau, Arthur de   69
God   6, 110
good   6, 7
Gordon, Lewis R.   2, 3
Gramsci, A.   180
Guadeloupe   17, 65, 83
guerrilla warfare   162
Guevara, Che   191
Guex, Germaine   51
guilt   25, 45, 56, 93, 125
Guinea   70

Habermas, J.   31
Haiti   7, 65, 77

Harlem renaissance poets   42
Hegel, G. W. F.   6, 15, 21, 27, 28, 32,
    33, 37–40, 50, 75, 76, 81, 92, 115,
    121, 137, 162, 163, 188–9
  and the Black   29–30
  F's critique of   30, 35, 73
  see also dialectics; negativity
hegemony   7, 106, 109
hierarchies   52, 149
Hippocratic oath   129
Hitler, Adolf   193
"homelessness"   62, 96
Honneth, Axel   188–9
"Hottentot" venus   22
Hountondji, Paulin   70
Hughes, Langston   42
humanism   6, 7, 12, 68, 94, 155
  F's unfolding view of   138
  ideology and   188–92
  new   104, 123, 124, 125, 175,
    177–205
  practical or ethical   181
  radical   29
  revolution and   160

identity   2, 11, 65, 67, 82
  Black stripped of   33
  corporeal   10
  ethnic   12, 13
  intellectual's reliance on   171
  national   8
  new sense of   68
  power and   7
  racial   12
  regional   12
  shift in   140
ideology   68, 70, 175
  colonial   79, 80, 81, 107
  contradictory   94
  humanism and   188–92
  lack of   147, 167
  liberal   79
  Manichean   171
imagination   46, 65, 127–8, 139, 152,
    203, 204
immanence   8, 76, 136
immediacy   35, 75, 128, 163,
    164
inadequacy   22, 50
inauthenticity   18–19, 26, 28

incompleteness 22
independence 1, 34, 38, 52, 55, 70, 76
  individual's development from
    dependency to 54
  real 124
individualism 131, 138
  bourgeois 82
Indochina 70, 98
inferiority complex 2, 3, 10, 11, 17, 18,
  24, 27, 29, 86, 169
  Black's, psychoanalysis and 42–60
  violence 120
inhumanity 101, 139
intellectuals 4, 6, 62, 79, 80, 148
  Black middle-class 79
  honest 134, 163, 166–71, 175, 190
  lazy 183–8
  masses and 11, 105, 174, 169
  and rural society 166–71, 176, 183–8
  vertiginous 171–5
  workers and 83
internalization 26, 28, 37, 39, 40, 44,
  52, 80
  inferiority complex 43
  unconscious 48
intersubjectivity 22, 26, 28, 172
  Merleau-Ponty's conceptualization
    of 27
intuitions 53, 69
Islam 10, 140, 141, 147, 233 n27
  F and 209–10 n30
  representation of 85
  Ulama 233 n27, 234 n6
  see also Muslims

Jeanson, F. 134, 231 n8
Jews 47
  Algerian 135
  and Black consciousness 18–24
  intellectualization 51
Jung, Carl Gustav 48, 49, 51

Kabylia 88, 89, 98, 99, 154, 162–3, 178,
  226 n44
Kant, Immanuel 6
Kasbah 100, 101, 108
Katanga 160
Keane, John 12
Kenya 121–2
  see also Mau Mau

Kojève, Alexandre 15, 28, 30, 36, 38,
  121

labor 57, 185–6
  exploitation of 85
  forced 15, 38, 55, 56
labor unions 36
Lacan, J. 3, 17, 44, 45, 51, 214 n2
Lacaton, R. 89–90
Lacoste (Minister-Resident, Algiers)
  100, 101
L'An V 5, 14, 93, 99, 127, 135–7, 147,
  159, 161
  see also DC
language 5, 29, 59, 63, 64, 149, 154
  and liberation 153–5
  muted and silenced 146
  of occupier 88
  of oppression 153
  philosophical 143
  psychoanalytic 44
  xenophobic or racial 112
Les Temps Modernes 15, 135
Lessing, Doris 45
Lévy-Bruhl, Lucien 85
liberation 2, 5, 11, 35, 40, 66, 72, 80,
  82, 103, 122, 126
  dialectic of 31, 168
  dreams of 110
  national 8, 9, 117, 118, 134, 138, 140,
    145, 147, 164
  philosophy of 57, 175
  struggle/fight for 100, 128, 132,
    133, 140, 145
  war of 89, 97, 99, 138, 147, 164
  women's 138, 139, 147
libido 22, 45
lived experience 3, 4, 5, 11, 16, 31, 52,
  54, 72, 76, 133, 162, 189
  as body subject 24
  dialectic as 10
  F's retelling of 159
  Merleau-Ponty, Sartre, and 24–9
  translated as "Fact of Blackness"
    212 n27
Liverpool 65
Lorcin, Patricia 162–3
love 32, 49–52
Lugard, Lord 108, 216 n15
lumpenproletariat 168, 169

Lumumba, Patrice 6, 102, 160, 162, 168
Luxemburg, Rosa 117
lynchings 23, 66
Lyon 5, 211 n7

Macey, David 102
McKay, Claude 42
Madagascar 16, 52–60
madness 66, 67, 89, 202
Mali 5, 127, 198
Malinowski, B. 44
Malraux, André 70
Manicheanism 1, 7, 13, 18, 21, 28, 30, 2, 37, 40, 49, 73, 86, 93, 103, 104, 111, 113–17, 137, 144, 152, 154, 162–6, 169, 174, 178–9, 191, 194, 181, 195
  after liberation 105, 148, 152, 195, 201
  Algiers School 91
  colonial 27, 52, 94, 108, 123, 128–33, 138, 158, 170, 172, 173
  racial 31, 159, 164
  reaction to 194
  self-understanding not restricted by 159, 189
  transcendence of 152, 195
  see also "reality", Manichean
Mannoni, Octave 42, 48, 52–60, 88
  Prospero and Caliban 48, 52–60
Marabout 119, 224 n22, 228 n15, 233 n27
Maran, René 51
Martinique/Martinicans 2, 4, 5, 9, 10, 17, 44, 46, 48, 49, 50, 54, 63, 64–5, 83
  Paris conference (1956) 99–100
Marx, Karl 3, 6, 16, 33, 36, 40, 41, 134, 136, 168, 184, 185, 186, 190, 195
  The Eighteenth Brumaire 82–3, 158, 187
  mental and manual labor 83, 190, 195
  see also humanism, new; labor; intellectuals, honest
masochism 23, 110
massacres 53, 55–8, 97

Massu, General Jacques 100, 102
master/slave dialectic 27, 28, 29–30, 31, 33–4, 57, 67, 75, 112
  risk 31, 38, 40
  see also Hegel; Kojève
Mau Mau 85, 121
Mauss, M. 92
MDRM (Mouvement de la Rénovation Malagache) 56
medicine 94, 129–30, 131, 132, 133, 135, 154–5, 160
  Western 129–30, 131, 133
  "traditional" 131–2
Memmi, Albert 104, 223 n18
Ménil, René 61
mental illness/health 90, 91, 125
Merleau-Ponty, Maurice 6, 15, 24–7, 28, 78
  phantom limb 25–6
Messali Hadji 97, 98, 122, 225 n43, 235 n6
middle-class society 3, 4, 78, 79, 113, 148, 172
  see also évolués; nationalism/nationalists, bourgeois
militarization 5
Mill, James 184
modernity 30, 31, 174
  and tradition 7, 11, 134
Mollet, Guy 102
Morocco 198
mothers 59
Mozambique 121
MTLD (Mouvement pour le Triomphe des Libertés Démocratiques) 225 n43, 235 n6
multiculturalism 136, 148
multilingualism 154
multiracialism 74, 154
Muslims 87, 88, 100, 101
  French Algerian civil status 84
  Jews and 135
mutual incomprehensibility 89
myth 49, 85, 110–11

Nairobi 85
Nantes 65
Napoleon Bonaparte 136, 162

Nardal, Paulette   42, 212 n2
national consciousness   3, 11, 12, 105,
   116, 127, 137, 151, 152, 153,
   192–200
   see also humanism, new
nationalism/nationalists   13, 55, 56,
   136, 142, 148, 177–205
   bourgeois   112, 113, 182–4
   F's conception   179–200
   narrow   98
   radicals among leadership   168
   rural masses and   166, 186–7
   three types of   179–83
   see also ideology; humanism, new
negativity   63, 66, 72, 76, 77, 81, 173,
   128–9
   absolute   38
   Césaire's negritude the embodiment
      of   71
   dialectic of   74, 162
   synthesis and   74
   see also absolute; Hegel
negritude   3, 4, 5, 7, 9, 54, 58, 61–78,
   171
   F's critique of   78–83
"Negro"   6, 7, 21–2, 33, 65, 79, 62
   White reactions to the word   48
"Negrophobia"   23, 48, 51, 52
neurosis   9, 17, 23, 25, 44–5, 52, 124
   abandonment   51
   clinical   43
   family structure   49
   individual   47
   obsessional   48, 52
   social origin of   46
"New World"   67
Nietzsche, F.   126, 152
Nyerere, Julius   188

object relations   51
Oedipus Complex   9, 31, 44, 45, 49, 53
ontology   24, 26, 28, 53, 73–4
organization   4, 109, 154, 157–76,
   200–3
   bourgeois   111–13, 182–3, 184
   decentralized   13
   philosophy and   175, 190–1, 193
   revolutionary   159, 166, 168, 175,
      186, 190, 196

"sclerosis" of   111, 154
   spontaneity and   148, 157–76
   Western   168, 182, 202
   underground   98, 101
"Orphic poetry"   62
Other   8, 17, 18, 20, 26, 28, 29, 30, 32,
   34, 37, 47, 48, 49, 50, 66, 75, 76, 78,
   94, 104, 119, 123
   absolute   21, 22
   White   22–3, 24, 44, 75
overcompensation   47
overdetermination   20

Pan-Africanism   177
Pan-Arabism   184
Paris   19, 29, 62, 83, 149
   Commune   136
   évolués   79
   First Congress of Black Writers and
      Poets (1956)   99–100, 181
Parti de Peuple Algerien   97, 234 n6
participatory democracy   148–56, 198
   African forms   155, 180, 202, 227 n5
   decentralization   178–9, 180, 188,
      190, 202
   see also Djemma; humanism, new;
      organization
peasantry   72, 85, 115, 167, 168, 184,
   187–8, 190, 191
persecution anxieties   54
personality   18, 42, 53, 103, 126, 140
   "African"   171
   culture and   45
   possession and disintegration of
      111
   weakness of   56
phenomenology   16, 24, 26, 31, 45, 82
   see also lived experience; Merleau-
      Ponty; the "real"; Sartre
Philippeville massacres   97
philosophy   16, 83, 121
   African and Africana   193
   conflictual and dualistic   26
Plato   39, 152, 191
police   109, 121, 144
political education   13, 147, 164, 165,
   192–200
Polynesia   65
Pontorson   87

popular culture 16
Porot, Antoine 85–6, 91, 222–3
Postel, J. 89
posttraumatic stress 120
poverty 54, 65, 66, 90, 132, 167
praxis 3, 16, 200
prejudice 49, 79
Présence Africaine 15, 57, 210–11 n3
projection 25, 48
  bodily 26
  sexual 23
proletarianization 167
psychiatry 85–91
  politics and 92–7
psychic energy 9
psychoanalysis 9, 16, 47, 87, 91, 96
  and Black's inferiority complex
    42–60
psychological mechanisms 54, 58
psychology 18, 45, 53, 79
  Adlerian 46–7
  of colonization 48, 53
  Jungian 47–9
psychopathology 89
psychosis 125

Rabémananjara, Jacques 57–8, 81
"Racism and Culture" (F) 99
radical mutation 10, 14, 113, 127–56,
    158, 173, 190
radio 148–56
Ranaivo, Flavien 58
rape 81, 85, 141, 142
rationalism 64, 71
  subverted 66
rationality 67
  instrumental 70
  irrationality 23, 66, 79, 80
Razanajao, C. 89
the "real" 57, 59, 79, 82, 91, 103, 110,
    128, 136, 150–1, 155–6, 193
"reality" 12, 33, 43, 44–5, 50, 51, 54,
    60, 64, 66, 77, 78, 97, 131, 136
  flights from 110
  Manichean 2, 9, 32, 90, 106–9, 113,
    125
reason 21–2, 31, 39, 66–7, 72, 79, 80,
    87, 114, 156, 165
  intuitive 69
  unreason 31, 80

reciprocity 16, 28, 29, 39, 50, 74, 86,
    89, 101
  absence of 40
  absolute 33, 34
  Blacks and 33–7
  dialectic of 32
  lack of 17
  mutual 26, 37
  see also Hegel; intersubjectivity
recognition 26, 33, 38
  absence of 30
  évolué looks for 51
  language and 153
  mutual 27, 28, 32, 34, 37
  nonrecognition 9, 24
  reciprocal 93, 115
  struggle for 27–8
  unilateral 28
  see also reciprocity
reformist parties 36, 112, 113, 121, 168
  see also nationalism/nationalists,
    bourgeois; organization, bourgeois
regionalism 99, 116, 201
regression 9, 40, 41, 146
  method of 31, 79
religion 6, 13
  see also Christianity; Islam; Jews
remembrance 63–8
repression 67, 81, 90, 116–17
  political and social 14
resentment 13, 50, 51, 164
resistance 4, 13, 64, 65, 75, 111, 129,
    153–4
  anticolonial 132, 142, 149
  colonial 138
  cultural 127
  ontological 26, 74, 140
revenge 1, 14, 98, 164
revolt 2, 73, 77, 132
  subjugated and ongoing history of
    20
Rhodesia 121
Rodin, A. 20
Roumain, Jacques 77–8
Rousseau, Jean-Jacques 126
Ruedy, John 84, 234–5 n6
Rwanda 105

sadism 23, 24, 90, 94, 96, 141
Sadji, Abdoulaye 50

Sahara 22
Saint-Alban 87, 89
Sanchez, F. 89
Sartre, Jean-Paul 1, 3, 6, 8, 15, 16,
  17–18, 24, 26, 27, 28, 32, 47, 50, 75,
  76, 78, 80, 104, 122, 124–5, 134,
  227 n2
  Orphée noir 71–3, 74
Sekou Touré, Ahmed 70
Sekyi-Otu, Ato 2, 3, 147
self
  awareness 64, 79
  certainty 31, 38–9
  construction 63, 143
  hatred 65
  knowledge 31, 164
  perception 48
  reflection 65
  understanding 159, 160, 189
self-consciousness 9, 31, 33, 34, 37, 38,
  74, 76, 77, 83, 115, 123
  "different ways" toward 123
  impossibility of 38
  recognition as an independent 34
self-determination 40, 55, 132, 134,
  163, 164–5
  see also Algeria; national
  consciousness
Senegal/Senegalese 5, 17, 48, 50, 59,
  60, 96
  see also Senghor
Senghor, Leopold 57, 58, 61, 62, 64,
  67, 79, 81, 82
  and negritude politics 68–71, 72,
  80
servitude 34, 35, 38
  see also master/slave dialectic
Sétif 56, 97, 116
Sharpeville 116
skepticism 38, 46, 105, 220 n59
skin color 20, 21, 25, 28, 35, 37, 51, 52,
  70, 71, 79
Skinner, Quentin 12
slaves 7, 9, 15–41, 64, 66, 75, 83
  "enfranchised" 112, 196
  see also master/slave dialectic
sociodiagnostic analysis 5, 9, 17, 43,
  46, 47, 52, 58
"Sociotherapy in a ward of Muslim
  men" (F and Azoulay) 87

solidarity 5, 72, 145–6
Songhais 82
Soummam conference (1956) 98, 99,
  100, 104, 122, 128, 147–8, 161
South Africa 121, 135
splitting 46
spontaneity 11, 117, 157–76
stoicism 38
struggle 8, 19, 29, 31, 52, 64, 77, 79, 99
  anticolonial 1, 4, 10, 12, 13, 31, 37–8,
    81, 82, 112, 121, 134, 142, 177, 178
  armed 105, 116, 119, 122, 124
  liberation 40, 100, 117, 128, 134,
    140, 145, 149, 164
  national 121, 134, 178
  physical 37, 39
  recognition 27–8
subjectivity 7, 8, 53, 58, 71, 105, 117,
  128, 151
subjugation 7, 92, 130
suffering 65, 67
superiority 22, 48, 56, 57, 136
  complex 46
superstitions 82, 134
surrealism 63–4, 65, 71

Tanzania 188
technology 70, 129, 133, 153, 194,
  205
Tempel, Placide 57
terrorism 97, 100, 101, 124, 126, 138
Third World 15, 30, 147
torture 5, 11, 60, 70, 92–7, 101, 102
Tosquelles, François 87, 89, 92
totalitarianism 7, 107, 110, 117, 120
Toussaint L'Ouverture 7, 65, 72
tradition 13, 81, 99, 110, 128, 129–30,
  131, 134, 208 n20
  distorted and disfigured 132
  modernity and 7, 11
  patriarchal 140, 147
trauma 44, 46, 125
tribalism 178, 196
truth 12, 18, 27, 39, 152, 153
  all-White 17
  objective 31, 75, 129–30
  social 50, 131
  subjectivity and 151
Tunis 89, 91, 102
Turner, Lou 98

unconscious   23, 43, 45, 47, 55, 56, 58, 59, 60, 69, 80, 151
Union Nationale des Femmes Algériennes   147
United States   20
universal brotherhood   18, 19
Universal Declaration of Human Rights (1948)   93
urban/rural dimension   158, 166–8, 176, 180, 190, 201

VE day (1945)   97
veiling tradition   10, 11, 22, 134
Veneuse, Jean   51–2
Vichy regime   4–5, 56
victims   25, 93, 95, 121–2
vigilantism   146
violence   1, 3, 5, 30, 64, 97–9, 100, 103–8, 118–26, 128, 138, 165
  absolute   80
  anticolonial   2, 14, 115, 118, 165
  as therapeutic   107, 118
  "Black-on-Black"   64, 86
  colonial   2, 7, 13, 93, 107, 113, 115
  humanism   120, 121–3
  interiorized   109–13
  language of   29
  national consciousness   116–17
  reciprocity of   135

simplistic understanding of   138
tragedy and   125
trauma and   125–6

WE (*The Wretched of The Earth*)   1, 2, 3, 4, 6, 9, 10, 39, 40, 74, 80, 81, 82, 90, 92, 93, 95, 96, 97, 99, 103–26, 131, 132, 137–8, 146, 147, 157–75, 177, 178, 180, 181, 182–94, 197–204
West Indians   63, 64, 65
Westermann, Diedrich   42
white supremacy   92, 93
Whiteness   19, 30, 47, 48, 50
Whites   5, 7, 8, 9, 16, 23, 32, 35, 50, 72
  support Algerian revolution   164–5
Wilayas   98
women   50, 51, 87, 135
  "absolute originality" of actions   139–48
  desires   113
  European   87
  liberation   139–48
  simple "Manichean conception" of reality   32
  veiled   138–47
  see also Capécia, Mayotte
World War Two   55, 56

Yugoslavia   63

CPSIA information can be obtained
at www.ICGtesting.com
Printed in the USA
LVHW080220100222
710760LV00020B/248

9 780745 622613